The Other Kaisers

The Other Kaisers

An Investigation Into the Proliferation of German Dynasties Throughout Europe

Oliver Thomson

AMBERLEY

First published 2010

Amberley Publishing Plc
Cirencester Road, Chalford,
Stroud, Gloucestershire, GL6 8PE

www.amberley-books.com

British Library Cataloguing in Publication Data.
A catalogue record for this book is available from the British Library.

ISBN 978 1 84868 357 0

Typeset in 10pt on 12pt Sabon.
Typesetting and Origination by FONTHILLDESIGN.
Printed in the UK.

CONTENTS

Maps and Illustrations

Maps

Family Trees

Black and White Plates

PREFACE

> In the hereditary monarchies there were at least eight out of ten who would not have been capable of running a grocery.
> Adolf Hitler, *Hitler's Table Talk* (N. Cameron, R. H. Stevens, H. R. Trevor-Roper)

> In the smaller states the costliness of a court, an administration, an army, in short the dead weight of taxation, increased in a direct ratio with the smallness and impotency of the state.
> Karl Marx, *Das Kapital*

Most of us are well aware that the current British royal dynasty is of German extraction, a mixture of Hanover, Saxe-Coburg-Gotha and various others. The late Queen Mother Elizabeth was the first non-German queen since Queen Anne, for even Queen Alexandra came from a German-Danish family. What we sometimes forget is that most of the other dynasties in Europe were also German in origin. That is still true of Denmark, Holland, Norway and Belgium as well as Britain. As a result of picking German wives, the Romanovs in Russia were ethnically almost 100 per cent German, which means, ironically, that the four emperors who were most responsible for the First World War, those of Germany, Austria, Russia and Great Britain were all basically German. In addition four other European dynasties which lasted into the twentieth century, those of Greece, Bulgaria, Romania and Portugal, were also German families. This book looks at the reasons why the Germans were such successful producers of royal dynasties that ruled other countries, though they themselves were late developers when it came to ruling a united Germany. It looks at the extraordinary power these families wielded, their great variety of lifestyles and their remarkable built heritage.

Spelling of Names

It is quite hard to be accurate, non-pedantic and readable at the same time, so I have not always been consistent. For example, Kaiser Wilhelm seems natural enough but Heinrich the Lion seems a bit pedantic, so I've used Henry. Gustavus Adolphus usually gets this latinised treatment, but I've tried to revert to Gustav Adolf. Then there are the Friedrichs and Frederiks, but we are used to Frederick the Great, the Karls, Charleses and Carols, some of whom change spelling as they cross borders. In most contexts Munich seems more acceptable than München, Hanover than Hannover, Brunswick than Braunschweig, Elsinore than Helsingfors. Generally I have used the spelling that seemed to ease the flow of the narrative, but have from time to time reminded the reader that there are alternatives.

INTRODUCTION

This is not part of a conspiracy theory, just an example of the extraordinary effects that can be produced in history as a result of fairly minor variations in customs and attitudes. Because German families were slower than nearly all other ethnic groups to adopt a system of primogeniture, the result was that for several centuries landowners kept subdividing their inheritances and the country was chopped up into over 300 small independent states. The rulers of these tiny states gave themselves fancy titles as princes and archdukes, so in the naïve snobbery of European royalty this meant that they produced a pool of marriageable spouses for real royal families in other countries. The result was that in due course most of the genuinely royal dynasties of Europe had been so infiltrated by relatively minor German families that Germans eventually took over their thrones. From London to St Petersburg, from Copenhagen to Athens the ruling royal dynasties in the eighteenth and nineteenth centuries were nearly all of German origin.

One of the ironies of history is that the Germans for many centuries proved the least competent people in Europe in terms of creating a sensible-sized nation state of their own. The Italians also failed over the same period but they had the excuse that their territory included the papacy, which led to constant interference in their efforts from outside. The reasons for the Germans' failure were several. With their reluctance to adopt primogeniture the princes and dukes kept dividing up their inheritances so that each of their sons could have a small principality of his own. In addition, their potential national leaders were too busy trying to recreate the Roman Empire to bother with their own nation, and later they were one of the few ethnic groups not to plump *en masse* for either Protestantism or Catholicism, but instead ended up with a religious patchwork.

Thus it was not till the rise of Prussia and the wars engineered by Bismarck that the bulk of Germans were finally united, and even then there were German-speaking areas like Austria, the east of Switzerland and pockets round the Baltic that were left out.

There was, however, one remarkable by-product of this chaos. Given the extraordinary snobbishness that existed from the Middle Ages till the last century, the sovereign princes and self-styled arch-dukes of even the tiniest and most idiotic of states were regarded as worthy husbands for non-German royal women, whilst their huge annual crop of marriageable daughters had a reputation as good breeding stock and provided a happy hunting ground for foreign kings in search of a queen.

Thus the Germans became the greatest exporters of royal blood-stock in Europe, and by the early nineteenth century, there were monarchs of German extraction in charge of a majority of the nations of Europe. The British had a German king from 1714 onwards and made sure the dynasty kept its German genes by constantly importing German brides or husbands for successive generations. While no one can be certain of the paternity of Tsar Paul of Russia (either the half-German Peter III or one of Catherine's Russian lovers), his mother Catherine the Great was pure German, and all subsequent tsars married Germans or ladies of German extraction, so the Romanovs were genetically at least 90 per cent German by 1917. Similarly, the Scandinavians had mainly Germanic kings from 1448, and the Dutch had Germanic Stadholders from the time when William the Silent moved from Nassau-Dillenburg. In the nineteenth century, there was a further boom in the export of German princelings who took over Belgium, Greece, Bulgaria, Romania and Portugal. In addition, three of the new dynasties that contributed to the pre-1914 instability of the Balkan region were German families. Ironically, therefore, all four of the emperors who did most to start the First World War, George V, Nicholas II, Wilhelm II and Franz Josef were all of German extraction and had German wives. Of the mainstream monarchies that still survive in Europe in the twenty-first century all but two have dynasties of German extraction, the two exceptions being Sweden and Spain, which have families originally from France. We should also remember that until the twentieth century many of these Germanic dynasties, particularly the British, Dutch, Belgian and Danish, also controlled substantial overseas empires, while the Germanic Romanovs held a vast land-mass stretching to the Pacific.

The purpose of this book is, therefore, to look at the extraordinary paths by which families from relatively small and often obscure German towns, like Nassau, Coburg, Oldenburg, Zerbst, Kiel and Brunswick, came to dominate European history for many years. We assess their ascent to power, their influence on affairs, their achievements and extravagances, the disasters for which they can be held responsible and the heritage they have left behind.

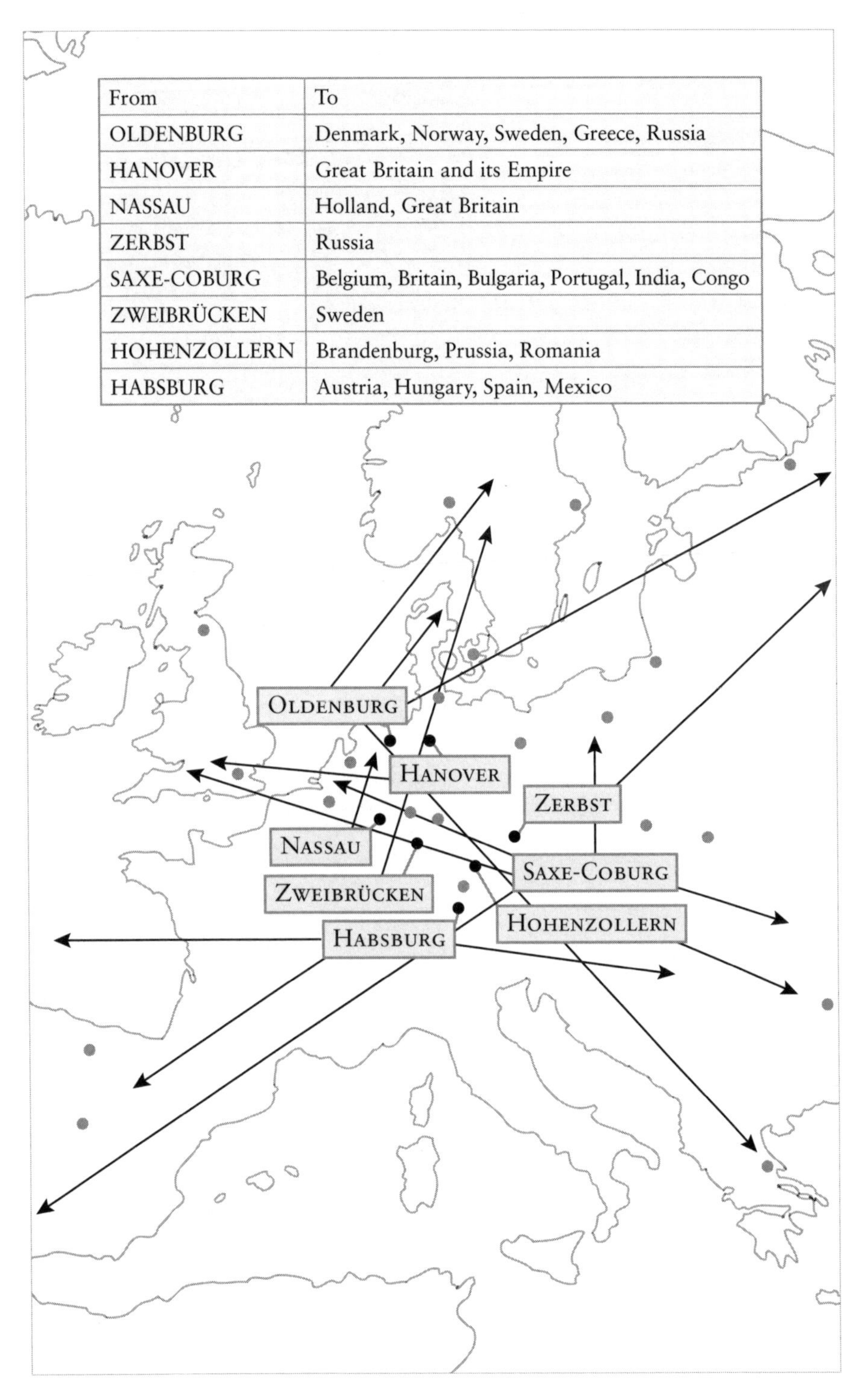

From	To
OLDENBURG	Denmark, Norway, Sweden, Greece, Russia
HANOVER	Great Britain and its Empire
NASSAU	Holland, Great Britain
ZERBST	Russia
SAXE-COBURG	Belgium, Britain, Bulgaria, Portugal, India, Congo
ZWEIBRÜCKEN	Sweden
HOHENZOLLERN	Brandenburg, Prussia, Romania
HABSBURG	Austria, Hungary, Spain, Mexico

The Main Migrations of German Dynasties

PART 1

The Families

CHAPTER 1

The Northbound House of Oldenburg

Oldenburg, once called Aldenburg, lies in Lower Saxony some forty miles east of the modern Dutch frontier and about the same distance from the North Sea. With a population now of around 160,000, it is only the fourth biggest city in Lower Saxony and dwarfed by its near neighbour Bremen, yet it is the original home of one of Europe's longest lasting dynasties. Luckily, despite its strategic position, it suffered relatively little damage during the two World Wars, so many of its historic buildings survive, including the moated Aldstadt, though not the original castle built here to guard the lowest ford on the River Hunte, which flows from here down to join the Weser. Small ships can still reach Oldenburg by the Weser and Hunte from the sea, and the area is good agricultural land, ideal for dairy cattle and arable crops, such as corn, kale and, recently, asparagus.

On the site of the old castle, built probably around 1108 by Eimar, the ancestor of this family who was then count of Saxony and Frisia, there is still the seventeenth-century Renaissance-style *schloss*. This was built to house his descendants, the Dukes of Oldenburg, after the main branch of the family had moved northwards to take over the crowns of Denmark, then Sweden and Norway. Not only did they achieve prominence in Scandinavia but they still hold the crowns of Denmark and Norway, they provided a short-lived dynasty for Greece, the penultimate Tsarina of Russia and possibly all the Romanov tsars after Peter III, the current Queen of Spain and five consorts* for British Royals, most recently Philip Duke of Edinburgh, so that the present British Royal Family has a significant portion of Oldenburg genes.

* The five are Queen Margaret of Scotland, wife of James III; Queen Anne, the wife of James VI of Scotland and I of Great Britain; Prince George, the husband of Queen Anne; Queen Alexandra, wife of Edward VII; and Philip Duke of Edinburgh from the Greek branch of the family.

A SMALL TOWN FAMILY

Like several other German families, the House of Oldenburg looked back to the Saxon hero Widukind as their ancestor of choice. Widukind had led resistance against the Frankish conquest by Charlemagne, so he had a heroic, nationalist image even though his efforts ended in failure. But it is three hundred years after Widukind's death that we find the first historically recorded member of the family, Eimar, Count of Frisia and Saxony (*d.*1108), and in 1189, his grandson was raised to be a prince of the Holy Roman Empire. Yet apart from the two small towns of Oldenburg and nearby Delmenhorst, the family's land holdings were very modest, and there was nothing to indicate that the counts might ever become more significant, though Count Otto I (1175-1251) had an unsavoury reputation for kidnapping and blackmailing the local farmers' wives. To make matters worse, with the usual German antipathy to primogeniture, they divided up what little they had amongst their sons, so the inheritances grew progressively smaller except when the cousins managed to marry each other, but then the process would start all over again.

In the end it was to be a remarkably obscure connection that brought about the extraordinary promotion of the Oldenburgs. Count Conrad I (*d.* about 1368), the first of the family specifically to designate himself Count of Oldenburg, married a princess from Holstein called Ingeborg. She came from Itzehoe-Plön just over one hundred miles to the north-east of Oldenburg on the other side of the Elbe, and on the surface there was nothing particularly remarkable about Conrad marrying a princess from a neighbouring county. Yet, unknown to Conrad, the bloodline of the old Danish Royal Dynasty, the House of Gorm, had begun to show signs of sterility. As it turned out, Conrad's new wife was the granddaughter of a spare Swedish princess, also called Ingeborg, who was herself a granddaughter of King Eric IV of Denmark (*r.*1241-50) and had married Count Gerhart of Holstein. No one could have predicted that such a remote connection through the female line would become significant eighty years after Conrad's wedding. But it did.

When Conrad died he followed the usual pattern of dividing his lands between his two sons, so this made the patrimony weaker. His elder son Conrad II died childless in 1401 and his younger son Christian V (*fl.*1399-1423) handed over to his own son Dietrich the Lucky (or Theodoric or Teudericus Fortunatus 1398-1440). He won his nickname by marrying a cousin so that he could get back some of the parts of the family estate that had previously been hived off to younger sons, specifically Delmenhorst. Despite this good fortune, even he cannot have foreseen that his family might be in line for a throne some eight years after his own death, but perhaps by coincidence, perhaps by design, he copied his grandfather in marrying a princess from Holstein, Hedwig (1398-1446), who had the bonus of additional royal Danish genes, for she was descended from King Eric V.

A double lack of fertility now by a strange quirk of fortune brought elevation to the House of Oldenburg. The Royal House of Gorm finally ran out of obvious heirs in 1448 when King Kristofer III of Denmark, Norway and Sweden (himself a Bavarian Wittelsbach – see p. 141 – it was to be 1654 before the Wittelsbachs made a Scandinavian comeback) died suddenly leaving no children by his wife Dorothea of Brandenburg. As the Danes looked around for a replacement king and found each male line disappearing in the sand, they turned to Holstein where two of the counts had married Danish princesses, yet here again there had been a dearth of male heirs. When the Danes offered their crown to Adolf VII, the Count of Holstein, he replied that he was too old for the job and, as he had no son, he pointed the Danes in the direction of Oldenburg. There, Dietrich the Lucky had indeed produced at least two sons, one of whom was Adolf's nephew Christian VI, the new Count of Oldenburg (1426-81).

Thus at the age of twenty-two Christian of Oldenburg was elected King Kristian I of Denmark and was crowned at Copenhagen. He had already inherited a large portion of Holstein from his mother. Two years later he also acquired the throne of Norway, which he invaded by sea in 1450, organized his own election as king and was crowned at Trondheim. Then seven years later he invaded Sweden, expelled the unpopular King Karl I Knutson (1409-70) and won his third crown. However, the Swedes did not like him much better than they did King Karl, so, after a few years, they drove Kristian out and reinstated Karl – only for the whole process to be repeated until Kristian finally lost a major battle in 1471.

Meanwhile, to ease his way into the Danish court Kristian had married the former king's feisty widow Dorothea of Brandenburg, a Hohenzollern – her first marriage to King Kristofer had only lasted three years – and this time she did produce children. One of their daughters became the bride of King James III of Scotland, the first of five Oldenburg consorts to come to Britain. Kristian, who had a poor grasp of finance, could not afford an immediate cash dowry, so he promised the Danish islands of Orkney and Shetland to the Scots if he should prove unable to raise the last 8,000 guilders of Margaret's dowry. He failed and as a result the two island groups were transferred to Scotland. But he had passed on his genes to the Stewarts, so that the ambitious James IV was his grandson, and all subsequent British monarchs can be traced back to him. The loss by Denmark of the Northern Isles was of relatively little consequence for they still held the Faroes and Iceland. Meanwhile, Kristian founded the University of Copenhagen before dying at the age of fifty-five.

The fashion that Kristian set for his new Danish dynasty by marrying a German wife was to continue for the next four centuries. Though he handed over the family's old patrimony at Oldenburg to his younger brother, he kept a foothold in Germany with his portion of Holstein and the family retained much of its German ethos, particularly its admiration for the German style of military training. When he died in 1481 after thirty-three years on the throne his son Hans (1455-1513) succeeded as King of Denmark and Norway after the obligatory election process in both kingdoms, with separate coronations in Copenhagen and Trondheim. He also became Duke of Schleswig-Holstein, and married Kristina of Saxony, so the 100 per cent German genetic mix was maintained. Genial and folksy on the surface he was in reality devious and ambitious, so he desperately wanted to regain the third kingdom, Sweden, and to consolidate his territories in north Germany. The first he managed by conquest in 1497 so that he could be crowned Johan II of Sweden, but the second ended in failure with his humiliating defeat by the people of Dithmarschen, a fertile area north of the Elbe that had been reclaimed from the sea – the people opened the dykes rather than surrender. This in turn led to him losing Sweden again in 1501. Nevertheless, despite these setbacks and waste of life he had certainly consolidated the hold of his dynasty, at least on Denmark and Norway, so that the election of kings became little more than a formality.

When the third generation of the dynasty took over then things, as so often happens, began to turn sour. Hans's son Kristian II (1481-1559), known as The Tyrant, took over the dual thrones of Denmark and Norway in 1513 and grabbed Sweden by force seven years later. There he made himself extremely unpopular by his ruthless culling of the Swedish nobles in the incident known as the Stockholm Bloodbath. It provoked a nationalist rebellion that led, in 1521, to the founding of a new Swedish dynasty by Gustav Vasa, so that the Oldenburgs lost Sweden for the next 230 years. He was not much more popular in Denmark itself where there was a revolt against his rule which forced him to flee to Holland after only ten years on the throne. Nor had he been popular with his wife, half-German princess Isabella of Castile, a Habsburg and sister of the Emperor Charles V, for he spent too much time with his mistress Hanne Dyveke, or Little Dove, an ambitious courtesan from Amsterdam. Her influence over affairs outraged Danish leaders so that, not surprisingly, she died suddenly in mysterious circumstances, and it is assumed from poison. After his expulsion in 1523 Kristian made numerous attempts to regain his thrones, spending much of his remaining thirty-six years in various prisons.

The self-destruction of Kristian II did no long-term harm to the Oldenburg dynasty apart from removing the possibility of their regaining the third of their crowns, that of Sweden. He was replaced in Denmark and Norway by his uncle Frederik I (1471-1534) who had served as Duke of Holstein where, despite his elevation, he continued to live at the family home of Gottorp. It was alleged that he never learned to speak Danish and was the only king of Norway never to visit it. He repelled his nephew Kristian's attempts to recapture Denmark and, somewhat dishonourably, lured him for talks in Copenhagen with the promise of a safe conduct only to lock him up in the dungeons. His only other military campaign, against Dithmarschen, was a disastrous failure. Like his father he married a German princess, Anna of Brandenburg (1487-1514), so there was still no question of diluting the German genes. Nor was there with his second wife, Sophie of Pomerania.

Frederik's son Kristian III (1503-59) took over in 1533 at the age of thirty and was mainly notable for his passionate conversion to Protestantism. He attended the Diet of Worms and suppressed the Catholic Church in Denmark after a civil war in which his aged grand uncle ex-king Kristian II attempted yet another come-back, posing in vain as the Catholic champion. Kristian III then organised the conversion of Norway and Iceland, arresting die-hard Catholics and confiscating the properties of the Church so that his own financial position was greatly improved. A pious, cautious but effective ruler he strengthened the centralised monarchy and naturally he maintained tradition by marrying a German princess, Dorothea of Saxe-Lauenburg.

When he died in his mid-fifties in 1559, their son Frederik II (1534-88) took over and had to spend most of the next seven years defending himself against his paranoid cousin Erik XIV of Sweden. He copied the latest German fighting styles and did succeed where his grandfather had failed in conquering Dithmarschen in north Germany, but after that his efforts to regain Sweden ended in disaster. Thereafter, his reign of nearly thirty years was mainly noteable for peace and rising prosperity, while he devoted himself to the pleasures of the flesh and the mind. He had the sumptuous Kronborg Castle built at Elsinore where he hired musicians from all over Europe and patronised the astronomer Tyco Brahe. He had married Sophia of Mecklenburg-Güstrow but was in his mid-forties before their son Kristian was born. One of his brothers, Magnus (1540-83), married the heiress of Livonia and briefly became its king with capitals in Kiel and Tallinn.

Kristian IV (1577-1648) was only eleven when he took over in 1588, but grew up tall and ambitious to make Denmark once more mistress of the Baltic. Like his father, he promoted technical education, worked hard, played hard, drank a lot and was promiscuous. He built up both his land and sea forces and was fairly successful in his first war against Sweden, the Kalmar War of 1611-13. His sister Anna had married James VI of

Scotland with whom Kristian corresponded in Latin, and she moved first to Edinburgh in 1590 as Queen of Scotland, then to London as Queen of Great Britain in 1603.

Kristian's niece, therefore, was James and Anna/Anne's daughter Elizabeth the wife of Frederick of Palatine who was given the dangerous throne of Bohemia in 1620. This gave Kristian the excuse he was looking for to interfere in the Thirty Years' War which then engulfed Germany, and so he snatched Hamburg and the bishopric of Bremen, two key cities lying between his family's German possessions in Oldenburg and Holstein. But, as Wedgewood puts it, 'he was a reckless rather than a gifted commander' and he was badly defeated by the imperial forces under Tilly at Lutter as he retreated back to Brunswick. While his campaign ended in failure, his Swedish rival Gustav Adolf achieved spectacular success in the same cause. After Gustav's death Kristian took the opportunity to attack Sweden where six-year-old Kristina had taken over as queen, but victory still eluded him.

Kristian had maintained tradition by marrying Anne Catherine of Brandenburg, another Hohenzollern, but he also kept a succession of mistresses, particularly Kirsten Munk with whom he had twelve children, twice the number he had with his wife. When his mistress was found to be having an affair with a German cavalry officer he had her tried for witchcraft, then exiled, and he transferred his affection to one of her former maids, Vibeke Kruse, who produced some more children for him. The consequential dysfunctional broods of children were to create unhealthy feuds in his later years and trouble for his successor. Meanwhile, he also acquired a gargantuan taste for food and drink exemplified by the bacchanalian orgies he enjoyed when he visited his sister and brother-in-law in London.

Despite all this, his work-rate remained high and he did his best to moderate the excesses of the Danish landowners and to improve the infrastructure of his country. The refurbishment of Copenhagen owed much to him, for he rebuilt Copenhagen Castle with its infamous Blue Tower, founded the Börse, with its twisted dragons spire, built Rosenborg, Holmenskirke, Proviantgarden and the five-sided Citadel of the city. He founded Kristiania as his new Norwegian capital after nearby medieval Oslo had been all-but destroyed by fire. Amongst his other foundations was Glückstadt in Germany, which he set up as a trading rival to the Hanseatic city of Hamburg, for he was passionate about increasing both Denmark's navy and its merchant fleet. In this connexion he was responsible for the first Danish colony in the East, Tranquebar in South India.

However, Kristian's vacillating and devious foreign policies irritated the other powers, particularly Sweden, and caused another outbreak of war in 1643. Though he was now into his mid-sixties he fought on and won popularity if not victory by sustaining thirteen wounds on his body and still urging on his men when his flagship the *Trinity* was attacked outside Kiel. Unfortunately, he lost the war. When he died in his early eighties he had been sixty years on the throne.

Kristian IV's second son Frederik III (1609-70) took over in 1648 unexpectedly, for his eldest brother had just died. The Thirty Years' War had finally come to an end and the Danish monarchy was at a low ebb, so Frederik, an introverted character more interested in science than politics, took a while to find his feet. He left the government to his brother-in-law Count Ulfeldt who had married his half-sister Leonora Kristina, daughter of his father's mistress Kirsten Munk. Eventually, Frederik staged an internal coup to get rid of Ulfeldt who was followed into exile by his feisty wife Leonora Kristina. She led an adventurous life abroad, sometimes having to dress up as a man and fending off the attentions of both sexes, before she was at last captured and interned for the next two decades in the Blue Tower, or Blätärn, of Copenhagen Castle. Even there she made a name for herself as a stubborn prisoner who survived numerous humiliations, yet used her time to write an informative journal and study the anatomy of the rats that lived in her cell.

Frederik, meanwhile, provoked yet another war with Sweden, which the Danes predictably lost, but there was a surprising outcome. When the Swedes counterattacked and besieged Copenhagen, Frederik showed unexpected courage and gained in confidence. He was thus able to shake off the controls that had been put upon him by the Danish nobles, so that from his time onwards the Danish kings no longer had to be elected but were hereditary and absolute monarchs. Thus though Frederik was a less colourful character than his father in his twenty-two years on the throne of Denmark-Norway he consolidated the Oldenburgs' control. He had married Sophie Amalie of Brunswick-Lüneburg, and his younger son George (1653-1708) was to be the Prince Consort of Queen Anne of Great Britain, so if it had not been for Queen Anne's sad inability to bear healthy children, he might have prevented the House of Hanover from ever setting foot in Britain.

Frederik's eldest son Kristian V (1646-99), born in Flensburg, took over in 1670 and was unremarkable except for one wasteful war to capture Skania. He married the obligatory German princess, Charlotte Amalie of Hesse, the daughter of George of Brunswick-Lüneburg, but had a habit of insulting her by parading his sixteen-year-old mistress Amelia Moth in court. Nevertheless he made progress in professionalising the government and introducing new legal codes for both Denmark and Norway.

Their son Frederik IV (1671-1730) took over in 1699 and waged an even longer than usual war against Sweden – the Great Northern War

(1700-30) – where ironically his two principal enemies were his distant relations King Karl XII of Sweden and Duke Frederick of Schleswig-Gottorp. Any success that he had was mainly due to the efforts of Tsar Peter the Great who defeated Karl XII for him at Poltava, but in the end his gains were modest, the recovery of Schleswig-Holstein. Regarded as one of the most intelligent of the Oldenburgs, he had the sense to abolish serfdom but any benefits from this for the peasants were undone later by his son. He married Louise of Mecklenburg who produced his heir, but he then went on to marry another two wives at the same time. His other major non-military extravagance was the building of two new Baroque palaces at Frederiksberg and Fredensborg. He was also responsible for the re-colonisation of Greenland – the original Viking settlers had long since died out.

His son Kristian VI (1699-1746), who succeeded in 1730, was obsessively religious but unhealthy, uncharismatic and not very humane. He negated the effects of his father's abolition of serfdom by having all peasants tied to the land so that they could more easily be conscripted for his army when required. His rigid pietism was unpopular and his autocratic pretensions were reflected in the building of three more palaces, Kristiansborg, Hirscholm and Eremitage. He married Sophia, a Hohenzollern princess from Brandenburg.

As so often happens, a rigidly pious father produces a licentiously retrograde son, and Frederik V (1723-66), who took over in 1746, was no exception. He was a compulsive womaniser – he produced five bastards with his main mistress – and an alcoholic whose one great virtue was that he avoided war. His only territorial acquisition was the Danish West Indies, which he bought in 1754. His first wife was Louise, the daughter of George of Hanover who later became George II of Britain, and she produced his heir, but his second wife Julia of Brunswick-Wolfenbüttel also produced a son who was to be significant in later years.

After seven fairly normal generations and straightforward handovers from father to son, the Oldenburg dynasty now began to show serious signs of dysfunctionalism. Kristian VII (1749-1808), the son of Frederik V and Louise, is reckoned to have suffered from dementia praecox from a fairly early age – his cousin George III of Britain later had similar symptoms – and this was exacerbated by the usual bullying by tutors that was recommended for European princes at this time, particularly those of German extraction. He was only seventeen when he succeeded his father in 1766, and the same year married his cousin, Caroline Matilda, the sister of George III. An extravagant Grand Tour, the stress of marriage and the demands of his pet whore, Storlete Catherine, proved too much for his delicate nerves and he came under the increasingly heavy influence of his German doctor Johann Struensee. This remarkable man became the queen's lover and may even have fathered her child as well as inaugurating a series of liberal reforms, which would have made Denmark a most progressive state for that time if they had been properly implemented. The Danish establishment, however, wanted nothing to do with them and engineered his downfall. He was accused of treason and publicly executed. The royal marriage was dissolved in 1772 and the queen was exiled to Hanover, while the wretchedly dissipated Kristian VII was thrust aside by his stepmother who acted as regent for the couple's young son. In 1784, Kristian was certified insane. He died in Schleswig twenty-four years later, in his fifties.

Kristian's legal, though possibly not genetic, son Frederik VI (1768-1839) acted as regent during his father's last two decades and was finally crowned only in 1808. Considering his background he was remarkably sane. As regent he had abolished the slave trade in the Danish colonies and finally removed the evils of serfdom in Norway and Denmark. He was unfortunate to be sandwiched between the conflicting demands of Britain and France during the Napoleonic Wars and so had to suffer the destruction of his fleet by Nelson at the Battle of Copenhagen and the bombardment of his capital by the British. He was punished after the war by having his dual kingdom split up, with Norway being forcibly hived off to the Swedes by the Treaty of Kiel. However, his cousin Kristian Frederik (1786-1848), who had been acting as regent in Norway, refused to obey the treaty and had himself briefly elected King of Norway until the Swedes invaded it and forced his abdication. He had, anyway, proved to be far too much of a liberal for the post-revolutionary climate. However, he was at least succeeded by another Oldenburg, Karl of Holstein-Gottorp (1748-1818), until the new Swedish dynasty of Bernadotte took over.

Meanwhile, Frederik VI and his German wife had failed to produce a male heir, and two decades after being forced off the throne of Norway his cousin Kristian Frederik succeeded him as King of Denmark. By this time he was a handsome man in his mid-fifties, had outgrown his youthful liberalism and was available to take over Denmark as Kristian VIII. His father had been Prince Frederik, the son of Frederik V and his second wife Juliana of Brunswick-Wolfenbüttel, so his Germanic antecedents were impeccable. He reluctantly continued the administrative reforms of his predecessor and granted some self-government to Iceland, but refused to deliver the expected constitution. His first marriage to his cousin Charlotte of Mecklenburg was a disaster but did provide him with a male heir. However, by the time he was approaching death in his early sixties he was, for whatever reason, fairly convinced that this heir, Frederik, was himself incapable of fathering a successor for he was well into his second marriage. So he instituted the process of scouring Europe for spare Oldenburg descendants to take over.

Meanwhile, the apparently infertile Frederik VII (1808-63) succeeded his father in 1848. He revived the liberal tradition, a hard drinking womanizer, who had a gift for mimicry and knew how to work the crowd, yet was a compulsive liar. However, unlike his father, he did go ahead with a new constitution that ended the absolute rule of the Oldenburgs, and this voluntary surrender of power earned him considerable popularity. Despite having three wives (Wilhelmine, not actually a German princess but an Oldenburg, so genetically almost pure German; Caroline of Mecklenburg; and Countess Danner, a dancer who had been his long-term mistress) he had a reputation for bi-sexuality and none of his relationships produced any offspring.

When he died childless in 1863 it might well have been the end of the Oldenburg dynasty after 400 years, but the screening process begun by his father had identified the ideal replacement, a distant relation in Glücksburg, so all was not lost.

THE SWEDISH AND RUSSIAN CONNECTIONS

Meanwhile, the branch of the Oldenburgs that had looked after the Holstein portion of the inheritance had also had a spectacular late flowering. In 1751, Adolf Frederik of Holstein-Gottorp (1710-71) became the elected King of Sweden, helped by previous marriages between his family and the Swedish royals. As the younger son of Kristian Augustus of Holstein Gottorp (1673-1726) he had been Prince Bishop of Lübeck, ruler of Eutin and had some Vasa blood as well as being an Oldenburg, for he was a direct descendant of Frederik I of Denmark. Two previous kings of Sweden, Karl IX and Karl X, had both chosen Holstein-Gottorp princesses to be their queens, and Duke Frederik IV of Holstein had married the daughter of Charles XI. Besides, there was political pressure from Russia for Sweden to choose a Holstein Oldenburg as king.

This Holstein-Gottorp branch of the Oldenburgs was to hold on, somewhat tenuously, to the throne of Sweden for the next four generations until 1818. Because of the strength of political factions Adolf Frederik remained in a weak position and, apart from occasional attempts to assert his authority, egged on by his aggressive Prussian wife Louisa Ulrika he spent most of his time making snuff boxes. In the end he succumbed to overeating after a particularly gargantuan banquet of lobsters, kippers, champagne and cream buns.

His first cousin meanwhile, Karl Frederik, son of Frederick, his father's elder brother, had become Duke of Holstein-Gottorp and in 1725 was married to Anna, the daughter of Tsar Peter the Great of Russia. The marriage did not last long for Anna died very soon after producing a son, Peter, born in Kiel in 1728, who came under the guardianship of Adolf Frederik until he was fourteen. Up to this time there was no obvious prospect of this boy being an heir to the tsardom, for Peter II had just taken over that role and might be expected to produce his own heirs. Besides, at the time the Holstein-Gottorp family were much more excited about their opportunities in Sweden than the unknown quantity of Russia. Certainly, the young Peter regarded himself as much more a German than a Russian.

However, in 1742, when neither Peter II nor the two empresses that followed him – Anna and Elizabeth – had produced any heirs, suddenly Peter was propelled into the limelight. Somewhat reluctantly, he headed for Russia designated as the next tsar, though his own preference would have been to stay behind and hope, instead, for the more civilized throne of Sweden. He took with him to Russia his obsession with the Prussian style of military training and a love of all things German that was later to prove his undoing.

It was perhaps no more than a coincidence, or a vague memory from the past, that when Elizabeth started looking for a potential bride for her nephew she picked on a relation of her late sister's husband. The sister of King Adolf Frederik of Sweden, Johanna Elizabeth of Holstein-Gottorp, who was a cousin therefore of the tsar-designate, had married Christian August of Anhalt Zerbst, a minor Prussian noble whose income was so low that he had to serve as a professional soldier in the Prussian army. While he was stationed as governor of Stettin in 1729 the couple produced a daughter called Sophie Fredericke. Not only was she half an Oldenburg through her mother but her father's ancestors had married Oldenburgs in two of the previous three generations. Sophie was thus chosen by Elizabeth to be the trainee tsarina and shipped to St Petersburg in 1745 with her name changed to Catherine.

The great unanswerable question about the marriage of Peter III and Catherine is whether their acknowledged son Paul was really Peter's or had been fathered by one of Catherine's early lovers, most probably Saltykov. Peter had certainly been impotent for the first few years of his marriage, and when that problem was solved by a minor operation, he much preferred the bed of his mistress to the one he was supposed to share with Catherine. If the future emperor Paul was Peter's son then Paul was 75 per cent German, the remainder made up of Russian and Lithuanian, but he was certainly both a Romanov and an Oldenburg of the Holstein-Gottorp branch. If, on the other hand, his real father was Saltykov then he was 50 per cent Russian but neither a Romanov nor an Oldenburg except for a few of his mother's Oldenburg genes. Either way, when he became tsar he ceded Holstein to his distant Oldenburg cousins but in return asked for Oldenburg itself and Delmenhorst to become part of Russia.

Of the Russian tsars who followed Paul, whether they were genuinely Romanov and Oldenburg-Holstein Gottorp or just Zerbst and Saltykov, the dynasty was technically Holstein-Gottorp and they deliberately almost all married German princesses, so genetically they were more and more German. The one exception was Alexander III who married Dagmar of Denmark who was, of course, an Oldenburg and therefore herself genetically almost pure German. Thus Pauk was paired with two German princesses, first Wilhelmina of Hesse-Darmstadt, then Sophia Dorothea of Württemberg, then Alexander I with Louisa of Baden, Nicholas I chose Charlotte, a Hohenzollern from Prussia, Alexander II had Marie of Hesse Darmstadt (probably the daughter of her mother's favourite courtier), Alexander III had Dagmar and Nicholas II had Alexandra, also from Hesse Darmstadt. Significantly, all the tsars from Peter III onwards indulged a slavish admiration for Prussian drill movements, uniforms and military tactics.

Meanwhile, in Sweden Adolf Frederik's son Gustav III (1746-92), a half-Hohenzollern with reactionary views, took over in 1771. He wrestled with the restraints of constitutional monarchy and several times tried to restore a degree of absolutism. He resorted to the old trick of distracting the attention of his parliament by starting a war with Russia. He even acquired a small Swedish colony in the West Indies, St Barthelemy, which was given a new capital, Gustavia. He was nevertheless typical of the enlightenment, a major promoter of the arts and a freemason. His marriage to Sophia Magdalena, an Oldenburg princess from Copenhagen, was tempestuous, perhaps because of his dubious sexual orientation. Even his own mother doubted that he was capable of producing offspring, and he had two strong male friendships. He was eventually murdered in the Stockholm opera house by a group of nobles dissatisfied with his policies.

His son Gustav IV Adolf (1778-1837) took over as a teenager, but there were doubts about his paternity, which in some circles was attributed to a Baron Munck. His rule proved reactionary and disastrously inept. To make matters worse Sweden suffered from a series of bad harvests in 1788-9. In 1805, he tried to distract attention by waging a totally ineffective war against Napoleon which led to Finland passing from Swedish to Russian control and Pomerania to the French, so he was compelled to abdicate in 1809 after a military coup; even his children by his wife Frederika of Baden were also excluded from the throne. Having earlier been somewhat prim and fanatically religious – he had rejected a Russian princess as his bride because she would not convert to Lutheranism – in later life his sexual demands became too much for Frederika and they divorced in 1812. He replaced her with a mistress but died alone in a Swiss hotel nearly thirty years after his abdication.

His successor Karl XIII (1748-1818) was his scheming and ambitious uncle who turned out to be the last of the line. Nearly sixty when he came to the throne, he had served successfully as an admiral, but by this time was prematurely decrepit after a lifetime of self-indulgence. He had married a cousin from Holstein-Gottorp but they had no children. She had an affair with Count von Fersen, while Karl simultaneously had one with Fersen's cousin Augusta. With the blessing of the allies, he invaded Norway and took over its crown from the Danish Oldenburgs, but he made little other effort and left the government to his designated successor the French Marshal Bernadotte. After five years on the throne he died, thus ending the dynasty's connection with Sweden.

DENMARK AND NORWAY

When the main Oldenburg line in Denmark ran out of immediate heirs in 1863 it might well have been the end of the dyasty, but Kristian VIII had foreseen his son's infertility and had initiated a search for a male heir in the wider family. This threw up another Kristian IX (1818-1906), son of the Duke of the ridiculously four-barrelled Schleswig-Holstein-Sonderburg-Glücksburg, who on his mother's side was a great grandson of Frederik V.

Born in Gottorp to this fairly impoverished branch of the family he had trained at the Copenhagen military academy and was selected as the heir as early as 1847 when it became clear that his predecessor was unlikely to produce one of his own. Ironically, just as the Schleswig-Holstein, still a quintessentially German branch of the Oldenburgs, was about to take over Denmark the German population of Schleswig-Holstein was wanting rid of a family that they now regarded as Danish and rebelled against their Danish overlords in 1862 asking Prussia for help. Kristian took some part in the subsequent disastrously one-sided war against Prussia, which ended with Schleswig passing into the hands of Bismarck. In his youth he had tried to woo the future Queen Victoria, but failed there and settled instead for Louise of Hesse-Kassel. In 1874, Kristian IX was the first Danish king to visit his province of Iceland and granted it semi-independent status.

Of Kristian's children two became kings and two became empresses. Frederik was to succeed him in Denmark, while George was chosen in 1863 to be king of Greece as Georgios I (1845-1913) after the deposition of his Bavarian predecessor. Of Kristian's daughters Alexandra became the wife of the future Edward VII of Great Britain and Dagmar became the Tsarina Maria when she married Alexander III of Russia, so that she was the mother of Nicholas II. Hence the extraordinary likeness of the two first cousins, George V of Britain and Tsar Nicholas II, who were both half Oldenburgs on their mothers' side.

Frederik VIII of Denmark (1843-1912) was in his sixties when he came to the throne in 1906 and had fought in the disastrous war of 1863 against the Prussians. For once in the history of this dynasty Frederik married neither a German princess nor a fellow Oldenburg but Louisa of Sweden, a descendant of the French Marshal Bernadotte. As in the previous generation, two of Frederik's sons became kings: Kristian in Denmark and Karl in Norway after the break up of the Swedish-Norwegian union in 1905.

Kristian X (1870-1947) was notable for defying the German invaders by riding through the streets on horseback till they imprisoned him in 1943. Soon afterwards, he granted full independence to Iceland. He married Alexandra of Mecklenburg-Schwerin in the Oldenburg tradition, but it did not affect his political judgement.

His younger brother Karl had been elected as Haakon VII (1872-1957) in 1905. He had graduated bottom in the Copenhagen naval academy but he had other significant advantages, such as some genes inherited from medieval Norwegian kings, a healthy son and an aunt/mother-in-law who was the Queen of Great Britain, for he had married his cousin Princess Maud, the daughter of Edward VII and Alexandra. Like his brother, he had to suffer the rigours of German conquest in 1940 and played a role in the military resistance.

The sons of these two both succeeded their fathers, Frederik IX (1899-1972) in Denmark and Olaf V (1903-91) in Norway. Frederik, who had served as a naval officer, took part in the resistance to Germany and later became a brilliant racing yachtsman. He married Ingrid of Sweden. When he died in 1972 the crown passed to his daughter Margrethe II (1940-), an archaeologist married to a Frenchman, Henri de Laborde de Monpezot. So over the past two generations the Germanic gene content has decreased rapidly.

Olaf of Norway similarly helped lead the resistance to the Germans and was chief of staff. He married Martha of Sweden so here too the Oldenburgs were ending their pursuit of German princesses, perhaps partly because as a species they were close to extinct. He was succeeded by his son Harald V (1937-) who forced his family to let him marry a commoner, a Norwegian called Sonja who became his queen. The heir to their throne is Haakon. As the twenty-first century dawned, the Oldenburg-Glücksburg dynasty in both Denmark and Norway had adapted sensibly to changing times and looked set to survive.

THE GREEK INTERLUDE

The transplanting of the Oldenburgs to Greece was much less successful. George of Oldenburg (1845-1913) had served in the Danish navy and was elected King of the Hellenes by the Greek national assembly in 1863 when he was only seventeen. His fifty-year reign saw the expansion of Greek power round Thessaly and Epirus, the Ionian Islands transferred from Britain to Greece but Crete still under Turkish rule. The country became embroiled in the Balkan War of 1912 and George was assassinated in Salonika the year after. He had married a Romanov princess, Grand Duchess Olga, niece of Tsar Alexander II, in 1867, and their son Constantine was born soon afterwards. George was, in his time, extremely well connected since one of his sisters, Alexandra, was Queen of Britain and the other the Tsarina Maria of Russia.

Constantine I (1868-1923) had an erratic career. He successfully helped create the first modern Olympic Games in 1896. He had fought not very successfully in the Turkish war of 1897, but had more success as a commander in the Balkan war of 1912 where Greece made significant gains. Despite pressure from both sides, particularly Germany, for like a true Oldenburg he had married Sophie, the sister of Kaiser Wilhelm, he insisted on keeping Greece out of the First World War, but in 1917 the pro-ally government led by Venizelos demanded that he abdicate in favour of his son Alexander. Three years later, he was restored by a plebiscite, but his comeback barely lasted two years and once more he had to abdicate, this time in favour of his younger son George (Alexander had died from a monkey bite), because of the country's poor performance during the Turkish War of 1922.

Meanwhile, his younger brother Andrew (1882-1944), who like him was half Oldenburg and half Romanov, had a spasmodic military career and took much of the blame, perhaps undeservedly, for the fiascos of the war in Asia Minor. True to tradition he had married a German princess, the saintly Alice of Battenberg, and after four daughters they produced Prince Philip (1921-) who was later to become the consort of Queen Elizabeth II. Philip was thus the fifth Oldenburg to become a consort of a British monarch. It was because of his Oldenburg genes and their Russian connection that his DNA was important in the identification of the remains of Nicholas II and his family. All four of Philip's sisters married German aristocrats. His mother, who was a great granddaughter of Queen Victoria, suffered a nervous breakdown, and his father lived with his mistress, Countess Andrée de la Bigne, on a boat in the south of France.

George II (1890-1947) had an even more erratic career than his father, for he was deposed within a year by a military junta, then restored again by plebiscite in 1935 working alongside the right-wing prime minister Metaxas. They managed to halt the Italian invasion of Greece in 1940 but not the German one that followed. George retreated first to Crete and then to exile in Britain. He was restored a second time in 1946 but died soon afterwards. Like a typical Oldenburg, he had married a German princess, the Hohenzollern Elizabeth of Romania, but they had no children and later divorced, so that he spent his last days with his mistress in Belgravia.

George was succeeded by his younger brother Paul (1901-64) who had been born in Athens and trained as a naval cadet. He shared the up-and-down careers of his father and brother, serving in the Greek navy during the 1922 Turkish war and as a staff officer in the Albanian campaign. Despite perhaps unfair rumours of bisexuality he ill-advisedly maintained the old Oldenburg habit of marrying a German princess, Frederika of Brunswick-Hanover, which made life difficult during the war. However, he managed seventeen years on the throne without succumbing to a military coup and handed the throne over to his son Constantine in relatively good order.

Constantine II (1940-) was less fortunate. Within three years of his succession he was faced by a right-wing military junta, the Colonels, and his only attempt to oust them ended in failure. So he was deposed in 1973 and a year later the monarchy in Greece was abolished. He had married another Oldenburg, Anne-Marie of Denmark, so their son Paul (1967-) is the theoretical heir with no immediate prospects of restoration. Their daughter Sophia married Juan Carlos, the Bourbon, who was, against all the odds, restored to the throne of Spain after the death of Franco.

CHAPTER 2

THE MATCHMAKERS OF HABICHTSBURG

In the year 1020, a minor German landowner called Radbot of Klettgau, whose brother was the bishop of Strasbourg, began building a white tower on the top of Wulpelsberg, a hill rising some 1,500 feet above sea level by the River Reuss just a few miles south of the modern German frontier in Switzerland. Nearby is the Aare River, which runs into the Rhine, and 2 miles downhill is the town of Brugg. Zurich is just 20 miles to the south-east. Because of its position the new castle was named the Castle of the Hawk, or Habichtsburg, later shortened to Habsburg.

This relatively modest castle has survived nearly 1,000 years and part of it is now used as a restaurant. The family that built it was to prosper extraordinarily, so that by the mid-sixteenth century it ruled a vast empire from the Danube to Peru. Later, as it neared its end, it was to play a major part in causing the Armageddon of 1914-18.

THE ROAD TO VIENNA

Bella gerunt alii, tu felix Austria nube
Others wage war, you lucky Austria marry

The early growth of the Habsburgs was like that of many other great dynasties: initially very slow. They gradually increased their holdings in the Aargau and took in towns like Muri, where Radbot had founded a famous monastery that still survives, and Zurich itself. Radbot's son Werner the Pious (1025-96) was followed by Otto II who fought for the emperor against the Turks but was murdered on his return in 1111. These first masters of Habsburg made themselves rich by exploiting the tolls on the Alpine passes and eventually achieved the rank of count for services to the emperor. Otto's grandson Albrecht the Rich (*d.*1199) held most of what is now German-speaking Switzerland as well as parts of Alsace.

It was quarter of a millennium after the family's foundation when one of the family, Rudolf (1218-1291), was unexpectedly elected as a stop-gap emperor in 1273 – partly because he was over fifty and not expected to last for long, partly because he was from one of the less powerful families and expected to be weak. He had made a good marriage to Gertrude of Hohenburg in what became a great Habsburg tradition of marrying heiresses, and used this as an excuse to seize considerable extra territories in Schwabia thus hugely increasing the Habsburg inheritance. Despite his age Rudolf unexpectedly managed a full seventeen years on the imperial throne, and at the remarkable age of seventy-three he defeated King Ottakar of Bohemia to take over Austria with its capital Vienna, an area that was to be at the heart of the family's fortunes for the next seven centuries. He at the same time persecuted the Jews, but mainly as a means of extorting money to pay for his campaigns. Meanwhile, he honed his image as a priest king, wandering the streets at night to feed the poor, ostentatiously handing over his horse to a priest who was carrying communion fare. It was excellent long-term public relations, even if Dante was not impressed, for he depicts Rudolf sitting at the gates of Purgatory, but it was to prove a false dawn. There was still strong prejudice against the imperial crown becoming hereditary in one family, and the Habsburgs were by no means the most powerful candidate dynasty.

There was a gap of six years before Rudolf's son, the one-eyed Albert/ Albrecht (1250 -1308), was elected emperor, and not until he had defeated and killed in battle his predecessor Adolf of Nassau. He had also driven his own younger brother, Rudolf, out of his possessions, thus reuiniting the now huge Habsburg inheritance that his father had divided between his two sons. Albrecht was less charismatic and is mainly remembered, perhaps unfairly, as the persecutor of William Tell, the legendary marksman of Altdorf. However, he did also make an effort to better the conditions of the serfs and desisted from the persecution of Jews. The most valuable contribution he made for the future of the dynasty was to become a martyr by being murdered. The guilty party was his nephew Johann the Parricide, son of the younger brother whom he had deprived of his inheritance, and it is one of the few examples of sibling rivalry in the Habsburg dynasty and an event used as an example to future members of the family to subordinate personal ambition to the overall success of the dynasty. To drive the point home, a thousand of Johann's supporters were massacred.

Success, however, eluded Albrecht's son Frederick the Fair (1289-1330) who despite great fame as a flower of chivalry failed in his efforts to become the next emperor and had to share even the Habsburg territories with his brothers, one of whom was the fun-loving Otto the Merry (1301-39).

After this there was a further gap of 100 years before the Habsburgs turned themselves into a genuine imperial dynasty. Meanwhile, they followed the German habit of splitting the inheritance between their sons, for instance Count Rudolf III had four brothers, all of whom successively had shares of the patrimony. The Habsburgs were, however, nothing if not determined and far-sighted. Typical of this was the energetic and highly intelligent Rudolf IV the Founder (1339-65), the first Habsburg duke born in Austria, who worked assiduously on the credentials of the dynasty though he died childless in his mid-twenties. He extended Vienna's Cathedral of St Stephan and founded Vienna University. More significantly, he had documents forged that gave the Habsburg counts the status of Electors in the Holy Roman Empire and at the same time invented the title of archduke to position the family as ahead of its peers. He also provided the dynasty with a family tree that went back to Noah and all the great heroes of the ancient world. Despite adding the Tyrol to the Habsburg domains he suffered from the squabbles of his three brothers who all had to be given their share of the inheritance.

Two decades later, the Habsburgs produced their second martyr; Rudolf's youngest brother Leopold XIII, Duke of Austria (1351-86) was killed fighting the Swiss at Sempach near Brugg. It was not a very glorious battle but it was enough for the Habsburgs to build a legend of heroism and self-sacrifice, which was exalted for them in the family shrine of Königsfelden. The theme of the family was that it would deserve imperial rank by superior virtue and holiness, so all young Habsburgs were taught to believe this. As Wheatcroft put it, 'This inner resilience was the key to their survival in the centuries that followed... the Habsburg myth of an imperial destiny.'

In 1438, after a gap of four generations the dynasty at last got its reward when Albert/Albrecht Duke of Austria was elected Holy Roman Emperor as Albert II (1397-1439). This tall, soldierly man had fought the Czechs and Turks, but, after only a year on the throne, he died in his early forties from dysentery contracted while campaigning near Buda. He had, however, embarked on the policy of predatory marriage, which was to be a characteristic of the dynasty, and in 1422 he chose the daughter of the Emperor Sigismund, a match that helped him secure the imperial throne. She also brought him the crowns of Bohemia and Hungary, from whose royal dynasty she was descended, as well as claims to Slovenia, which were to lead to Austria's later dangerous inroads into the Balkans. He left two daughters and an unborn son, Ladislas the Posthumous, who was instantly made head of the House of Habsburg and later inherited the thrones of Hungary and Croatia, but obviously he could not be elected emperor.

Though there was still no acceptance of the hereditary principle for the Empire, at least the preferred candidate was another Habsburg, a cousin of Albert's, Frederick of Styria (1415-93), who also held Carinthia and

Carniola but was perceived as fairly weak: ideal material so far as the Electors were concerned. Thus in 1440, he was elected King Frederick IV of Germany and then crowned in Rome, the last emperor to be so, as Emperor Frederick III (just to make matters even more confusing he was Duke Frederick V of Austria) and was to reign for a remarkable fifty years, long enough at last to establish the Habsburgs as the automatic choice for the imperial throne. This remarkable man's father was Ernest the Iron, self-styled Archduke of Styria (1377-1424), son of the martyr Leopold III, and his mother was the legendary Polish princess Cymburgis who could allegedly crack nuts between her fingers and had the fat pendulous lower lip which became a genetic characteristic of the dynasty.

Despite his impressive parentage Frederick, born in Innsbruck, was unathletic and unwarlike, contributing little to the expansion of the Empire. In fact, for a time after 1462 he even lost Vienna to his aggressive younger brother Albert, always a thorn in his side. He could not defeat him in battle but outwitted him by holding his nephew, the young Ladislaus the Posthumous, theoretical head of the family, as his prisoner. He was chronically short of money and was referred to as 'a collector of horse droppings'. Yet he transformed the dynasty by organising two remarkable weddings. The first was his own to Eleanor of Portugal, a princess nearly twenty years younger than himself, whose dowry was sufficient to remove his financial worries for at least a reasonable period even though in the short term she brought no extra territory. The second, even more spectacular, was of his son Maximilian to Mary the heiress of Burgundy in 1477. This was to lead to the extraordinary increase in Habsburg influence that saw them not only encircle Germany itself but also potentially France. Frederick thus epitomised the adage '*Tu felix Austria nube*', the idea that the Habsburgs did not need to fight but would expand their empire by marriage. He was also obsessed with image and reputedly devised the cleverly acronymic slogan A.E.I.O.U. (*Alles edreich ist Österreich Untertan* or *Austriae est imperare orbi universo*) and he founded the Knights of St George, which came to symbolise the spiritual aspirations of the Habsburg dynasty as one that meant to give more than it took. He was close to eighty when he died in agony after his septic leg had been amputated, and his personal motto was 'happiness is to forget what you cannot recover'.

Frederick's other great achievement was to be emperor for so long that by the time of his death the Electors had almost forgotten what it was like to hold a diet (or electoral meeting) and so he achieved what no previous Habsburg had managed: he arranged for his own eldest son, Maximilian, to succeed him; thus at last re-establishing the habit, if not the principle, of hereditary rule of the Empire.

THE ROAD TO MADRID

The Emperor Maximilian (1459-1519), who was ethnically half Portuguese, became joint ruler with his father for the last decade of Frederick's life and then took over sole control on his death in 1508. He was to continue his father's empire building using the same technique: well thought-out weddings. He had been trained from childhood to be the new German Hercules, the last knight of chivalry with a mission to unite Europe against the Infidel. His reign laid the foundations for the dynasty's massive expansion. By himself marrying the Valois heiress of Burgundy he acquired the Netherlands for his dynasty, even though after his wife's early death in 1482 he ceded most of Burgundy itself to the French. A multi-lingual workaholic, he reorganised Germany itself and imitated his father by setting in train a further series of marriages that would give his family a stranglehold over Europe. His stroke of genius was to arrange the marriage of his eldest son Philip, who had been made Duke of Burgundy, to Juana, the daughter of Ferdinand and Isabella of Spain, at the same time organising his daughter Margaret's wedding to Juan of Aragon, in case the first plan failed. Thus within a few years the Habsburgs absorbed three major dynasties, the Valois of Burgundy and the two great Spanish kingdoms of Castile and Aragon.

With his own second marriage to Bianca Sforza of Milan he also claimed the overlordship of Milan, much to the disgust of the French, so that he caused a series of wars against the French in Italy. In addition, he organised the double marriage of two of his grandchildren into the Hungarian and Bohemian royal dynasty so that those two areas would come within the Habsburg portfolio as they finally did in 1526. Though not a great war leader he did introduce a new breed of professional soldier, the Landsknechts, who became the finest mercenaries of the era, and he also brought in a fashionable and extravagant new fashion in armour, which imitated the latest trends in male clothing. His one great military failure was his comprehensive defeat by the Swiss at Dornach in 1499, resulting in the Habsburgs losing the homeland from which they had sprung, but to make up for it he bought control of the Tyrol from his cousin Sigismund.

At the same time he employed the finest artists and writers of the day to create awe-inspiring propaganda for the dynasty so that his empire not only became more powerful, but also looked the part. One of his triumphal engravings was the largest ever undertaken, requiring ninety sheets of paper. Yet he still had time to father eleven bastards.

There was one other setback. Maximilian's eldest son Philip the Handsome of Burgundy, a philandering playboy with little obvious aptitude for power, died before him, of typhoid, having just six months earlier become King of Castile after the death of his mother-in-law Isabel in 1504. His widow, the allegedly Mad Juana, the heiress of Spain, became a neurotic recluse, according to the propaganda of the day constantly reopening her husband's coffin.

Thus when Maximilian died the imperial crown was to skip a generation to his young grandson Charles (1500-58) who was only nineteen, born in Ghent and brought up mainly in Burgundy. His father Philip had died when he was only six, so he inherited the rump of Burgundy at that stage. At this point, his distraught mother Juana – technically Queen of Castile – had been locked up by her father Ferdinand so that he could continue ruling Spain without having to refer to a supposedly unstable daughter. So Castile was kept tightly within the family, and when Ferdinand himself died in 1516 young Charles treated his mother just as badly as her father had done and for the same reason: power without interference. He visited her a couple of times in her cell but did nothing to improve her wretched conditions despite the fact that she lived for another four decades. So the entire Spanish Empire, which included Naples, Sicily and most of the newly-discovered American colonies, passed to Charles/Karl/Carlos at the age of sixteen. Three years after that when Maximilian, his other grandfather, died he took over Austria and the Holy Roman Empire after a perfunctory election process in which King François of France had put himself forward as a rogue candidate. Thus Charles became, without question, the most powerful monarch in the western world.

Charles V had been brought up as a French speaker, very much in the spirit of Burgundy where the Order of the Golden Fleece based at Dijon formed his character as the ideal serving knight. Illogically his younger brother Ferdinand, who had been born in Aragon and spoke Spanish, was sent to Austria to be his deputy there. The two brothers did not meet until they were in their teens and could hardly communicate as they had been brought up to speak different languages.

Despite, or perhaps because, of his massive inheritance at such an early age, Charles was not content. He may have inherited a little of his mother's bipolar tendencies and the Habsburg genes were also that way inclined. In addition, he was epileptic and his enlarged lower jaw, inherited from the Habsburg side, made it hard for him to chew, so he suffered frequently from indigestion and never ate in public. Furthermore, in later life he suffered from gout or arthritis. Even before that he was physically ungainly, uncharismatic, dull but conscientious and an emperor who preferred backroom planning to campaigning on the battlefield. Yet having inherited huge power he was ambitious for more and realized that even to hold his inheritance together he needed to keep up the momentum of aggression. The crushing of Montezuma and the Aztecs of Mexico by Cortes from his base in Cuba within a year of his accession gave him the dream that he had a divine mission to rule the world and eliminate paganism. The areas of Panama, Nicaragua and Venezuela soon followed, and when the remnants of Magellan's fleet struggled back home in 1522 it proved that Spain could circle the world. Charles was the new Hercules whose pillars (Gibraltar and its opposite number across the strait) decorated the new pieces of eight, now renamed in Flemish as thalers or dollars.

Such understandable delusions of grandeur were soon offset by awkward realities. He had to put down rebellions in Ghent, the city of his birth, and in Spain. Then he was faced by the wave of Protestant heresy that had begun to sweep across Germany since Luther had nailed his ninety-five theses to the door at Wittenberg in 1517. The Inquisition was brought into the Netherlands from Spain three years after his accession and the first two heretics burned in 1523 with an estimated 30,000 executions during the rest of his reign. It was not that Charles was deliberately cruel, even in what he regarded as a just cause, but he failed to restrain his henchmen and virtually ignored the genocide which his subjects inflicted in the Americas.

He also had to continue the war with France begun by his father. There was not just the existing quarrel over who should control Italy, but the French were, for the first time, hemmed in on three sides by a single superpower. Burgundy was a particularly sensitive issue. Thus Charles pursued an expensive vendetta against King François, eventually defeating and capturing him at the battle of Pavia with the help of the Constable of France whom he had lured into changing sides but then cheated of his promised reward. Yet he was cheated in his turn by François who reneged on all the promises he had made whilst a prisoner. Two years later, in 1527, Charles sacked the city of Rome more ruthlessly than the pagan Goths. For this he won another crown: that of Italy.

He also devoted much time to the fruitless suppression of the German Protestants and to the defence of Vienna from the threat of capture by the Turks. Cynically, however, he and his brother had grabbed their share of Hungary after its last king had been overwhelmed by the Turks at Mohacz in 1526. The conquest of Mexico in the first year of his reign was followed by that of Peru in 1531; yet, despite all the treasure amassed, he was still overstretching the primitive finances of his enormous empire. Making war on several fronts at the same time meant huge expenditure on mercenaries and equipment.

In the gaps between his other wars, as in 1535, he did pursue his vision of a crusade by attacking and capturing Tunis from the Muslims but he still spent more time fighting Protestants. In 1547, his army decisively defeated the Protestant rebels in Germany at Mühlberg, but the bold image of him by Titian showing him on a charger was a propaganda exercise, for by this time he was so arthritic that he had to be carried on a litter. In the end, his persecution of Protestants both in Germany and the Netherlands served only to make them more fanatical and left sectarian divisions that were to last for centuries.

Meanwhile, like a good Habsburg, Charles had married the heiress of Portugal, his cousin Isabella, and spent his honeymoon in the Alhambra at Granada where he built a magnificent new palace. The marriage produced only the one son, Philip, who survived to adulthood, but Charles had several mistresses, including the Bavarian singer Barbara Blomberg who gave birth in 1547 to his best-known bastard the charismatic Don John Austria (1547-78). His best-known bastard daughter was Margaret of Parma (1522-86) who later served as his regent of the Netherlands.

By his early fifties Charles was beginning to sink into depression, perhaps exhausted by over thirty years of supreme stress but certainly plagued by crippling gout and chronic dyspepsia, so he began a slow process of abdication, which led to the division of his empire into two halves, with the huge Spanish portion going to his son Philip while Austria and the Holy Roman Empire went to his brother Ferdinand. It was another three years before he managed to shed all his duties; yet when he at last retired to the monastery of Yuste in Estremadura this remarkable man was confined to a wheelchair and lasted barely a year. He left his heirs a deficit of thirty-six million ducats.

SPLIT BETWEEEN TWO CAPITALS

Philip or Felipe II (1527-98), born in Valladolid, was the only surviving son of Charles V and his Portuguese queen Isabella. He was just under thirty when he became the King of Spain in 1556 and, like the rest of the Habsburg family, he was to attempt to use marriage to extend and consolidate his empire. His first marriage to Mary of Portugal ended with her early death after producing the ill-fated and unstable Don Carlos. His second marriage, two years before he took over Spain, was much more politically motivated, for it was to Queen Mary of England and if she had been fertile could have brought England into the Habsburg Empire. But Mary was eleven years older than Philip, whose interest in her was spasmodic, and no heir was forthcoming, so England did not, after all, become a Habsburg appendage after her death.

Ethnically speaking, Philip, though a Habsburg, was primarily Portuguese and Spanish with only a small portion of Germanic genes left. He inherited his father's religious zeal with even greater fanaticism. Like Charles he appeared to deplore violence, yet condoned it on a massive scale.

However, he was much less confident than his father, less decisive, reluctant to start wars or initiate plans for conquest, a martyrish workaholic who was prone to get bogged down in detail and reluctant to delegate. In the words of one ambassador, 'he pays less attention to augmenting his own greatness than to hindering that of others.' Whereas his father had been unpopular in Spain for promoting Flemings, Philip was just as unpopular in Aragon for favouring Castillians.

Philip's half-brother Don John of Austria was a totally different character, a charismatic womanizer and a natural leader. The son of Charles V's Bavarian mistress, he was acknowledged by Philip but never treated as royal. He won the dramatic naval victory of Lepanto against the Turks in 1571 at the age of twenty-four but, sadly, died of typhus in his early thirties.

Meanwhile, Philip was the new Apollo, rather than Hercules, and rebuilt the Temple of Solomon in the Escorial, which was to house 6,000 saintly relics, a clutch of soft-porn Titians and the tiny study where the workaholic king poured over every detail of his empire. In his passionate drive to rid the world of heretics he exhausted his resources in a wasteful effort to suppress the Dutch Protestants, at one point letting his commander condemn the entire population to death. He began the ethnic cleansing of the Muslims in Spain and indulged in a fruitless attempt to conquer England after his second wife's death in 1558. He drained his already over-stretched treasury to pay for wars that achieved very little, his fleet was badly mauled by Drake and the Protestants in Holland survived his worst efforts. The same could not be said of the millions of aboriginal inhabitants of his colonies in South America and the West Indies, a huge proportion of whom died from over-work or European infectious diseases.

By the time Queen Mary died Philip's only surviving son, Don Carlos, was showing signs of severe instability and had sadistic tendencies: he liked watching young girls being whipped it was rumoured. So that most Catholic of kings decided that the interests of the dynasty came first, and despite papal disapproval married his son's fiancée Elizabeth de Valois who was eighteen years his junior. He helped nurse her through smallpox and numerous pregnancies, but the result was a series of miscarriages or infant deaths. His fourth wife was the woman who had taken over the role of his son's fiancée, Anna of Austria, a Habsburg cousin, so the tendency for inbreeding intensified. They had five children but it was only the fourth of their sons who was strong enough to outlive his father. This was the future Philip III.

By the time of his death the size of Philip II's empire had increased to some two billion acres, for he had acquired Chile in 1554 and had added the crown of Portugal and its colonies, including Brazil, to his portfolio in 1580.

Felipe III (1578-1621) became King of Spain, Portugal and Naples at the age of twenty. Not only was he a Habsburg on both sides but, unlike his predecessor, he had more German genes than Spanish Philip, and was 'a pallid and anonymous creature' according to Elliot who inherited all of his father's religious fervour and financial extravagance, so that he allowed Spain to slide further into economic and agricultural decline. Unlike his father, he was far from industrious, and Wedgewood describes him as 'an undistinguished and insignificant man'. He maintained the Habsburg habit of either marrying a prominent heiress or, if there was none available, then another Habsburg, so the genes were not diluted – a very mixed blessing. His choice was Margaret of Austria who died shortly before him having produced the requisite heir, who was thus back up to an 80 per cent quota of Germanic genes.

BACK IN VIENNA

Meanwhile, the Habsburgs back in Austria were also handicapped by their religious fervour. Ferdinand I (1503-64) had taken over from his brother Charles V as emperor in 1558 and though a staunch Catholic had been somewhat more conciliatory than Charles to the German Protestants, recognising that violent suppression might never bring peace. He was already a well-experienced ruler having run the eastern half of the empire as Archduke of Austria for over four decades. This partially explains the fact that when his ailing brother abdicated Ferdinand refused to let him pass the double empire of Spain and Austria over to his own son Philip, but insisted instead that he and his son should inherit the eastern half.

By his marriage too he had very much strengthened his position for he chose Anne of Bohemia and Hungary who bore him fifteen children. When her brother the King of Hungary and Bohemia was defeated and killed by the Turks at Mohacz Ferdinand became king as successor of his brother-in-law, taking in all of both the kingdoms, including Croatia that had not been surrendered to the Turks. Thus he committed the empire to a multi-ethnic future and an ultimately vulnerable presence in the febrile Balkans. His worst crisis came with the two attacks by the Turks on Vienna itself in 1529 and 1533. He kept out of harm's way in Prague but his armies managed to repel the attacks. After all that his six years as emperor were something of an anticlimax.

His son Maximilian II (1527-76) was already in his late thirties when he took over and an experienced administrator who had fought in several campaigns for his uncle Charles V. He was much more tolerant of Protestants, in fact he almost became one himself but had to continue repositioning the Habsburgs as the bastion of Catholicism just as did his cousin Philip II of Spain. He married Philip's aunt, Maria of Spain, a daughter of Charles V, with whom he had sixteen children, including two emperors and his daughter Anne who became Philip II's fourth wife and the mother of the next Spanish king. It was all beginning to verge on the incestuous. The atmosphere at Graz where the Habsburg children were raised was cold, Jesuitical and ascetic. The place where they were eventually buried the Kapuzinergruft in Vienna became another national shrine.

Maximilian's eldest son Rudolf II (1552-1612) who took over as emperor in 1576 had been educated in Spain and was similarly tolerant of Protestants but did not have the will to implement his views and simply allowed the religious crisis to deepen. On the one hand he was a generous patron of the arts and did much to develop Prague as a cultural centre, but he also dabbled extensively in the occult. He mounted a fairly ineffective crusade against the Turks, the backlash from which led to a revolt in Hungary, and his Albanian general Georgio Basta was guilty of genocide amongst the Magyars of Transylvania. Rudolf was probably bisexual, allegedly having a series of affairs with members of both sexes, and certainly refused to marry even for the sake of the dynasty. Latterly he became such a recluse and so ineffective as a ruler that there was a demand for his brother Matthias to take over the real power. Matthias staged a military coup that effectively dethroned him shortly before his death.

When Rudolf died at the age of sixty in 1612 his much abler brother Matthias (1557-1619) took over the title as well as the duties but was by this time already in his late fifties. To the annoyance of some of the Catholic princes, he continued the policy of conciliating the Protestants. He had married a cousin, Ann of Austria, and they had no children, so this meant that two emperors in a row had produced no direct heir.

This turned out to be very unfortunate, for the imperial crown now went to a cousin Ferdinand of Styria (1578-1637), a product of the Jesuit regime at Graz. As Archduke of Styria before his elevation he had persecuted the Protestants there quite successfully and imagined that he could follow the same tactic throughout the empire. By insisting that his territories, particularly Bohemia, should be cleansed of heretics he precipitated a series of rebellions, which in turn led to one of the most unpleasant civil wars in world history. Thus the reign of this dangerous fanatic coincides with the first eighteen years of the Thirty Years' War, which was made even worse by the fact that various neighbouring countries chose to join in. The interference, particularly of Sweden and France, led to massive consequential suffering. The war was not just long but devastatingly brutal for civilians as well as soldiers and it achieved very little. As a man, Ferdinand was described by Wedgewood as 'small, cheerful, a good family man, fond of hunting, kind to the poor so long as they were good Catholics, but utterly ruthless in every other way'.

Ferdinand had married a good Bavarian princess, Maria Anna, and they had seven children. His son and successor Ferdinand III (1608-57) was just under thirty when he took over in 1637 and eminently more sensible than his father. Though himself an experienced soldier who led the defeat of the Swedes at Nordlingen, he had grasped the futility of the war, which had begun to run out of energy by this time, but it still took nine years of diplomatic wrangling to arrive at a proper peace. However, Ferdinand did do much to end the religious squabbling that had split the empire, and he created space for himself to spend time on his music, at which he was very proficient, and to patronise most other art forms. He had three wives, the first one his first cousin Maria of Spain with whom he had six children, the second with his second cousin and the third with an Italian.

BACK IN MADRID

Ferdinand was three years younger than his cousin Philip or Felipe IV of Spain (1605-65) who had succeeded his father in 1621 when he was fifteen. In a strangely incestuous dynastic partnership, Ferdinand had married Felipe's sister Maria Anna of Spain and their daughter Mariana married Felipe, so that she was his aunt and cousin as well as wife. It is quite possible that it was this repetition of inbreeding that presaged the end of the Spanish Habsburgs. Unlike Ferdinand, King Felipe did little to stabilise the Habsburg dominions under his control. While more intelligent than his father, as Elliot puts it 'he shared his absence of character'. As the 'Planet King' he patronised artists like Velasquez and Zurburan, but he left affairs of state to his chief minister Olivarez and presided over a rapid decline in Spanish power, both territorial and economic. With one sister married to Louis XIII of France and another to the new Holy Roman Emperor he should not have been short of allies, but in 1640 he lost Portugal and its colonies to a group of rebels, in 1648 he lost the Netherlands and in 1659 he lost the Flanders fortresses.

Now came the time for the Habsburgs to be hoist by their own petard. For two centuries they had used marriage as a means of enhancing their dynastic power. But there must always come a time with such a strategy when the result of marrying foreign heirs and heiresses is not to gain territory but to lose it. This was now about to happen to the Spanish Habsburgs. None of Felipe's children by his first wife Elizabeth de Bourbon survived and his only surviving son, Carlos, was born to him and his much younger second wife

Mariana of Austria in 1661 when he was in his late fifties. Not only was this boy still only four when his father died, but it was rapidly evident that he was mentally and physically retarded. Should he prove incapable of ruling and of producing children of his own then this meant that the Habsburg Spanish inheritance would pass to Felipe's sister Anne of Austria who had contracted the apparently advantageous hand of Louis XIII of France. This meant that instead of possibly gaining France the Habsburgs could lose Spain to the French. And despite a protracted war that, in the end, was what happened.

VIENNA

Meanwhile, the Emperor Ferdinand had died eight years before his Spanish cousin and son-in-law. He was succeeded in 1658 by his second son Leopold the Great (1640-1705) who was King Felipe's nephew and who was half a Spanish Habsburg. Like so many second sons in dynasties Leopold had been educated to play a junior role, but his elder brother died unexpectedly of smallpox just before his father, and so the short, ungainly, sickly, awkward Leopold, with his exaggerated version of the Habsburg lower jaw, was thrust suddenly on to the imperial throne at the age of eighteen. To compound his virtually incestuous relationship with the Spanish Habsburgs, Leopold had as his first wife Felipe's daughter, the blonde Maria Theresa who was thus his niece and cousin as well as his wife. Perhaps luckily, there were no children from this marriage, and it was not till he acquired his third wife, the Dusseldorf-born Eleonore of Neuburg, that he produced his heirs, Joseph and Charles.

Despite his aloofness and lack of physical presence, Leopold, by hard work and longevity, made a real success of his reign, hence the addition of Great to his name, though probably he started that fashion himself just to keep up with his rival Louis XIV who did the same. Though very much a desk-bound commander-in-chief he was more or less permanently at war during a reign that lasted nearly fifty years, fighting the Ottoman Turks for control of the Danube, using Polish help to save Vienna from capture in 1683, fighting alongside William of Orange and later Marlborough against Louis XIV who was, of course, also his cousin, to stop the Habsburgs losing Spain to the Bourbons, a task which ultimately failed.

MADRID

The first four decades of Leopold's reign matched fairly closely the lifespan of his unfortunate Spanish cousin Carlos II (1661-1700) who took over the crown of Spain in 1665 at the age of only four. Not only was he already showing signs of instability but, perhaps as a result of inbreeding, he had such an extreme version of the Habsburg protruding jaw that he could not chew his food (mandibular prognathism). He also was possibly epileptic and suffered from a bone disease – acromegaly – and given that so many of his ancestors had married close relatives, and that they were often aunts or uncles as well as first cousins of each other, it was perhaps not surprising. As a result he was regarded as incapable of education and was not even trained in personal hygiene. In addition, he was something of a sadist, for he apparently enjoyed a whole day spent watching the burning of heretics; on one occasion twenty-one victims suffered at the stake in his presence. Such was his eccentricity that he soon acquired the nickname El Hechizado, or the Bewitched.

Since Carlos was the only surviving male member of the Spanish Habsburgs it was critical for the dynasty that he should father an heir, but extremely doubtful if he was capable of doing so. Carlos was still the nominal ruler not just of Spain, the southern Netherlands and most of Italy but also of a vast empire that stretched from Mexico to the Philippines, from Florida to Argentina and Chile. So in a final attempt to preserve the dynasty his Austrian-Habsburg mother procured him an attractive wife in the faint hope that a Spanish-born heir might be produced. The unfortunate bride was a spare Bourbon princess, Maria Luisa of Orleans, who died of depression after ten years of humiliating failure. For a second attempt the determined queen mother sent for her brother's German sister-in-law, the pretty but empty-headed Maria Anna of Neuburg who also failed in her main role, though she did her best to extract Spanish wealth for herself and her relations.

Thus in the end all efforts to save the Spanish Habsburgs were in vain and the closest heirs were the French Bourbons. The dreaded Louis XIV was not only the son of Felipe III's sister, Anne of Austria, who had married Louis XIII, but he had himself also married Felipe IV's sister. The Austrian Habsburgs and the British were aghast at the prospect of France taking over Spain and its empire, so there were endless negotiations to try to arrive at a compromise. Louis XIV realised the risks but let his ambassador persuade the dying Carlos to make a will leaving Spain to the Bourbons, but if they rejected the inheritance then it would revert to the Habsburgs in Vienna. When Carlos died Louis could not possibly allow himself to be encircled by Habsburgs, so he forced the issue by sending one of his grandsons, Philip, to claim Spain for the Bourbons. This and other aggressive actions led to a war that lasted thirteen years and cost many lives, but in the end the Habsburgs never recovered their Spanish crown.

Back to Vienna

Leopold the Great's last five years were spent fighting the War of Spanish Succession, and his main objective was for his second son Charles to succeed as the Habsburg candidate for the Spanish throne, while his first son Joseph would take over Austria and the Empire. He died before the matter was resolved but could do little in the meantime to prevent the young Bourbon Philip from enjoying most of his Spanish inheritance despite the fact that he was twice ejected from Madrid before the French armies finally saved his throne for him.

In 1705, Leopold's son Joseph I (1678-1711) took over as Holy Roman Emperor but only lasted six years during which his main achievement was the suppression of Hungary. He died of smallpox in his early thirties. He had married a good German princess, Maria Amalia of Brunswick-Lüneburg, but she produced only daughters, so under Salic law the imperial crown went in 1711 to his younger brother Charles, the erstwhile would-be King of Spain.

For the previous eleven years Charles VI (1685-1740) had never expected to become emperor and had spent his time instead fighting to grab the throne of Spain as the preferred candidate of his dynasty. Once he was emperor his motivation to persist in the vain struggle for Spain was finally removed and the objectives of the War of Spanish Succession withered away. By this time, the Bourbon King Felipe of Spain was well settled in and sufficiently disconnected from his relations in Paris for France no longer to seem set on world domination. So Charles settled down to being a normal, if unexceptional, Habsburg emperor. Like his brother, he married a Welf princess, Elizabeth of Brunswick-Wolfenbüttel, and the overwhelming problem of his final years was that, like his brother, he only produced female heirs. He had a desperate struggle therefore to preserve the Habsburg inheritance and called in numerous favours from neighbouring states to protect Maria Theresa, his daughter and designated successor, as the head of the dynasty if not the empire.

Maria Theresa (1717-80) was twenty-three and pregnant when she inherited her titles as Queen of Hungary and Bohemia, and Archduchess of Austria. She handled the situation with great skill. Playing on her role as a mother and a vulnerable woman, she had a warm, outgoing personality, hardworking, frugal, with a sense of humour and a Viennese accent, all of which helped to make her popular. After an interlude during which a non-Habsburg, Charles, the aggressive husband of her cousin Maria Amalia, stood in as emperor, Maria Theresa's own husband, Francis of Lorraine, was elected and she could claim the title of empress. Francis I (1708-65) was the second non-Habsburg in succession to hold the imperial crown but at least both of them had Habsburg wives.

Needless to say, the neighbouring heads of state who had promised not to take advantage of a female head of the Habsburgs did exactly that, particularly the ambitious Frederick of Prussia (see p.103). Despite his destructive inroads. Maria Theresa kept the Habsburg estate reasonably intact, losing Silesia to Frederick and bits of Italy to the Bourbons but adding bits of Poland (Galicia and Ludomeria), bits of Bavaria to the west and Bukovina to the east to offset her losses. In other respects she achieved a great deal by encouraging agriculture and industry, reducing taxes and greatly aiding the economic recovery of the empire, particularly Austria itself. Along with all this she bore ten children who all survived to adulthood. Her palace at Schönbrunn, with more than a thousand rooms, was built to rival Versailles and was one of her few extravagances; even there she kept the heating to a minimum.

When her husband Francis died suddenly after attending the opera in 1765 the imperial crown passed to their son Joseph II (1741-90) who, although genetically half French and technically the first of a new dynasty, Lorraine-Habsburg, was very much a Habsburg. He thus formed a partnership with his mother for the next fifteen years as she retained her roles in Austria and Hungary while he ran the empire. When she died he assumed the double role for a further decade but with increasing frustration. Sometimes known as 'the revolutionary emperor', he was a hard-worker who resolutely pursued radical reforms, such as the abolition of serfdom, and introduced a degree of religious toleration. However, the multi-ethnic empire was beginning to suffer from separatist aspirations of its component nations, such as Hungary, the Netherlands and even Tyrol, all of which rebelled during the French revolutionary period. He ruined his health in fairly fruitless wars against the Prussians and Turks and died before he was fifty, perhaps now more often remembered as the somewhat reluctant patron of Mozart ('too many notes') or as the brother of Marie Antoinette whose execution he did not live to see. Haydn composed the Kaiser Quartet for him in 1790, including the tune which became the national anthem of Germany in 1922. His greatest fault as a Habsburg was that, like his grandfather, he left only daughters despite two wives, Isabella of Parma and Maria Josepha of Bavaria.

So once more the imperial succession passed from brother to brother. Leopold II (1747-92) enjoyed only two years on the throne. He had spent most of his career to date in Florence as Duke of Tuscany where he seems to have been happy, easy-going, popular and known as Pietro Leopoldo. Mozart had composed *La Clemenza di Tito* for his wedding to a more-or-less Italian princess, Maria Luisa of Spain, daughter of the Bourbon King of Naples and his Saxon wife, Maria Amalia. Their son Francis was twenty-four when Leopold died shortly before his tragic sister Marie Antoinette was sent to the guillotine, an outcome which he would have been helpless to prevent.

The End of One Habsburg Empire and the Beginning of Another

Francis II (1768-1835), born in Florence, was to prove more than almost any other member of his long-lasting family its extraordinary ability to adapt and survive. He had become Holy Roman Emperor in his early twenties in 1792 and lacked the experience to cope with the massive turbulence caused by the French Revolution. His aunt and uncle Marie Antoinette and Louis XVI were both executed early in his reign and he himself soon lost the Austrian Netherlands and Lombardy to the French army in 1797, but gained Venice and the coast of Dalmatia. Yet he knew how to make himself popular by letting his subjects wander in to see him every morning. Wearing just a simple uniform he would do walk-abouts and developed the Holy Alliance as a sort of dynastic protection league. However, after only twelve years in post he was disastrously defeated by Napoleon at Austerlitz and Vienna was captured by the French. The Holy Roman Empire ceased to exist in 1806, and more territory was lost in 1809, including Salzburg, Carinthia, Trieste and Croatia, but Francis bought some time by allowing his daughter Marie Louise (*d.*1847) to marry the upstart new Emperor Napoleon. With his own empire destroyed he had to abdicate, the first of his dynasty to do so, but this was not the end.

As Wheatcroft puts it 'Like a lizard that has torpidly been lying in the sun for hours on end it could move with great speed when threatened.' Two years before abdicating in 1806 Francis had ingeniously appointed himself to the new post of Emperor of Austria. In the act of losing one imperial crown he simply replaced it with a new one, a piece of dynastic chicanery to match any of his predecessors. Thus overnight he transformed himself into the Good Kaiser Franz I of Austria, one of the first European monarchs to know how to work a crowd. Eight years later he shared the victory over Napoleon at Leipzig and, with peace at last, recovered Lombardy, Venetia and Galacia.

Francis/Franz had two wives, Elizabeth of Württemberg and Maria Teresa of Naples, who produced several sons as well as the new wife for Napoleon. His youngest brother the epileptic Rudolf (1788-1831) was a major patron and talented pupil of Beethoven's.

Franz's heir Kaiser Ferdinand I of Austria (1793-1875), who took over in 1835 in his early forties, was sadly one of the least able of all the Austrian Habsburgs. Since his parents were double first cousins – he had only four great grandparents – his genetic pedigree was highly suspect. Plagued by frequent epileptic fits, probably impotent, and feeble-minded though sometimes witty, he was known as the Benign (*Gütige*) and a lover of apricot dumplings. He was totally out of his depth when revolution spread through Europe in 1848, and he was persuaded to take the blame for the repressive policies of Metternicht and his other ministers. So he abdicated and retired to Prague Castle – Bohemia had always been his favourite part of the empire – where he died nearly three decades later in his early eighties.

The survival of the Habsburgs was touch and go as one after another the numerous ethnic minorities of the Austrian Empire rebelled against its authority. Since the marriage of Ferdinand to Maria of Sardinia had proved infertile, probably because he was impotent, the next in line for the throne was Ferdinand's younger brother Franz Karl (1802-78), but many of those at court, including his own wife Sophie of Bavaria, described at this time as 'the only man in the Habsburg family', did not think he was energetic or charismatic enough to take on the difficult role of restoring stability. Instead she manipulated affairs so that Franz Karl would stand aside in favour of their teenage son Franz Josef who was less tainted by the old regime.

Franz Josef (1830-1916) had been put in a Hussar uniform at the age of five, was made to learn Hungarian as well as German, loved playing with toy soldiers and was sent to Italy to train with Radetzky when the troubles of 1848 began. When he heard from his mother that she had persuaded both his uncle and father to step aside he apparently muttered 'farewell my youth' and dedicated himself to saving the dynasty. As A.J.P Taylor put it 'The Habsburgs were the tightest organisation in the history of modern Europe.' The rebellion in Hungary was suppressed and thirteen Austrian generals faced the firing squad. Radetsky marched the Italians back into line and the crowds of Vienna were cowed.

Like many of his predecessors, Franz Josef was immensely hardworking and dedicated his life as 'the first servant of the people' having himself painted as the 'Last Cavalier'. He tried his best to be *Kaiserlich und Königlich*, sometimes rudely abbreviated to 'kaka' (sounded like German slang for excrement). He was faced with the awesome task of trying to hold together a multi-ethnic empire that included a number of rebellious regions, not least Hungary and parts of Italy. As his grandfather had said, 'It is a worm-eaten edifice so that if you remove one piece you do not know if it will fall down.' The Hungarian problem he did almost resolve by the Ausgleich in which the crowns were separated and Hungary gained some devolution. But crucially he lost control of Germany itself to the Prussians after the Battle of Sadowa in 1866, and but for Bismarck's restraint he might have lost his empire altogether.

Franz Josef's long life was plagued with personal as well as political disasters. While Vienna danced away to the infectious music of the Strauss family, he felt compelled to rise at dawn to do his endless paperwork. His wife and cousin the beautiful Elizabeth of Bavaria was high spirited and so bored with the repressive court life of Vienna that she liked to disappear to Hungary or abroad, but she did take the trouble to find her husband a compliant mistress, Catherine Schratt, before she did so. Eventually, Elizabeth was murdered by an anarchist in Geneva. Three of Franz Josef's brothers came to sorry ends: one of them, Maximilian, was shot after making himself Emperor of Mexico; another, Karl Ludwig, was poisoned in Palestine; and a third, Ludwig Victor, was exiled in disgrace for his flagrant homosexuality and transvestite habits. Franz Josef's son and heir Rudolf famously rebelled against the austere discipline of court life and committed suicide with his mistress at Mayerling in 1889. This left Franz Joseph's second brother Karl Ludwig as heir to the throne, but he was persuaded to stand aside in favour his son the Archduke Franz Ferdinand (1863-1914). Finally, and most disastrously, Franz-Josef's nephew and newly designated successor Franz Ferdinand was shot by the Serbian nationalist Gavrilo Prncip at Sarajevo in 1914. Franz Josef himself may not have been entirely displeased by the murder as he believed that Ferdinand had married beneath him and was in danger of 'contaminating the dynasty' but naturally he had to pretend to be outraged, and this feigned rage against the Serbs was to end up costing many millions of lives.

Already, Franz Josef had dabbled disastrously in Balkan politics, most rashly taking over Bosnia-Herzegovina in 1908 and ineffectively trying to suppress Serb nationalism. Now, at the age of eighty-four, this embittered old emperor and his compliant ministers manoeuvered themselves into a position where they would corporately punish the Serbs, thus provoking Russia to retaliate on the Serbs' behalf. This would in turn bring Russia's ally France into the war and then Austria's ally Germany. The Germans would then have to invade France through Belgium and that would bring in the British. Perhaps the only thing that he might not have foreseen was that to starve out the British the Germans would use their submarines to sink American ships and so bring the United States also into this absurd war. The chain reaction from the murder of one Habsburg thus led to the downfall of three of Europes' largest dynasties and the deaths of over forty million people.

Franz Josef died two years before the war ended. His grand nephew Karl I (1887-1922), son of Archduke Otto Franz of Austria and Maria of Saxony, took over but was deposed two years later as Germany and Austria surrendered to the allies, dying in Madeira a few years later. Thus ended one of Europe's most conscientious and business-like dynasties, one that had lasted six and a half centuries. At one time it had controlled two substantial empires at the same time. It had kept power within the family with remarkably few sibling quarrels and with only one female head of family in thirty generations. Within two years, three of Europe's most remarkable dynasties, the Habsburgs, Hohenzollern and the Romanovs all came to an abrupt end. Most of the multi-ethnic empire of the Habsburgs was divided up into four main nations – two old ones, Austria and Hungary, and two newly created composites, Czechoslovakia and Yugoslavia – neither of which were destined to survive.

THE MEXICAN ADVENTURE

Having, in the tradition of Germanic dynasties, succeeded in acquiring a throne outside Germany, that of Spain in 1516, but lost it and its vast worldwide empire in 1700, the activities of the Habsburgs outwith German-speaking areas had been restricted to their expansion into Italy, the Balkans and towards the Black Sea. However, the dynasty had one final flirtation with the new world in 1863 when Maximilian (1832-67) was offered the throne of Mexico by its assembly and was backed by Napoleon III of France who had invaded Mexico to collect debts from the previous government. The younger brother of the Emperor, Franz Joseph, had served harmlessly as an admiral in the Austrian Navy and was married to Charlotte, a Saxe-Coburg and daughter of Leopold of Belgium. Unfortunately for the new Emperor Maximilian, a large number of Mexicans preferred the regime of their liberal ex-President Benito Juarez and forced the withdrawal of French troops. The Empress Charlotte headed back to Europe to seek help for her husband, but the strain was too much for her and she suffered a nervous breakdown. With an army of only 8,000 Maximilian did his best to survive and fought off the republicans at Queretaro. He could have still made his escape but chose to remain with his supporters. In 1867, still only thirty-four, he was captured and faced a firing squad.

CHAPTER 3

THE UPWARDLY MOBILE HOUSE OF ORANGE

The tiny city of Nassau has a population now of under five thousand and lies in the picturesquely wooded Lahn valley where the Taunus Mountains rise to a height of nearly three thousand feet. There still exists Nassau Castle, an exotically tall tower with quaint Gothic turrets, on the spot where Count Heinrich first established a tiny new state on land previously belonging to the Archbishop of Trier. Nassau soon became linked with the nearby village of Dillenburg on the River Dill near Giessen, and it was in Dillenburg that was born the man who took this family to a new level when he inherited the princedom of Orange and soon afterwards was elected Stadholder of Holland. This remarkable family provided William III of Orange who, but for his wife's damaged fertility, might have founded a new British dynasty, as well as a succession of modernising monarchs who have adapted well to change and survived many difficulties to retain the crown of the Netherlands into the twenty-first century.

THE BEGINNINGS

This family seems to have been founded by two brothers, Drutwin (*d.*1096) and Dudo Count of Laurenburg (1093-1117), who built the first castle. Like our other families, the House of Nassau made slow, erratic progress for its first few centuries, hampered as ever by the Germanic habit of dividing up its patrimony amongst each of its sons. This happened when the first Count Heinrich the Rich (1180-1250) split his fairly small territory between his sons Walram (1220-76) and Otto. Despite that, one of Walram's sons, Adolf of Nassau-Weilburg, was elected King of the Romans soon afterwards and Emperor in 1292, not because he was regarded as a strong candidate but the reverse. Unfortunately, he was never officially crowned emperor in Rome and was killed in battle in 1298 at Gollheim by the one-eyed Albert of Habsburg (see p.34) who replaced him. So, as with the Habsburgs, the Nassau family's early experience of royalty was no more than a false dawn. In fact, he had followed a Habsburg who was expected to be weak but had failed to live up to that promise. His son Gerlach divided up his portion of the inheritance, and so his grandson Johann (1309-71) became the first of the new Nassau-Weilburg wing of the dynasty that five centuries later was to acquire the grand duchy of Luxembourg. Meanwhile, by marriage the family had also acquired neighbouring Arnstein, with its imposing hilltop monastery.

THE MOVE TO HOLLAND

It was a descendant of Emperor Adolf's, Engelbert I of Nassau-Dillenburg (1370-1442), who by marrying a Dutch heiress first gained some small estates in Holland at Breda, thus establishing a tiny foothold in the area where the family were just over a century later to achieve power. His grandson Engelbert II (1451-1504) gave some indication of the future when he was chosen Stadholder of Flanders, while another grandson, Johann V (1455-1516), fathered the man who was to begin the total transformation of the family fortunes. This was Heinrich III of Nassau-Breda (1483-1538 – the Nassau inheritance had been spilt as usual) who for his second wife acquired a French lady, Claudia of Châlon (1498-1541). She was a sister of the Prince of Orange and settled with Heinrich at his home in Breda where they produced a son, René, in 1519. So when her brother Philibert Prince of Orange died childless in 1530, this eleven-year-old boy became the heir to the princedom of Orange.

The princedom of Orange had been founded around 1180 by Bertrand of Baux, that extraordinary hilltop castle in Provence which is still surrounded by its medieval ghost town, and was a small enclave of the Holy Roman Empire in the south of France. However, over the years, by a series of good marriages it had acquired considerable properties in the border area between the Empire and France: Brabant, Luxembourg, Franche Comté, the Dauphiné and Charolais. Young René had to change the family names from Nassau-Breda to Châlon as a condition for his inheritance, but that was a small price to pay for becoming one of the richest landowners in Europe.

René, however, was killed at the age of only twenty-five in 1544 whilst fighting for the Emperor Charles V at the siege of St Dizier. He and his wife had produced a daughter, but she died soon after birth, so René, his mother and daughter all lie buried in the Grote Kerk at Breda. Since René had no brothers, this meant not only that there was no direct heir to the House of Nassau-Breda but also to the princedom of Orange. That is why, by a twist of fate, both the huge property portfolio of Orange and the little Dutch enclave of Breda went to René's cousin, Wilhelm/Willem/William of Nassau-Dillenburg (1533-84) who at the time was aged eleven. He had neither any French blood nor any Dutch and he was a Roman Catholic, albeit not a fanatical one.

THE FIRST WILLIAM OF ORANGE

The early career of William, known later as Willem de Zwijger, or the Silent was unexceptional. He was the son of Willem of Nassau-Dillenburg the Rich (1487-59) and inherited Nassau later when he was twenty-six. His nickname seems to have reflected the fact that he was slow in voicing controversial decisions and kept his own council.

As a relatively minor prince of the Holy Roman Empire, like his late cousin he owed allegiance to the Habsburgs, and when the Emperor Charles V abdicated it meant that Philip II of Spain took over the Dutch part of the Empire.

Willem, therefore, entered the service of Margaret of Parma, the king's half sister who was acting as his regent in the Netherlands. At the age of twenty-two he was appointed Stadholder of Holland, Zeeland and Utrecht, based mainly in Brussels, but as a Lutheran sympathiser he found the policies hard to uphold. Thus in his early thirties he became disillusioned in the Habsburg service, particularly when Philip introduced a policy of extreme religious intolerance and replaced the moderate Margaret with the ruthless Duke of Alva who brought with him the Spanish Inquisition. Willem resigned his post as Stadholder in 1567 and returned to the family seat in Nassau. Whilst there he became a committed Protestant, and when he refused Alva's command to return to Brussels he was condemned as an outlaw. Soon he found himself supporting the Watergeuzen or Sea Beggars, groups of armed men waging an informal war of liberation on the sea coast, a war that was to last for eighty years.

Five years after his retreat to Nassau, Willem returned with an army to drive the Spanish Habsburgs out of Holland. Despite many difficulties and reverses, he was able to create a small independent state known as the United Provinces in 1579, though he did not attempt to make himself king as the nation was founded as a republic. Three of his brothers were killed during the fighting. Then, when there was a temporary lull in what came to be known as the Eighty Years War, he had time to found Holland's first university at Leiden.

Though Willem was a German prince only one of his four wives was German. With his first wife the Dutch Anna of Egmond he produced, among others, Philip, the next Prince of Orange, though he was never able to be Stadholder because he was kept as a hostage in Spain. After an affair with Eva Elincx, which resulted in a bastard son, William married his second wife, the neurotic Anna of Saxony. She produced the brilliant Maurits/Maurice who did succeed him as Stadholder and eventually after Philip's death as Prince of Orange. Later, he divorced Anna on grounds of insanity, and with his third wife Charlotte of Bourbon, a former nun, he had six daughters. Then with his fourth wife, another French woman, Louise de Coligny, he produced Frederik Hendrik who was the only one of his three immediate successors to produce an heir. In total he had fifteen children. He was honoured as Father of the Fatherland, and the Dutch national anthem *Het Wilhelmus I* celebrates his achievements, as does the mnemonic national colour, orange.

William the Silent was fifty-one when, at the peak of his powers, he was assassinated in Delft by a Spanish agent. Philip, his eldest son (1554-1618), became Prince of Orange but died a broken man soon after being released from Spanish captivity. He had married a French Bourbon but they had no family. Philip's half-brother, Maurits/Maurice (1567-1625), the son of William's German second wife, had taken over as Stadholder at the age of only seventeen. Born in the old family seat of Dillenburg and educated at Heidelberg he continued the task of driving out the Spaniards, and with some British support achieved brilliant victories in the 1590s that led to the recognition of the Dutch Republic in 1609 and a truce for twelve years. In 1618, he succeeded his half-brother Philip as Prince of Orange and enhanced his own supreme authority when his rival Oldenbarnevelt was executed. Maurice, however, was not dynastically minded, for while he produced several illegitimate children with his mistress Margaretha van Mechele he never married and died in his sixties leaving the princedom to another half-brother, Frederik Hendrik.

THE GOLDEN AGE

Frederik Hendrik (-1647) thus took over in 1625. Described by Wedgewood as 'the generous ruler of Holland's golden age', he created the backdrop for a period of dynamic economic development and exploration as well as extraordinary artistic output. In 1639-40, the great Dutch admiral von Tromp defeated two massive Spanish armadas to secure Dutch dominance at sea, so that Holland took over parts of Brazil from the Portuguese, had settlements in North America, such as New Amsterdam at the mouth of the Hudson River, and acquired a considerable empire based round Surinam, the areas now known as Indonesia, with a colony en route at the Cape of Good Hope. All this made Holland one of the leading colonial powers of the day and

Amsterdam became a city of great wealth. Rembrandt (1606-69) made his name there in 1631 and painted *The Night Watch* a few years later.

Frederik Hendrik had reverted to custom and married a German wife, Amalia of Solms-Braunfels, whose family home was very close to Nassau and who had spent much of her life as an aide to Elizabeth Stuart, the Scots-born wife of the Elector Palatine in Heidelberg. Their son William (Willem II 1626-50) who succeeded briefly both as prince of Orange and as Stadholder in 1647 was ambitious to conquer the remainder of the Spanish Netherlands. This meant that he had to arrest some of his political opponents and besiege his own city of Amsterdam. He was perhaps on the verge of success when, after only three years in office, he died of smallpox in his mid-twenties. Perhaps because of his mother's long connection with the Stuarts he had married Mary, the daughter of Charles I of Great Britain, the brother of the Electress Palatine. Mary was pregnant with the future William III (1650-1702) when her husband died, and his royal Stuart genes were to have a considerable role in shaping his future.

There followed twenty-two years in which there was no Stadholder from the House of Orange, and young William led a fairly uneventful life. But in 1672 a French army was sent by Louis XIV to invade the United Provinces and the Grand Pensionary de Witt was assassinated. So the Dutch needed a new leader and picked young William III as Stadholder, despite his lack of military experience. He learned his trade rapidly, and in the face of almost overwhelming odds he opened the dykes to stop the French invasion with cold seawater. Ironically, Holland had recently lost its colony of New Amsterdam due to the naval exploits of the British admiral James Duke of York, William's uncle and soon afterwards his father-in-law, after whom it was renamed New York. Yet now, as Britain abandoned its anti-Dutch policy and instead faced up to the danger from France, the Duke of York's daughter Mary was selected in 1677 as bride for William, her first cousin. So the Orange family had two Stuart wives in succession, both of them called Mary. Since at this point neither Charles II nor his brother James had produced any legitimate sons both Mary and William, in his own right, were very close to the throne of Britain.

The Move to London

Meanwhile, William had halted the French invasion and achieved the Peace of Nijmagen in 1678. Seven years after that in 1685 his father-in-law and uncle James Duke of York took over as King of Great Britain. Soon rumours were reaching Holland that James was trying to turn Britain into a Roman Catholic autocracy. Within three years the rumours were becoming even more toxic, for James and his new Italian wife had at last produced a baby son who could be brought up as the next Catholic king of Britain. For the Anglican majority in parliament, and outside, this was the last straw. Famously, the 'Immortal Seven' invited William to invade Britain and bring with him his wife as its potential new queen. For William it represented an enormous risk, for not only did James II have a substantial professional army ready to defend his shores, but William risked having his own heartland of the Netherlands invaded by the French whilst he was out of the way. Given the dangers it is hardly surprising that William insisted on being made king in his own right as a half-Stuart alongside his wife. Nevertheless, the potential rewards were also huge for not only would he become king of a major international power but he would be able to call on considerable extra resources in his long-term aim of establishing Dutch independence and freedom from the threats of France.

As it turned out the conquest of Britain was much easier than might have been expected, for James panicked and senior generals like Marlborough went over to William's side. Even during the final showdown on the River Boyne the Jacobites made serious errors and William, who at the time had an asthmatic attack, had an unexpectedly easy victory.

So for the first time since the Emperor Adolf the House of Nassau had a king in the family. Yet in some respects it was another false dawn, for William and Mary, despite a couple of pregnancies, produced no living children and Mary, after two miscarriages, could not try again. So when William fell from his horse, allegedly, according to Jacobite gossip, startled by 'a little gentleman in black velvet', it was the end of the House of Orange as a British dynasty and a huge blow to their nebulous tradition as more or less hereditary Stadholders in Holland. It was to be forty-five years before the family fully regained its position there.

THE SECOND WIND

The man who rescued the dynasty was Johann Willem Friso (1687-1711), a descendant of William the Silent's brother and head of the Nassau-Dietz branch of the family who were hereditary Stadholders of Friesland and based at Leeuwarden. He was designated the new Prince of Orange in 1702 and led the Dutch army under the command of Marlborough. At the age of only nineteen he led the Dutch contingent with great courage at Oudenarde. Winston Churchill gives a glowing account of his abilities at Malplaquet where he had two horses shot from under him and 'would not be denied'. However, he never became Stadholder of all the provinces for he was drowned when his ferry sank in the Holland Diep during a storm. As Churchill put it, 'he must have used up all his luck at Malplaquet.'

Johann Willem had only been twenty-four, and six weeks later his wife bore a son, Willem Karel Hendrik (1711-51). After inheriting the post of Stadholder of Friesland as an infant, Karel Hendrik/Charles Henry spent the next thirty years gradually adding more regional stadholderships to his portfolio. Then in 1747, there was another French invasion and in such a crisis he was at last chosen to the overall position and renamed himself Willem/William IV. Sadly he died a mere four years after obtaining his ambition, but at least he was in a position to make sure that his son took over as Stadholder. In addition, he had inherited the properties of two other branches of the family, Nassau-Dillenburg and Nassau-Siegen, so earlier splinterings were rectified. He had married Anne, the daughter of George II of Great Britain, a German princess born and brought up in Hanover. In fact, for the next two centuries most of the consorts of the House of Orange were to be Germans.

Their son Willem/William V (1748-1806) became hereditary Stadholder of all seven provinces at the age of three, and his mother Anne of England acted as regent till her death seven years later. William then passed into the control of the Duke of Brunswick and remained so, ineffectual, lazy and insensitive to the new political mood even after he came of age in 1766. Disgusted by the unrestrained depredations of British privateers during the Seven Years' War he instead sought the alliance of Prussia and married Wilhelmina, the much more strong-minded sister of King Frederick William of Prussia. When he supported the Americans during their War of Independence he had to suffer attacks from the British privateers again, and then found himself hemmed in by his own revolutionaries when they caught the bug from France. As a result he was driven into virtual exile in Guelders and had to be restored to the Hague by a Prussian army in 1787. Seven years later he was driven out again, this time by the French, and Holland was turned into the Batavian Republic. He spent his remaining years as an exile in England, dying, in his late fifties, a disappointed man.

Thus William V did not live long enough to see the restoration of his son William VI (1772-1843), a much more aggressive character who had mounted a failed attack to recover Holland from the French in 1799. On inheriting the princedom of Orange he only had the tiny principality of Nassau-Orange-Fulda to rule for his first six years. Then in 1813 Holland was at last freed from the control of Napoleon, but its economy had suffered badly. In the post-revolutionary atmosphere William was invited back as hereditary prince and the concept of a republic was abandoned. Two years later after the crisis of Waterloo, William accepted the revised title of King of Holland and became Willem/William I, at the same time also becoming Grand Duke of Luxembourg. However, the ethnic and religious diversity of his expanded kingdom started to cause strains, and in 1830 the Catholic French-speaking Belgians began to voice their feelings as an oppressed minority. To make matters worse the Dutch had done well out of the far eastern colonies but this wealth had not percolated through to the Belgians. Famously, after hearing the opera *La Muette de Portici* about the uprisings in Naples the audience burst onto the streets of Brussels and demanded independence. The Dutch army went to put down the rebellion but French intervention allowed the rebel Belgians to win their freedom.

Like his father, William had married a Hohenzollern princess, Wilhelmina, and on her death seems to have lost heart, depressed also by the loss of Belgium, the reduction of his powers in the latest constitution and the fact that, ironically, he now wanted to marry a Belgian Catholic, Henrietta d'Oultremont. So he abdicated in 1840 and retired to Berlin where he married in his late sixties but died suddenly three years later.

His son, William II (1792-1849), had fought in both the Prussian and British armies, fighting in the Peninsula and at Waterloo under Wellington who regarded him as somewhat extravagant with his soldiers' lives. He was briefly engaged to Charlotte, the daughter of the future George IV, but she refused to marry him, perhaps sensing the bisexual tendencies for which he was blackmailed in 1819. So he married instead Anna Pavlovna, the sister of Tsar Alexander I, and, though a Romanov, she had a very high proportion of German genes.

Having made his early home in Brussels he took Belgian separatism as something of a personal insult, especially as he led the army that was trying to stop it and had the humiliation of having to back down when faced by French intervention. He had a further humiliation in 1848 when faced by revolutionary crowds and famously confessed 'I changed from conservative to liberal in one night in 1848'. A year later, he died at the age of fifty-seven.

His son, King William III (1817-90), took over reluctantly in 1849 as the tide of revolution receded and held the crown uneventfully for four decades, threatening to abdicate on several occasions. He married his own first cousin, Sophie Emma of Württemberg, whose mother Catherine Pavlovna had been another spare Romanov grand duchess. The marriage was somewhat turbulent as he was conservative in his attitudes whereas, surprisingly, she was not. He was also regularly unfaithful and described by the *New York Times* as 'the greatest debauchee of the age' whereas Queen Victoria regarded him as an 'uneducated farmer'. The other downside of this marriage was that it produced no surviving sons, so that he was the last Dutch king for three generations. When Sophie eventually died he scurried around looking for a replacement until he was accepted at last by a woman forty years younger than himself, Emma of Waldeck and Pyrmont, a minor German princess, with whom the old rake was happy and who provided him with a healthy daughter. Ten years later, he died at the age of seventy-three.

Under Dutch law the couple's daughter Wilhelmina (1880-1962) could inherit Holland, Surinam and the other Dutch colonies, but the Grand Duchy of Luxembourg was a part of the former Holy Roman Empire and only men could inherit there, so Luxembourg went to a sideways branch of the Nassau Orange dynasty and remained so with Bourbon accretions.

Wilhelmina succeeded her father at the age of ten and behaved impeccably as a constitutional monarch for the next fifty-eight years. Despite marrying a German, Hendrik Duke of Meckenburg-Schwerin, a minor Hohenzollern, in a union that was dutiful rather than romantic, she won much popular acclaim by her stubborn resistance to Hitler and, though she had to seek exile in England, remained a symbol of defiance.

In 1948, Wilhelmina began the new custom of voluntary abdication to freshen up the face of the dynasty. Her successor Queen Juliana (1909-2004) was also a model constitutional monarch, though she too had a German husband, Prince Bernhard zur Lippe-Biesterfeld (1911-2004), who, though a charismatic pilot and active resistance fighter, later caused some embarrassment by a financial scandal with the Lockheed Corporation. Juliana and Bernhard had four daughters and when Juliana (like her mother) abdicated in 1980 at the age of seventy-one, her eldest daughter Beatrix (1938-) took over. She married Prince Claus and they produced the first male heir in four generations, Prince Willem van Oranj (1967-), who broke all the moulds by marrying Maxima, an Argentinian of Italian extraction. The House of Nassau Orange has adapted well to twentieth- and twenty-first-century conditions and shows no obvious signs of disappearing. Ironically, it lost Orange to the French in 1672 and Nassau to the Prussians in 1866.

CHAPTER 4
From Welf To Windsor

The small south German town of Weingarten was formerly known as Altdorf but is first heard of in the days of Charlemagne when Welf Isenbart became Count of Altdorf. It lies in the valley of the River Schussen near Ravensburg. This became the replacement seat of the Welf family after the castle at Altdorf was destroyed in 1056 and was replaced on Martinsberg by the famous Benedictine abbey of Weingarten from which the town took its new name and which itself more recently became a teachers training college. Both towns are just north of Lake Constance or the Bodensee and lie in the area now known as Bad Württemberg. The family of Welf (or Guelf) were to have a long and erratic road to the top for they were prominent in papal politics in the Middle Ages and came very close to winning the crown of all Germany in the twelfth century, only to slide right back down the greasy pole.

For many years afterwards their bases were Brunswick and Lüneburg, and then towards the end of the seventeenth century they put on a spurt to become Electors of Hanover, and soon afterwards, in 1714, as a result of a lucky marriage and because of their staunch Protestantism, they became preferred candidates for the throne of Great Britain. A hundred and twenty years later they merged with another German family, that of Wettin and Saxe-Coburg (see below), and changed heir name to Windsor during the First World War.

The First Few Dawns

The path of the Welf family from their beginnings in Altdorf till their arrival in London took nearly nine hundred years, and their upward progress was plagued by false dawns. The first Welf, Isenbart (*c.*750-806), born in Metz, built his castle at Altdorf and made a very good marriage, and this was to be the technique by which they achieved most of their successes but it was a very up and down process. Each time they appeared to be on a winning streak they suffered disaster. Welf's bride was Hedwig,

Duchess of Bavaria, who was also the Abbess of Chelles, so Welf added large tracts of Bavaria, an area just conquered by Charlemagne, to his patrimony. Such was his enhanced prestige that their daughter Judith was chosen as his second wife by the Emperor Louis the Pious (778-840), the son of Charlemagne. However, it was far from an easy life for Judith, as her stepchildren consistently plotted against her and her two ambitious brothers Conrad and Rudolf. One of her bastard stepsons accused her of committing adultery, arrested her and had her two brothers compulsorily shorn as monks.

Despite this setback, Conrad's career survived and his grandson Rudolf (859-912) went on to found a new mini-dynasty, which held the crown of Burgundy for four generations till Rudolf III the Pious, or Ineffective, died childless in 1032. However, it was one of Conrad's younger sons Welf I Count of Alpgau and Linzau in Schwabia (*d.*876), whose successors kept the family going and sent it in a new direction. One of the family, another Conrad (900-75), was declared a saint after returning from Jerusalem with a piece of the True Cross for his new monastery at Kreuzlingen. Welf II (*d.*1030) was a less saintly rebel who brutally sacked the city of Augsburg. His grandson Welf III (*fl.*1047-55) was made Duke of Carinthia by the Emperor Henry III and he also held land in Italy as Margrave of Verona, responsible for guarding the southern frontier of the Holy Roman Empire.

Welf III never married and instead devoted his energies to building the new Benedictine Abbey at Altdorf on the site of the original Welf castle. As he lay dying at his new castle of Ravensburg by Lake Constance he left his inheritance to his nephew Welf IV (-1101), the son of his sister Chumiza (Cunigunde). She had moved to Italy and married Alberto Azzo, Duke of Milan and Lord of Este, so the family acquired a strong Italian connection, which was to be significant for several generations. Welf IV further expanded the family's portfolio by marrying a Bavarian heiress, Ethelinde, and became Duke of Bavaria but was to die at Paphos on his way to the crusades in 1101.

A dozen years earlier Welf IV had become deeply involved in the murky politics of the Holy Roman Empire, a strong opponent of the Emperor Henry IV and supporter instead of the emperor's *béte noir*, the ambitious Pope Gregory VII. In addition, he divorced his Bavarian wife and replaced her with Matilda, the widowed sister of William the Conqueror. To further his disruptive activities in Italy he had also organised the marriage of his seventeen-year-old son Welf V (1072-1120), later known as The Fat, to a widow more than twice his age. This remarkable woman, the feisty Margravine Matilda of Tuscany, or La Gran Contessa, was forty-three and had previously been married to her own stepbrother, so she brought the family, at least temporarily, large additional tracts of Italian land.

Matilda was an obsessive plotter on the Pope's behalf and even persuaded the Emperor's own son, Conrad, to rebel against his father. Though the Emperor Henry IV had captured several of her castles she held the vital pass over the Alps at Canossa and continued to defy him.

Six years later when young Welf was twenty-three and his wife nearly fifty they had, unsurprisingly, produced no children, so he divorced her. Both he and his father who had for so long been fighting against the Emperor Henry IV now changed sides and fought for him so as to secure his consent for their continued dukedom in Bavaria. The wily Matilda contrived to make sure that all her property was transferred to the church, not snatched by the Welfs, though they later got some of it. Despite the two mens' change of heart, the pattern had been set and the Welf family came to symbolise the anti-imperial side in the long feud that split the cities of Italy for the next couple of centuries. The other side were known as Ghibellines, and amongst their better known adherents was the poet Dante.

Welf V remarried but left no children. For the next three generations the heads of the Welf family were all called Henry, the first one, Heinrich the Black (1075-1126), being Welf's now middle-aged younger brother. He had been based in Italy but had married a Saxon heiress, Wulfhilda, so after fighting off his rivals there he acquired substantial properties in Saxony to add to the Bavarian and Italian portfolio. However, he did not live long to enjoy it and abdicated his own duchy of Bavaria so that his son could marry the heiress of the Dukes of Saxony. Soon afterwards he retired as a monk to the family monastery of Weingarten and died there.

His son Henry the Proud (1108-39), or Heinrich der Stolze, took over as Duke of Bavaria in 1126 and of Saxony ten years later, adding also the title of Margrave of Tuscany, so he was unquestionably the greatest landowner in Germany. As such he was a natural candidate for the crown of all Germany, but his youthful arrogance upset too many of his potential supporters, and despite having all the regalia ready in his vaults, he was never elected to the post. Even the fact that he had married the previous emperor's daughter Gertrude, who brought Brunswick as her dowry, did not help. He was about to make war on the successful candidate, Conrad III (1093-1152, crowned emperor in 1138), when at the age of only thirty-two he was stuck down by illness and died at the monastery of Quedlinburg. His younger brother Welf VI (1115-91) kept the family tradition going by running Tuscany and making himself duke of Spoleto, though he also kept the family seats in Swabia. Their sister Judith married the Duke of Swabia, head of what had now become the new ruling dynasty of Germany, the Hohenstaufen. This was soon followed by the collapse of the Welf presence in Italy, and Welf VII (1135-67) died of malaria before his father – while campaigning – and left no heir.

THE RISE AND FALL OF HENRY THE LION

The third of the Henries was Henry the Proud's ten-year-old son, later known as Henry the Lion (1129-95), or Heinrich der Löwe, born at Ravensburg. He was, therefore, still only a vulnerable thirteen when Conrad III decided to snatch away the family's duchy of Bavaria, and he had already lost Saxony. Along with his uncle Welf VI, he rebelled, but by this time the Hohenstaufen were becoming well established and the Welfs still excited too much jealousy amongst their peers. Conrad did eventually restore Saxony to him but he had to wait till 1156 after Conrad's nephew Frederick Barbarossa had taken over the crown before he was restored to Bavaria.

So once more the head of the Welfs was the largest landowner in Germany. In 1147 Henry had used the excuse of a so-called crusade against the pagan Slavs to extend his territory eastwards into Pomerania, and the same year added Swabia to the list by marrying its heiress Clementia, but he divorced her after fifteen years, bribed with a few Saxon fortresses by Barbarossa who did not like the intrusion into his own Swabian heartland. Thereafter, with the help of Barbarossa whose diplomatic policy it suited, he married Matilda, the daughter of Henry II of England and sister of Richard the Lionheart who became an ally of the family. The next marriage between the Welfs and a princess with British blood, Sophia of Palatine, had to wait for nearly 500 years.

Like his father Henry the Lion was much too ambitious, rich and powerful to be the sort of man whom the other German princelings would chose to have as their king. He was also too powerful a subject for any emperor to be able to relax when his back was turned. As Whitton puts it, he had extended his estates 'by ruthless trespass upon the rights of others'. He also got the psychology wrong, for a humbler approach might have worked better. Instead, when he commissioned an elaborate copy of the gospels for his new church in Brunswick dedicated to St Blasius, he had a picture included of himself and his new wife being crowned by Jesus Christ – something of a presumption, particularly as, in contrast with the conventions of that time, he was depicted as the same size as Jesus. In addition, at great expense, he bought a piece of the so-called True Cross to enhance still further his image of omnipotence. Some of his wealth he used wisely, for he founded what became two major cities, Munich and Lübeck, while he greatly expanded Stade and Lüneburg. But he devoted most of his attention to his own capital Brunswick, the city added to the Welf portfolio by his royal mother Gertrude. There he built the massive Dankwarderode Castle, a palace larger than that of the emperor himself, and outside it set up his iconic bronze lion, the first bronze statue to appear in northern Europe. He also began Brunswick Cathedral where he and his successors were to be buried. At Munich he built a new bridge over the Iser and deliberately created a bottleneck to trap customs dues from the salt traders and make a profit from his new town.

Meanwhile, Henry had become reconciled with the Emperor Frederick Barbarossa and supported him through many of his somewhat wasteful wars in Italy, but eventually became disillusioned in 1174, particularly as there was no restoration of the Welf lands in Italy. This desertion of the colours gave Barbarossa the excuse to have him charged with treason and in 1180 he was declared an outlaw. He attempted to raise an army against the emperor, but his allies failed to rally to his side in this crisis, and a year later he surrendered, spending the next four years with his English relations in Normandy and England. He made a brief comeback in 1185 but three years later was exiled again, only able to return when Barbarossa headed off to the Holy Land to join the Third Crusade.

On his return Henry took out his spite on the city of Bardowick which had been disloyal to him, destroying it totally. After Barbarossa's death he continued his fight to have his duchies restored to him, but the new emperor Henry VI was too strong for him and five years later he had to make peace. All that he was given in return was the small, newly concocted dukedom of Brunswick-Lüneburg, which was to be the family's base for the next four centuries. He had taken the family to new heights only to fail when the prize of the German crown seemed almost within his grasp. Even worse the mini-empire that had taken a century to build up was snatched away. He had nearly been a great man and to some was a hero. Ironically, when Hitler had his body exhumed in the hope of finding a Nordic giant, instead there were the remains of a shortish man with dark hair.

THE BRUNSWICK ERA

With the death of Henry the Lion Brunswick was no longer the capital of a mini-empire, but he had built it with the infrastructure of a major medieval city, which sea-going ships could reach up the River Oker. So it continued to prosper with trade links to England, Flanders and Russia. In addition, the other town retained by the Welfs after their recent downfall was Lüneburg, which stood astride huge salt deposits that soon made it one of the wealthiest cities in Germany. Thus in due course, when the dust had settled, it was Henry the Lion's grandson Otto (1204-52 son of William of Winchester) who acquired what was left of the vast Welf inheritance and became the first Duke of Brunswick-Lüneburg. He was to continue the line that eventually led first to Hanover, then Windsor, but in the short term the family had suffered a huge set-back and its leaders were to make matters much worse before they got better.

Meanwhile, there had been one last flurry of medieval Welf grandeur for Otto's uncle, another Otto (1175-1218), Henry the Lion's second surviving son did, by a series of chances, succeed where his father had failed. Ironically, Henry the Proud and Henry the Lion had both missed out on the crown because they were too successful, too powerful and perceived as too much of a threat by the princelings who elected the king. Otto, on the other hand, was chosen because by his time the Welfs were very much weaker. In addition, Otto was popular with the pope because of the Welfs' long tradition of supporting popes in their struggles against German emperors. Thus when he was only twenty-three, Otto, born in Normandy and educated in England, was chosen as a rival king to Philip of Swabia. He was crowned at Aachen with fake regalia as his rivals the Hohenstaufen held the real thing. Things were not easy for him, however, and he was defeated in battle by Philip and badly wounded in 1206, so that he had to retreat to Brunswick. Two years later, however, Philip died and Otto was able to make himself sole king. He became Holy Roman Emperor a year later but then proceeded to break the promises he had made to the pope not to invade Italy. He was excommunicated but still persisted in attacking Sicily – such was the lure of the South for German princes. By this time his new rival, Barbarossa's grandson, young Frederick II, was sixteen and Otto's supporters began to drift away to him. Two years later Frederick's army attacked Otto, defeated him and he was deposed. He was left in Harzburg Castle to be beaten to death by priests as he confessed his sins over and over again. Despite two marriages, he had no children, hence the continuation of the Welf line by the sons of his surviving brother William of Winchester. Otto was only forty-three, so it was yet another false dawn for the Welf dynasty.

William of Winchester (1184-1213), known as Long Sword, had been Henry the Lion's youngest son, born and brought up in England. He had died before he was thirty but had married a Danish princess and left a single son, Otto the Child (1204-52), who in due course claimed the stump of the Welf inheritance. Both the great dukedoms of Bavaria and Saxony had gone to rival families but Otto took over Brunswick-Lüneburg from his father's other brother Henry, who had no family. Even then he had to withstand a savage attack on his lands by the maverick Emperor Frederick II and only survived it by appealing to his mother's Danish relations. He fought alongside the Danes at Molin in 1225 and at Bornhorst in 1227, after which he was taken prisoner and immured in the fortress of Rostock.

On his release from captivity Otto passed through Brandenburg and fell instantly in love – for once it does not seem to have been a politically arranged proposal – with Matilda, daughter of the Margrave. Despite its non-political motivation the marriage that followed was very politically astute. Seven years later Otto was at last made Duke of Brunswick-Lüneburg by Frederick II, as well as being made a Prince of the Holy Roman Empire.

This might have been a sound foundation for a Welf revival, but for the next four centuries the Welf family not only produced too many male children but reverted to the traditional German distrust of primogeniture and tried to give each boy an independent inheritance. This resulted in the fragmentation of the already truncated Welf territories and a succession of ducal twosomes and threesomes, an extravagance that added considerably to the governmental overheads of the ever smaller sovereign states. Thus, for a start, the duchy was divided in two by the sons of Otto the Child, Albert the Tall (1236-79) and John (*d.*1267). The period 1279-1318 saw three fraternal dukes sharing the spoils in different rotations, followed by Otto the Mild (1318-44) who took over after the disastrous famines of 1315-8.

By the time that Albert II the Fat's son Magnus the Pious (-1369) took over the Lüneburg-Wolfenbüttel section of the duchy it was in dire straits due to a war against the Archbishop of Magdeburg. His son Magnus II with the Necklace (Torquatus 1328-73) lost both Lüneburg and his life in a battle near Leveste. Besides, his career coincided with a particularly miserable period in German history, for 1351 saw a major outbreak of the Black Death, which wiped out a third of the population, and in retaliation the survivors tried to wipe out the Jews.

It was Magnus' younger son Bernhard I (1358-1434) who from our point of view is the key figure, for it was from him that the future electors of Hanover were descended rather than his elder brother Frederick. Bernhard held the Lüneburg half of the duchy with his capital at Celle. It was he who built a new ducal schloss on the banks of the River Aller and had a canal dug to turn the town into a fortified island.

Meanwhile, the elder brother Frederick of Brunswick (1357-1400) who had been brought up by his guardian Otto the Evil conquered Lüneburg in 1388. He achieved another false dawn for the dynasty, for in 1400 when the incompetent Emperor Wenceslas was deposed, he was chosen by one faction as the replacement. It was a very brief period of glory, for within a year he was murdered on the orders of the Archbishop of Mainz, and it was his rival Ruprecht III from the Palatinate who came out on top.

THE CHANGE OF FAITH

After that the Brunswick-Lüneburg branch of the family plodded uneventfully through the next century, but the constant subdividing of ducal estates made it hard for the dukes to live in the style to which they reckoned they were entitled. Thus when Ernst I (1497-1546) took over as one of the Dukes of Brunswick-Lüneburg based in Celle his finances were at a low ebb. He had studied at Wittenberg University and there came into contact with the latest Lutheran theology, but it may well have been his poverty that provided the main motivation for his attack in 1520 on the wealth of the local Catholic churches. It suited him to work with the local firebrand preacher Wolf Cyclops, and as a result of his zealous attack on the Catholics he acquired much needed cash and the nickname Confessor (Der Bekenner). The fact that he cast his lot with the Protestants was, of course, to be of immense importance for the family nearly two centuries later when the British were looking around for a Protestant alternative to the Stuarts.

THE MOVE TO HANOVER

Despite his increase in wealth after the dissolution of the local monasteries Bernhard had four sons to provide for, and in so far as it is our task to trace the line that produced the Electors it is the youngest of the four, William the Mad or the Younger (1535-92), that matters. William married a Danish princess, Dorothea, but had to share the Brunswick-Lüneburg inheritance with his brother Henry. He then suffered a series of nervous breakdowns, during which his resources were plundered by corrupt underlings. Despite this he did, in his turn, father fifteen children and it was his sixth son, George (1582-1641), who was given the Callenberg portion of the patrimony and thus the first of the family to make his home in its principal town, Hanover/Hannover. Founded originally on the River Leine as a village for ferrymen and fishermen, Hanover had become a walled town in the fourteenth century and now, in 1636, became the capital of a minor dukedom.

George's life coincided with a downward spiral amongst his Brunswick-Wolfenbüttel cousins who were fighting each other. One of the Dukes of Brunswick-Lüneburg, who had become an alcoholic, was deposed in 1622 by his own mother, Elizabeth. Wolfenbüttel itself, founded on a virtual island in the Rover Oker 9 miles south of Brunswick, became a residence of the Dukes of Brunswick in 1432 and was to remain so till 1753. It was the scene of a Swedish victory over the Habsburgs during the Thirty

Years' War and became the home of the famous ducal library where the philosopher Leibniz supervised the collection of rare books.

George, like his father, had four sons for whom he had to find an inheritance and the youngest of them, Ernst August (1629-98), as is the way with youngest sons, was palmed off in 1662 with the bishopric of Osnabrück, while his three elder brothers shared the dukedom of Brunswick-Lüneburg. However, four years earlier he had made a marriage that was quite unexpectedly to raise the family to an entirely new level. His bride was a minor Protestant princess, Sophia of Simmern (1630-1714), born in the Hague and the youngest daughter and twelfth child of the exiled ex-king Frederick of Bohemia, whose resistance to the Empire in 1620 had caused the Thirty Years' War. Both Sophia and Ernst August were grandchildren of King Christian III of Denmark, an Oldenburg. However, of much greater importance in the longer term, though it is doubtful if anyone could have foreseen this, was that her mother was Elizabeth (1596-1662), the daughter of James VI of Scotland and I of Great Britain.

Sophia had, a few years earlier, remarkably turned down marriage to her rakish cousin the still exiled Charles II. As it was, she and Ernst had the first of their five sons, George Louis/Ludwig, in 1660. Not only was she thus the ancestress of the British royal line, but, since her daughter married Frederick of Prussia, she was also the ancestress of all the German Kaisers.

Sophia turned out to be a highly intelligent woman, fluent in both French and German, who had been brought up in the sophisticated environment of Leiden, patronised Gottfried Leibniz and later took a great interest in the gardens at Herrenhausen. She lived to the age of eighty-three, dying, in the end, just a few weeks before her cousin Queen Anne and outliving her husband by sixteen years.

Meanwhile, her husband, Bishop Ernst August, had another stroke of fortune. His eldest brother, Christian (1622-65), had inherited the Callenberg part of the dukedom in 1641 but in 1648 had been awarded Lüneburg as well, so he had passed Callenberg on to the second brother George William (1624-1705). Then, in 1665, when Christian died without any sons, George William took over Lüneburg and passed Callenberg to the third brother, John Frederick (1625-79). This latter was something of a maverick, for he converted to Roman Catholicism. After many years living with his mistress who had borne him a daughter, Sophia Dorothea, he decided to marry the mistress and legitimise the daughter so that she might at least inherit some of the income from his lands. Meantime, he spent huge sums himself building the magnificent palace and gardens of Herrenhausen in imitation of Versailles and employing the polymath Leibniz to collect books for his library. He died, however, in his early fifties, so at last Ernst August, the youngest brother, won his share in the duchy.

Thus Ernst August Prince Bishop of Osnabruck at the age of fifty took over the territory of Hanover and Göttingen, and three years later to make sure that none of its wealth seeped away to the late duke's daughter Sophia Dorothea of Zell he arranged her marriage to his own eldest son George. His daughter Sophia Charlotte married the future first King of Prussia, Frederick I. With this background of enhanced wealth and prestige he shortly afterwards became a candidate for office as one of the elite electors who chose future Holy Roman Emperors. As part of the preparation for this honour he at long last introduced primogeniture and, to the disgust of George's brothers, abandoned the policy of subdividing the patrimony amongst all the sons. To enhance his prospects of promotion further he went to join the Emperor Leopold's army in his war against the Turks, and in 1692 was at last given the rank of Prince Elector. Six years later he died at Herrenhausen without ever having officially undertaken the office of elector, but the position had been secured for his son to inherit.

Three years later the widow Sophia, now aged seventy-one, was recognized as heir apparent to the throne of Great Britain after her cousin Anne.

PREPARING FOR THE MOVE TO LONDON

Ernst August's son George (1660-1727) was thus in his late thirties when he inherited the duchy of Brunswick-Lüneburg and became Elector of Hanover with lands covering most of lower Saxony. He had been born in Osnabrück where he and his young brother were known in the family as Gorgen and Gustchen. Their mother, the half-Stuart Sophia, went off for a year in Italy when they were both infants but came back to produce another four brothers. As a youngster of fifteen George had been given his first taste of fighting in the Franco-Dutch war against Louis XIV. He also fought for the emperor in the Great Turkish War of 1683, where his father did well at the siege of Vienna and his second son Frederick August was killed.

In that same year of 1683 George's new wife, his first cousin Sophia Dorothea of Zell, now aged fifteen, with whom his relationship never seems to have verged on the warm, produced their first child, the future George II. They had a daughter four years later but their marriage had ceased to function. George spent most of his time with his mistress Melusine von der Schulenburg with whom he had two daughters 1692-3. Sophia became involved with the Swedish Count Philip Christoph von Königsmark who was murdered, probably on George's orders and at his expense, and his body dumped in a sack full of stones in the River Leine. George had his marriage dissolved on grounds of desertion in 1694, and Sophia was sent for the rest of her long life – another thirty-three years – to Ahlden Castle on Lüneburg Heath. Strangely, her fate echoed that of her distant relative Caroline Mathilde, the Danish queen caught in her affair with Struensee (see p.25) who was walled up in nearby Celle.

It cannot be assumed that in any way the Elector George, now in his early forties, was waiting impatiently for the crown of Great Britain. In 1702, it had passed to Queen Anne and, though her healthiest child had died at the age of twelve in 1700, she was herself still under forty and might yet produce a healthy heir, though perhaps the Act of Settlement of 1701 assumed that this was unlikely. Besides there was no certainty about the shifting tides of political favour, and there was young James Edward, son of James II, waiting expectantly in Paris. Anyway, at this point if the British crown did head for Hanover it was not for George but his mother Sophia.

Meanwhile, George continued to consolidate the Brunswick-Lüneburg inheritance, so that by 1705 all the splintered territories were back in one pair of hands except for Wolfenbüttel itself. That year he also organised the marriage of his heir George (1683-1760), with whom his relationship was at best cool, to Caroline of Ansbach, a fringe member of the Prussian Hohenzollern dynasty. George also bolstered the cultural reputation of his court at Hanover by employing two major celebrities. Leibniz (1646-1716), the polymath who had invented calculus at the same time as Newton and developed his optimistic world philosophy, lived in Hanover for his last thirty years and had been supported by George's mother and uncle. The newer addition was the *kapellmeister* George Friederic Handel (1685-1759) who came to Hanover briefly in 1710 before later moving to London.

In 1714, Queen Anne died in London a few weeks after George's half-Stuart mother Sophia, but even at this point there was no certainty that George would be invited to take over the British crown. The Tory ministry of Bolingbroke and Harley had fallen, but Bolingbroke was still flirting with the Jacobites and if young James had agreed to give up his Catholic faith it was quite possible that Anne might have bequeathed her crown to him. Nor when the summons did arrive was George in any hurry to head for London. At fifty-five the prospect for him of moving home from his beloved Herrenhausen to London was not necessarily all that attractive. He spoke no English and whereas his princedom in Hanover could be run on comfortably despotic lines this was not the case with the British, who could be hard to handle and had rid themselves of two kings in the previous century. So there is the sense that it was duty rather than anticipation of pleasure that motivated him. He might have otherwise delegated the task to his surviving brother if that brother had been half-intelligent. So he had made little advance effort to canvas for support before Anne died and afterwards just waited to see if there were any signs of vigorous opposition. When this did not materialize, after a suitable interval he set off for Britain leaving his son, thirty-one-year-old George with whom his relationship was still acerbic, to stay behind briefly in Hanover.

No foreign king, short of stature and in his mid-fifties is likely to become an instant hero with his new subjects and George I was no exception. His greatest asset amongst opinion formers was that he was a Protestant. He was not without ability, for he had risen to the rank of commander-in-chief Upper Rhine in the imperial army and had fought with some show of courage in several battles, losing two brothers in the process, but he was far from charismatic. As J.H. Plumb put it, 'It was almost impossible for a monarch to be dull, however stupid.' With the bulbous blue eyes of his family he had a bad temper, loved the opera and was obsessed with military uniforms. He had left his ex-wife incarcerated in Ahlden, so there was no queen, but he brought with him his two mistresses, the stoutish one known as the Elephant and the thinner one known as the Maypole. He did his best to avoid court ceremonial, disliked meeting his new subjects and appearing in public. But despite his reputation to the contrary he did learn to speak passable English for a middle-aged German and during his reign of thirteen years he did nothing to make the Hanoverian dynasty any less popular than it had been before he arrived. One major advantage for him was that his only rival, young James Edward Stuart, was even less charismatic than he was and very much less of a soldier, so the Jacobite rising of 1715 was defeated with relative ease. He returned regularly to Hanover, which remained his favourite residence, but without overt signs of authoritarianism managed to keep a tight control of affairs, especially after 1721 when Robert Walpole became his chief minister shortly after the stock market collapse known as the South Sea Bubble. He died at the age of sixty-seven.

George II (1683-1760) was in his mid-forties when he took over in 1727 and like his father in many respects, though they shared a mutual hatred dating back, probably, to the usual Germanic paternal bullying. He was short, quick-tempered, vain, humourless and self-centred. He was an experienced soldier who had seen service in a number of wars, but although he was the last British king to lead his own army, he was not an able general. Having been brought across to Britain soon after his father's accession he had a dozen years to acclimatise himself before his elevation, but had lost any possible relationship with his eldest son Frederick who had been left behind in Hanover when they moved to London.

Despite all this, George was to reign for a third of a century without committing any major errors, although some of that may have been due to the intelligence of his wife Caroline of Ansbach, the well-read patron of Leibniz who did most of his strategic thinking for him. As the ballad put it, 'You may strut dapper George but t'will all be in vain. We know tis Queen Carole not you that doth reign.' One of her key achievements was to persuade him to retain the services of his father's able minister Robert Walpole whom he wanted to sack on principle on his first day as king. It was to be a feature of his reign that he lacked genuine self-confidence and generally bowed to the judgment of ministers, like Walpole and later Pitt, who had stronger characters than he had. Walpole went on to provide one of the most stable, if not the least corrupt, parliament-based executives that Britain had so far produced. So the country enjoyed peace and prosperity until the frustrated opposition parties niggled him into an absurd war twelve years later with Spain, the War of Jenkins' Ear. There was then George's last military escapade at Dettingen when he was sixty, the last time a British king took charge of his army, followed by the scare when Bonnie Prince Charlie unexpectedly reached Derby, but George's personal contribution to affairs was superficial. Walpole commented 'Our master, like most peoples' masters, wishes himself absolute', but the Hanoverians simply did not have the necessary drive. As Plumb, somewhat unkindly, put it of the first two Georges, '... fortunately they were crassly stupid... though obstinate, domineering and excessively prone to interference in detail, [they] were incapable, totally incapable, of forming a policy.'

Later, when the Elder Pitt took over as prime minister he let the elderly George bask in the glory of a succession of brilliant victories. His kingdom now took in most of Canada, the east coast of North America, much of Bengal, a substantial portion of the West Indies and slave bases in West Africa. Scotland and Ireland were both secure and even Hanover had been expanded. Thanks partly to the wars, industry and agriculture were both booming.

Like his father, George liked music and, unlike him, enjoyed ceremonial so two of Handel's best-known pieces under his patronage were the *Royal Fireworks* and the *Water Music*.

Just as his father had hated him so George in turn hated his own eldest son Frederick Prince of Wales (1707-51). Frederick was regarded by both of his parents as beneath contempt; they had been ordered to leave him behind in Hanover when he was seven and did not see him again until he had come of age. In the meantime they had a large new family into which he did not fit, and they nicknamed him the Griffin. Caroline later said 'our first born is an ass' and wished him dead. They were even convinced that he was impotent and could not believe it when he apparently fathered a daughter with his wife Augusta of Saxe-Gotha (1719-72), the first but by no means the last of this family to link with British royalty (she was the daughter of Frederick the Duke of Saxe-Coburg-Altenburg – see p.123). They had married in 1736 when she was sixteen and went on to have seven more children, including the future George III. The prince was so angry with his parents that when Augusta was in labour for their first daughter he moved her from Hampton Court to St James to get away from them, so they became even more outraged. Frederick responded to his parents' rejection by supporting the parliamentary opposition to his father and a large coterie of anti-government writers, artists and musicians, which only made matters worse. In the end the unhappy situation was resolved when Frederick died in his mid-forties after being hit by a cricket ball – cricket was one of the many enthusiasms he had acquired in his efforts to seek popularity. 'Here lies poor Fred who was alive and is dead. Had it been his father I'd much rather.'

George II outlived his first son by nine years and his beloved, or at least much valued, wife Caroline by twenty-three. He was in his late seventies when he himself suffered a stroke and died. His favourite son and the one more like himself had been his second son William Duke of Cumberland (1721-65), a not incompetent general who lost Fontenoy but won Culloden and was commemorated by Handel's *Judas Maccabeus*.

Thanks to Frederick's premature death the crown skipped a generation and went on George II's death in 1760 to his grandson George III (1738-1820), an immature young man of twenty-two who, even at this stage, showed signs of instability. He had not learned how to read till he was eleven, yet despite several breakdowns he was to remain king for sixty years.

The key characteristic of George III, or Farmer George as he came to be known, was his constant search for someone who could be both a personal friend and a prime minister, a person upon whom he could rely both emotionally and politically at the same time. The first of these was ironically a descendant of the old Stuart dynasty, John Stuart Earl of Bute, a politician of very limited experience who had been kept in the political wilderness during the previous reign but had met George at the races and become so friendly with his widowed mother that there were rumours of an affair. They shared a passion for gardening which resulted in the expansion of Kew and many additions that included the Chinese Pagoda. Augusta, who had been a widow since she was thirty-two, died three decades later of throat cancer. Eighty years later the Saxe-Coburgs were to add even more of their genes to the British royal bloodstock.

George's relationship with Bute bordered on infatuation. They both had a slight touch of paranoia, and Bute, though not incompetent, found it hard to cope with the glories achieved by the overbearing Pitt in the previous decade. He could win little glory just by bringing the Seven Years' War to a peaceful and sensible conclusion, as it was not easy to promote peace after a series of successful, empire-building wars. Thus when George had to accept that Bute could not survive as prime minister he suffered the first of his mental breakdowns. Nevertheless, as king most of the time he at least looked the part: Horace Walpole described him as 'tall, full of dignity...florid and good-natured.'

Meanwhile, just after his grandfather's death, and almost with a streak of masochism, George had married a fairly uninspiring German princess, Charlotte of Mecklenburg-Strelitz (1744-1818). This was apparently on the rebound, for there is evidence that he had contracted an earlier marriage with a Quaker from Wapping called Hannah Lightfoot and even had three sons by her, one of them allegedly the George Rex who was sent off to South Africa in 1797 with strict instructions never to marry in case his children might be seen as alternative candidates for the throne. George Rex did have children, but out of wedlock, and died at Knysna.

Young George was also allegedly in love with Lady Sarah Lennox, descended from one of Charles II's bastards, but it was made clear that his duty was to marry a German, albeit one considered attractive, for she was skinny and very dark-skinned, this latter perhaps due to her descent from Alfonso of Portugal and a Moorish mistress. It is said that at the wedding ceremony the doddering Earl of Westmorland did homage to the wrong woman. As it happened, given the King's temperament Charlotte turned out to be the ideal wife, providing him with emotional security and bearing him fifteen children, an effort which, unlike most of his forebears, he rewarded by being totally faithful. So with four generations of Hanoverians resident in London all the eldest sons had kept the bloodstock 100 per cent German and, as we shall see, this trend was set to continue.

One result of George III's large family was that he had to buy a larger home, Buckingham House, later Buckingham Palace. His domestic life may have been virtuous but it was far from easy, especially when his sons grew up to be extravagant ill-disciplined boors. His only other hobbies seem to have been music and farming.

Of George III's sisters two had made interesting marriages. Caroline married Kristian VII, the King of Denmark, one of the Oldenburgs (see p.24 – Oldenburg is just miles from Hanover, so the two dynasties had emerged from neighbouring cities) who, coincidentally, was even less mentally stable than George. Therefore she became infatuated with the notorious minister Struensee (Kristian's equivalent of Bute) and was punished by imprisonment near Hanover for the rest of her life. Another sister, Augusta, married Karl Duke of Brunswick, so it was a double Welf fixture. George's brother William Duke of Gloucester married Maria Walpole, the product of one of the former prime minister's affairs, which caused scandal and the introduction of a new law preventing royals from marrying without approval. The couple produced a son of the same name known as Silly Billy or Cheese who married his cousin, one of George III's daughters, Mary, but produced no grandchildren for him.

George III's most unfortunate choice of minister was Lord North, a character even weaker than himself, whose policy with regard to the American Colonies he shared with the resultant humiliation of losing them. Not only was the king now suffering regular bouts of insanity, perhaps related to the porphyria, which came down through his Stuart genes or perhaps from the Welf connection (see p.70), but as the century closed he was becoming both blind and deaf. Ironically, at this point his title was changed from being King of Great Britain to that of United Kingdom and Ireland.

His eldest son George (1762-1830), soon to act as regent, was deeply in debt to the disgust of his frugal father. He had at long last married Caroline of Brunswick-Wolfenbüttel (1768-1821) in 1795, so not only was she a German but even a descendant of the Welfs like himself. However, he had been spoiled by a succession of mistresses, actresses like Mrs Robinson and the exotic Catholic widow Mrs Fitzherbert whom he had perhaps married secretly and who was the love of his life, so the homely German princess lived up to none of his expectations.

Like his father and the previous three generations of the house of Hanover, George had a very poor relationship with his parents. Whilst George III was still alive, George favoured Whig politicians like Fox and Burke, not so much for reasons of principle but just to irritate his father. Thus he pushed George III further to the right than he might otherwise have gone, but once he succeeded to the throne himself in 1820, when he was in his late fifties and free from the need to provoke his father, he favoured Tory ministers for most of his reign.

In one respect at least his habits as regent were maintained when he became king: his over-indulgence and his extravagance. He had spent huge sums of money on buildings, including the Brighton Pavilion, Buckingham Palace and Windsor Castle. He prided himself on his good taste in clothes and architecture, patronised John Nash and added extensively to the royal collection of valuable paintings and books. As his obesity became more obvious he began to cut down on public appearances, but he did make the effort to visits parts of the realm where his predecessors had failed to venture, Edinburgh and Dublin, as well as making the obligatory trip to Hanover.

His marriage to Caroline of Brunswick had in theory lasted nearly twenty-five years but he had abandoned her many years earlier after the birth of

Charlotte (1796-1817), their only child. He found his wife unattractive and allegedly unhygienic whilst her later extramarital friendships, though probably unconsummated, were enough to cause some scandal. Yet the fact that he kept her a virtual prisoner in Shooters Hill and made hypocritical attempts to divorce her caused him considerable unpopularity, which was only partially relieved when she died unexpectedly in 1821.

Both of them had shown little interest in their daughter who nevertheless grew up to be the most popular member of a now much more unpopular dynasty. She was married off to Leopold Duke of Saxe-Coburg-Saalfeld, much to the disgust of her dotty old grandfather who thought the Saxe-Coburgs were not good enough. Yet it seems to have been a love match and went ahead despite the early objections.

Sadly, Charlotte died in childbirth in 1817, thirteen years too early to share the fortune of her husband who then became the first King of Belgium (see below) and thirteen years too early to succeed her father. Had she lived, however, it is hard to believe that the great powers would have allowed her to be queen of both Britain and Belgium.

Apart from producing the one daughter, George, as Regent, had shown no interest in the survival of the dynasty, and whilst he made no further effort to produce an heir he also made little effort to persuade his brothers to help out. Despite having twelve surviving children (Octavius, Alfred and Amelia all died as infants) George III so far had only the one officially legitimate grandchild and she was now dead. It was as if his surly sons had reacted perversely against the saintly domesticity of the previous generation. However, at this point there was a panic and George III's rebellious sons were called on to do their duty as studs. For two them it was too late. The second son Frederick, Duke of York (1763-1827), was married to Frederika of Prussia but childless, while the scar-faced fifth son Ernest Duke of Cumberland (1771-1851) had chosen a twice widowed German princess suspected, unkindly, of doing away with both her previous spouses. The next two sons were middle-aged bachelor dukes who were now made to marry the usual German princesses in a double ceremony at Kew Palace. Neither of the couples had known each other for more than a few weeks.

The elder of the two, and currently third in line for the throne, was William Duke of Clarence (1765-1837) who was already in his fifties and had conducted a long-running affair with the popular actress Dorothy Jordan. She had borne him ten children, all known as Fitzclarences, who lived appropriately in Clarence House. As the third son of George III he had joined the navy as a teenager in 1779 and seen service over some thirty years, rising to the rank of admiral of the fleet in 1811. He had a reputation for ignoring authority, famously sailing into Plymouth harbour when he had been ordered to stay in the West Indies. His chosen bride was Adelaide of Saxe-Meiningen (1792-1849) from the House of Wettin who was twenty-seven years his junior. She produced two daughters for him but they both died.

The younger of the two bridegrooms at Kew was Edward Duke of Kent (1768-1820), a considerably less attractive character who was such a martinet during his military career that he had caused mutinies through his sadistic punishment of his men and had been removed from the army in 1803. He had been married once before and had enjoyed a long-term (twenty-eight year) affair with his mistress Madame Saint Laurent, but neither relationship had produced any issue. In addition, he was chronically short of money, so the usual grant awarded to newly married princes was a considerable attraction for him.

His new bride was Victoria of Leiningen (1786-1861), a widow with two children. She was from the Saxe-Coburg-Saalfeld family and sister of Leopold, the man who had been married to the luckless Princess Charlotte and it was he who found Edward his new mate. Typically, the duke could not bear to warn his mistress of his impending desertion, so that she first heard about it in the morning papers. This caddishness earned him the family nickname of Joseph Surface (the cad in *She Stoops to Conquer*). Edward was fifty and Victoria was thirty-four, and two years later, in 1819, their daughter Victoria was born at Kensington Palace, a healthy legitimate grandchild at last for the now fast fading George III.

There were, however, some challenges to this birth story perhaps inspired by Edward of Kent's remarkable lack of issue during his previous relationships and the fact that he died only eight months after his daughter was born. The fact that Duchess Victoria famously fell out with William her brother-in-law after he became king and was suspected of a love affair with her aide Conroy lent some credence to the theory, as did the fact that young Victoria and her progeny seemed to have inherited none of the porphyria strain that characterised George III and the Stuarts, but instead acquired the strain of haemophilia that had not been evident before. Despite all this, Victoria bore a reasonable resemblance to her Hanoverian forebears, so the odds are against this rumour and there is the possibility that the haemophilia was the result of Edward being somewhat old for paternity, whilst the porphyria may have continued, for signs of it were noted in Princess Charlotte of Wales and William of Gloucester.

Just to make sure of the dynasty, George III's seventh son Adolphus Duke of Cambridge (1774-1850), who sported a blond wig and lived a bachelor existence in Hanover, was also persuaded to marry a German princess, Augusta of Hesse-Cassel. They produced a son George in 1819 (later to inherit Hanover from his uncle Ernest) as well as two daughters, one of whom, Mary Adelaide, married Francis of Teck, a German prince, and bore Mary of Teck who was to be the wife many years later of George V. (see p.87 and p.161)

This left still one bachelor son of George III's, Augustus Duke of Sussex (1773-1843), but he, at least, was a man of principle. He had already had one unauthorised marriage to Lady Augusta Murray whom he met in Rome and by whom he had two not quite legitimate children. He now refused to abandon his second long-term mistress, or secret wife, Lady Cecilia Underwood. Many years later, Queen Victoria allowed the old couple to marry officially.

After a decade on the throne, the obese George IV died at the age of sixty-eight. The next brother, the Duke of York, had died childless in 1827, so the third brother William Duke of Clarence took over as William IV at the age of sixty-five. He was the fifth of the Hanoverian dynasty and, like all his predecessors, had a German wife, Queen Adelaide. He fitted the image of the bluff, simple sailor who defied authority and ignored convention, so he was not unpopular. His main ambition as king was to live long enough for his young niece Victoria to come of age and for his hated sister-in-law and her favourite Conway, therefore, to have no chance to act as regents. Politically, like his siblings, William had been almost liberal before his elevation, but after it swung sharply to the right, opposing the first reform Act of 1832 until it became clear the position was untenable. He then mellowed towards liberal reform and managed to live long enough to see his niece's seventeenth birthday. As Sir Sidney Lee, rather unkindly, put it 'the throne has been successively occupied by an imbecile, a profligate and a buffoon.'

The first three Hanoverian monarchs had all remained princes and electors of Hanover, but in 1803 it was conquered by Napoleon and soon afterwards the Holy Roman Empire, for which they had been electors, ceased to exist. After Napoleon's fall in 1814 George III became King of Hanover as did both George IV and William IV. However, under Salic law William's female heir Victoria could not inherit Hanover, so its crown was passed to his surviving younger brother Ernest Augustus who therefore headed off to Germany in 1837 and thus removed one of the new queen's uncles who might otherwise have resented her accession.

Two features stand out in considering the large family of George III. The first is the amazing reluctance of his children to marry or their inability to attach themselves to partners of suitable rank to satisfy their parents. Of his daughters, all died spinsters or childless: Charlotte after marriage to Frederick of Württemberg, Elizabeth after marriage to Frederick of Hesse-Homberg, Mary after hers to Silly Billy of Gloucester, while Augusta and Sophia had never married. Two of his sons married voluntarily but had no children. Four had been living happily with mistresses till their middle age and one of them would not change his status even under pressure. The generational switch from uxoriousness to permissiveness was marked and the same kind of reaction was to be evident with Victoria's children.

The second feature was the sudden drop in overall fecundity of a dynasty that at one point seemed to have heirs aplenty and then suddenly, in 1817, found itself struggling. This lesson was not lost on young Victoria who was to take very seriously the task of marrying off her nine children and making sure that the other halves were good breeding stock, preferably German. It was this obsession that was to cause a proliferation of her Germanic grandchildren round the courts of Europe. As if competing for attention from their grandmother they felt obliged to display themselves in military and nautical finery, to have bigger yachts and navies than each other, to have smarter and better-drilled armies. This all contributed, in no small way, to the mutually aggressive stances adopted by the great powers in 1914.

VICTORIA AND THE SAXE-COBURGS

Victoria was crowned at he age of nineteen in 1838, already showing signs of a fiery temper and knowing her own mind. Her relationship with her mother had deteriorated rapidly as the desperately ambitious Conway tried to dominate them both and secure a position of influence under the new regime. She was determined to stop him and relied on the Whig prime minister Lord Melbourne who became a substitute father-figure for her. Meanwhile, yet another father substitute was her uncle Leopold of Saxe-Coburg, now King of Belgium, who tutored her in the ideas of constitutional monarchy and paraded his nephew Albert (1819-61) in front of her as a suitable consort. She was also conditioned to favour the Saxe-Coburgs by her longterm duenna Baroness Lehzen and Leopold's agent, the assertive Baron Stockmar.

On her part, Victoria, who was essentially very lonely at this point, greatly admired Albert's looks, and after their second meeting, and some discrete indications of an affirmative response, she proposed marriage to him. They married in 1840, and after his early death from typhoid at the age of forty-two he was looked on retrospectively as the ideal husband. In the way that sons often react against their fathers, Albert's response to his lecherous and extravagant father was to become prudishly moral and financially cautious, so this suited Victoria who had a similar background.

Thus Victoria, whose eight great grandparents had all been born in Germany, continued the Hanoverian habit of procuring a spouse from Germany. In addition, she married her own first cousin from what had been previously the relatively obscure family of Saxe-Coburg-Gotha (see p.117). So to date, after five generations, the mainstream Hanoverian dynasty still had not married outwith the pool of German mini-royalty from which it sprang and this was set to continue. With Victoria and Albert it was not just a question of having the heir and a spare marry German spouses, but creating a whole network of Germanic sons and daughters-in-law spread throughout Europe. And to advise them they had their guru Baron Stockmar. Thus when, in 1844, the young couple already had four children under the age of four they were already planning a very Germanic future for their family.

Their eldest daughter Victoria, or Vicky (1840-1901), was, at the age of four, earmarked to marry the heir to the Prussian throne Frederick, or Fritz (later Kaiser Frederick 1831-88), a union that was to produce by far the most dangerous of Victoria's grandchildren, Kaiser Wilhelm II. The second child Albert Edward, known as Bertie, was destined to be the next British king and expected to marry a good German. Much to his parents disgust and disappointment he reacted to their earnestness by going to the opposite extreme, devoting himself to sport and mistresses and failing to agree to any of the pure German princesses on offer. However, he did eventually more or less comply in 1863 by marrying the beautiful Alexandra of Denmark whose father Kristian IX came from German stock and whose mother was from Hesse-Kassel. This at least meant that the next generation of Hanoverians would be ethnically German.

Of the next two babies Victoria's second daughter Alice (1843-78), later diagnosed as a carrier of the dreaded haemophilia, was at first picked out by her big sister Vicky to marry another Prussian. The queen, however, was not keen and invited the young Prince Louis of Hesse-Darmstadt, a nice red-faced, simple German, to Ascot – a blind date that led to their marriage in 1860. This union later produced the second most dangerous of Victoria's grandchildren, the Empress Alexandra of Russia, who passed their haemophiliac inheritance to her luckless son the last Tsarevich. Of Alice's other children one was another Victoria who married a Battenberg, resulting in the general elevation of the Battenberg/Mountbatten clan, which included the mother of Prince Philip, Duke of Edinburgh.

Queen Victoria's second son, the newly born Alfred, or Affie (1844-90), was expected to take over Albert's Coburg inheritance, so it would be even more natural for him to marry a German. In fact, he ended up as a prematurely bald naval officer, in 1873 marrying Marie, the only daughter of Tsar Alexander III so she was nearly 90 per cent German. Alfred almost certainly drank himself to death, and their son, another Alfred, allegedly caught venereal disease whilst serving in the German army and shot himself in 1899 after an unsuitable marriage.

After Alfred, Victoria still had another five children for whom to find spouses, and in the end only one of her nine offspring married a British partner, and this was one of the least successful marriages, for Louise (1848-1939), something of a feminist and a would-be sculptor, separated from Archibald Marquis of Lorne (1845-1914) and they had no family. Of the rest Helena, or Lenchen (1846-1923), married Kristian of Schleswig-Holstein (1831-1917); Arthur (1850-1942) married Louise of Prussia (1860-1917); the sickly Leopold, another haemophiliac, wed Helena of Waldeck-Pyrmont; and the youngest of all, Beatrice (1857-1944), married Henry Liko of Battenberg (1858-96).

Leopold and Helena's only son Charles Edward (1884-1954) was born the same year that his father died, so he became an almost instant Duke of Albany and perhaps suffered most from Victoria's love of the German heritage. For when the two Alfreds, her son and grandson, died in quick succession there was no direct heir for Saxe-Coburg, which was now inside the new German empire, so she sent Charles Edward to be the replacement duke with the result that the unlucky man was caught on the wrong side in both the World Wars and caused much embarrassment by groveling to Hitler.

Thus the marriage-broking of Victoria led to a very complex network of relationships in which members of the family found themselves on the opposite side in potential conflicts, and their attitude to each other was often conditioned more by a sense of rivalry than of comradeship. This was, ironically, particularly evident with the German marriages, especially when the Prussians, under Vicky's father-in-law Wilhelm I, chose to annex Hanover after their victory over the Austrians in 1866. For the Hanoverians to lose Hanover and for Queen Victoria's cousin, the wretched George King of Hanover (1819-78), to lose his throne was a humiliation, even if Victoria's daughter Vicky was destined to be the Empress of Germany. George had succeeded his father Ernest Augustus as both King of Hanover and Duke of Brunswick-Lüneburg, but had lost one eye through a childhood illness and the other from a teenage accident, so he was totally blind. His mother was a Mecklenburg-Strelitz so he had spent his childhood in Berlin, but despite his handicaps he was determined to defy the Prussians and ignored the sensible advice of his parliament to make peace, so he could blame no one but himself for his dethronement.

Meanwhile, Queen Victoria did have some compensation, for before her daughter could be raised to imperial rank she was herself given that bonus when Disraeli declared her Empress of India in 1876, replacing the last of the Moguls who had been forced out after the Indian Mutiny. During her very long reign, her popularity ebbed and flowed. She spent such a long time making herself a British institution that most of the anti-German feeling wore off. She had a bad patch after the death of Albert when she went into an almost catatonic state of grief and later came close to making a fool of herself with her ghillie Mr Brown, yet she became an ever more iconic figure, representing the moral values and aspirations of an age. She outlived Albert by forty years and died at the age of eighty-one.

Edward VII (1841-1910) was thus sixty when he at last took over from his mother and technically speaking was the first of a new British dynasty the Saxe-Coburgs. A chain smoker, serial womanizer, lover of cards and horseracing and a gargantuan eater, he symbolised a totally different lifestyle from Victoria and Albert which was nevertheless not unpopular with his new subjects. His sub-poena in the Mordaunt divorce case and his involvement in the baccarat cheating scandal caused much more worry to his mother than to the general public. Yet perhaps because he had always been made to feel inadequate by his perfectionist parents and his obsessive tutor Baron Stockmar, he just wanted to be liked, could not control his temper and turned to rebellion. Whether it was to compensate for the Germanic stance of his parents – both Victoria and Albert were pro-Prussian – or his well-known streak of rebelliousness against their tastes and those of his tutor Baron Stockmar or simply his preference for the French style of enjoyment, Edward cultivated the French assiduously; without interfering overtly in politics, he did help create the mood which resulted in Britain's Entente Cordiale of 1904 and, by a chain-reaction, this in turn led to the Anglo-Russian agreement of 1907 – two alliances that involved later disastrous consequences.

There may also have been an element of inter-family animosity, for though he was eighteen years older than his nephew Wilhelm II (1859-1941) the latter had irritatingly become Kaiser thirteen years before his own elevation and often flaunted his seniority. Besides, Wilhelm with his withered arm tended to overcompensate with unnecessary aggression and even succeeded in upstaging Edward during Victoria's last illness. He had also been unnecessarily offensive to the British during the Boer War. So there is an extent to which Edward's attitude towards his upstart nephew motivated him to cultivate the French and Russian alliances, thus unwittingly helping to create the psychological framework for the start of Armageddon in 1914.

Another factor in moulding the attitude of Edward, and later his sons, was the background of his wife Alexandra, for though he may not have been the most faithful of husbands, he could not help but be influenced by her. She was so beautiful that she offered at least some competition to the string of mistresses with whom he was associated (Sarah Bernhardt, Lillie Langtry, Alice Keppel and others). Alexandra (1844-1925) had been born in the Yellow Palace, Copenhagen to the German-speaking Glücksburg branch of the Oldenburgs, her impoverished father Kristian having moved from Holstein for employment – her mother was Louise of Hesse. In 1847, when she was three, Kristian was, surprisingly, selected as the heir to the throne of Denmark, which at that point still encompassed the Oldenburg territories of Schleswig-Holstein. Yet soon afterwards Kristian's original patrimony of Holstein-Gottorp-Glücksburg came under threat, for its German speaking population objected to their Danish overlords, rebelled and appealed to Prussia for help.

Her father was thus involved in a one-sided war to save his homeland from the Prussians soon after she first met her future husband Edward Prince of Wales on a carefully arranged blind date at Speyer Cathedral. They married in March 1863, her father became king six months later and the next year the Prussians conquered Schleswig-Holstein, thus substantially reducing the size of his inheritance. Her brother had taken part in the fighting so whilst she would not be anti-German she would be anti-Prussian and from 1870 onwards that became the same thing. Moreover, as her sister had married Tsar Alexander III of Russia she was likely to be pro-Russian. Edward himself was outraged by the attack on Denmark and wanted the Royal Navy sent out to frighten the Prussians, but neither Victoria nor her ministers took him seriously. He adopted a similar stance when Bismarck later attacked Austria and France. Personal relationships all came into it, for after the Schleswig war he had visited his sister Victoria in Berlin and been riled by her tactless crowing at the victory and her pride that her somewhat ineffective husband Fritz, the crown prince of Prussia, had won a medal for his part in it.

To some extent Edward's personal involvement in developing what became the 'special relationship' with the United States also became part of the framework for 1914 diplomacy, as did his nurturing of the friendship with Japan. It was not that he overstepped the mark of constitutional monarchy by dictating foreign policy, but simply that by his general bonhomie he cultivated friendships that presented politicians with a background in which they might forge alliances with dangerous consequences that could not yet be foreseen.

For the second half of his reign he worked with a radical Liberal government which put in hand a number of the most far-reaching reforms attempted by any ministry since 1832. In particular there was Lloyd George's budget, which redistributed wealth more drastically than ever before and was only forced through the House of Lords by the king agreeing to swamp the upper chamber with new peers unless they passed it.

Like all his dynasty, Edward was unnecessarily hard on his sons who grew up to fear or hate him and expect, in turn, to be feared or hated by their own sons. His eldest son Albert Victor, or Eddy (1864-92), who inherited the elongated neck of the Oldenburgs, was perhaps too intelligent and open-minded to fit the restricted job specification and sufficiently eccentric to inspire allegations of an affair with a Calcutta laundry boy, an association with a homosexual brothel in Cleveland Street and even the suspicion, without any real evidence, that he might be Jack the Ripper. Perhaps worst of all he wanted to marry a Catholic, Helene d'Orleans. Luckily, perhaps, for the monarchy he died of 'flu/pneumonia before he was thirty, so it was the next son George (1865-1901), a safer if less charismatic pair of hands, who became Prince of Wales in 1901 when his grandmother died.

Prince George had meanwhile very conveniently taken over his late brother's fiancée Mary of Teck (1867-1953) as his potential bride. She was to be the first Hanoverian consort born in Britain, but she did have a German father, Francis Duke of Teck, who had married Mary Adelaide of Cambridge, the grand daughter of George III's whose mother was Augusta of Hesse-Cassel, so Mary's genes were virtually 100 per cent German. She had been chosen as the perfect steadying influence for the unreliable Eddy, and dutifully transferred herself to George when his elder brother died.

George V succeeded when Edward died of a predictable bout of bronchitis. He was forty-five, three years older than his first cousin Tsar Nicholas II of Russia to whom he bore an uncanny resemblance – their mothers Alexandra and Maria were sisters. Nicholas had already been tsar for sixteen years, already suffered one revolution and one serious defeat in war against the Japanese. His wife Alexandra from Hesse-Darmstadt was also George's cousin, another of Queen Victoria's grandchildren. Both George and Nicholas were made to feel inadequate by George's uncle Wilhelm II who was only six years his senior but had been emperor already for twenty-two years with an ever increasing arrogance that compensated for his withered arm. George had served as an officer in a navy that had for many years been without a serious competitor anywhere in the world but now had the German navy with its Dreadnoughts hot on its heels, so this made for an uneasy personal relationship.

In addition, since George had been somewhat bullied by his father and since his late elder brother Eddy had been his mother's favourite, George was shy, anxious to please and extremely short-tempered when others failed to please him. Like his father, he was a heavy smoker and unnecessarily hard on his own sons but unlike him avoided sexual entanglements. He set a fashion by wearing his trousers creased at the sides, not at the front and back.

George inherited his father's prime minister Herbert Asquith, and the Liberal government continued with the radical reforms already started during the previous reign. It was just beginning to address two of the remaining most controversial issues of the day, female suffrage and self government for Ireland, when the Sarajevo murder precipitated such a major crisis that everything else had to be thrust aside. As A.J.P. Taylor put it, 'Formally speaking the war came as though King George V still possessed the undiminished prerogative of Henry VIII. The meeting held at Buckingham Palace that committed Britain to the First World War was attended only by the king himself, one minister and two court officials. The Cabinet had agreed that the neutrality of Belgium should be defended but was barely consulted on the declaration of war.' It was not that the King interfered, but he and his father had helped create an atmosphere which would not allow a tolerant attitude towards German aggression. Nevertheless, the war against Kaiser Wilhelm must have caused him and his wife acute embarrassment, since both of them had so many German genes. Thus, in 1917, he finally took the step of altering their family's official dynastic surname from Saxe-Coburg to Windsor. It must have been galling too when George did his best to support generals like Robertson and Haig whilst they presided over huge troop losses and then, due to political pressure, had to backtrack on some of his support. It must have also been very embarrassing for George after the war when his first cousin Nicholas II sought political asylum in Britain. He had initially offered refuge but then changed his mind as he came to realise that the revolutionary fervour might be contagious and that his own position could be threatened. In 1917-18, Europe lost three emperors, all of them ethnically German, and George did not want to be the fourth.

Generally George V did a reasonably professional job as king. He was the first Hanoverian to visit India as its emperor and attended the famous Delhi Durbar of 1911, but he did not travel to the dominions. He accepted the granting of independence to the Irish Free State in 1922, which meant that his title had to change to King of the United Kingdom and Northern Ireland. He was also the first British monarch to ask a Labour government to take office and presided over the extraordinary charade by which the British Empire managed to transform itself into the British Commonwealth with the monarchy as its main justification. He was the first British monarch to broadcast regularly on radio and had a Christmas message written for him by Rudyard Kipling.

George celebrated his silver jubilee on the throne in 1935 and died soon afterwards. Unfortunately, as in all Germanic dynasties, his sons had been pressurized by him in their youth and had all reacted in different ways. The eldest, Edward, was able and charismatic but only superficially confident, perhaps because he had been beaten too often by his tutors or bullied as a naval cadet. He was never allowed to share any of the real hardships of the Front Line during the Great War, though not for want of asking. He seems, like his grandfather, to have had a reluctance to accept conventional monogamy. Thus when he inherited the throne as Edward VIII (1894-1972) in 1936 he was already forty-two and a bachelor. He appeared to have a preference for older, married or divorced women, and in the case of Wallis Simpson one who was not only a commoner, a double divorcee and an American but also, at forty, unlikely to produce an heir for the dynasty. It was a sign of the declining enthusiasm of the old Welf dynasty that had lasted a thousand years that he preferred Mrs Simpson to the title of King Emperor, and chose rather to abdicate than be crowned. He was to spend the last thirty-six years of his life in comfortable but unsatisfying exile with the love of his life, from whom, ironically, there was no escape.

Edward's younger brother Albert Duke of York (1895-1952) had neither expected nor wanted the promotion when he was suddenly asked to take over the throne as George VI in 1936. Since he was expendable he had served in the navy at Jutland and later joined the fledgling R.A.F. In 1923, he had broken with tradition at last by marrying a genuinely British wife, Elizabeth Bowes Lyon (1900-2001), but he was, after all, only second in line to the throne. She thus became the first ethnically British queen since Anne died in 1714.

In 1926, as Prince Albert, the new king had played tennis at Wimbledon and next year with his wife was the first British royal to visit Australia. Yet he still had to struggle with a debilitating stammer, his naturally retiring nature and, like the two generations of kings before him, his very short temper.

George V and Mary of Teck had produced three other sons: the third, Henry Duke of Gloucester (1900-74) who was prone to alcoholism; the fourth, George Duke of Kent (1902-42), to ambivalent sexual adventure; and the fifth, Prince John (1905-19), to epilepsy. He was educationally retarded, kept in the background and died as a teenager.

The war against Hitler and in particular the bombing of London helped George VI and his wife to position themselves as much less aloof than all their predecessors and win a kind of backs-to-the-wall and family-comes-first popularity that set a new tone for the dynasty. However, George was the last Emperor of India, which became independent in 1948. He remained King of Canada, Australia and New Zealand and those former colonies with a mainly white population, but other major ex-colonies became republics.

George VI died suddenly in his late fifties and his elder daughter Elizabeth II (1926-) became queen at the age of twenty-six. She inherited the sense of duty and family decorum that had characterised the previous two generations. She aimed to hold together the vague entity of the

Commonwealth by means of frequent air travel, trips on the Royal Yacht, a constant stream of public engagements and television broadcasts. She married Prince Philip, a nephew of King Constantine of Greece, one of the Glücksburg-Sonderborg branch of the Oldenburg dynasty originally from Holstein in northern Germany. His mother was a Battenberg (see p.156).

The eldest of their three sons, Prince Charles (1948-), was pressurised, like so many of the first born in this dynasty, with harsh training and, in his case, a rigid public school education and arduous service in all three of the armed services. At the same time he was obliged to mate with a blue-blooded virgin so that the line would be preserved. Charles was perfectly trained in every conceivable facet of his future job but never given an opportunity to practice it. He acquired every accomplishment, yet still fundamentally lacked confidence and was never given a subsidiary role in which he might have developed it. In 1981, at the age of thirty-three he at last married the untested Lady Diana Spencer and apart from producing an heir and a spare their marriage was one of the most humiliating disasters for this dynasty since the crowning of the prince regent.

Not only did Charles undergo a messy divorce but had to watch his ex-wife have a succession of affairs with replacement partners which only ended with her death in a Paris underpass. Even in death Diana continued to wreak her revenge on a dynasty that had never, at least in her mind, fully accepted her as an equal. Her very defiance had made her such a popular figure that her ghost was able to force the Windsor dynasty to its knees.

Her two sons came out of this mess relatively unscathed and honed their image by imitating their dead mother as much as their living father. In 2008, Prince Charles reached the age of sixty, the age at which Edward VII had at last succeeded his elderly mother in 1901. Despite his intelligent stance on many world problems and his addiction to sensible good works the prospects of his reign being anything but an anti-climax looked remote.

The House of Welf

Welf Count of Aldorf *d.*876

Duke Welf III of Carinthia *d.*1055

Azzo of Este = Kunigunde

Welf the Crusader, Duke of Bavaria *d.*1101

Welf V *d.*1120 — Henry the Black, Duke of Bavaria *d.*1126

Henry the Proud, Duke of Bavaria and Saxony *d.*1139

Henry the Lion *d.*1195

Emperor Otto — William of Winchester, Duke of Brunswick-Lüneburg *d.*1213

Duke Otto the Child *d.*1252

Duke Albert the Tall *d.*1279

Duke Albert the Fat *d.*1318

Duke Magnus the Pious of Lüneburg-Wolfenbüttel *d.*1369

Duke Magnus the Necklace *d.*1373 *(splits Duchy into three)*

Duke Bernard I of Lüneburg *d.*1434

Duke Frederick the Pious *d.*1478

Duke Otto V the Magnanimous *d.*1471

Duke Heinrich IV *d.*1532

Duke Ernst I the Confessor *d.*1546

Duke Wilhelm the Mad *d.*1592

Bishop (later Duke, later Elector) George *d.*1698 = Sophia of Wittelsbach/Stuart

Elector (later King) George I *d.*1727 = Sophia Dorothea of Zell

King George II *d.*1760 = Caroline of Ansbach

Prince Frederick *d.*1751 = Augusta of Saxe-Coburg

King George III *d.*1820 = Charlotte of Mecklenburg-Strelitz

ng George IV *d.*1830 — King William IV *d.*1837 — Edward Duke of Kent *d.*1820 = Victoria of Saxe-Coburg-Gotha

Queen Victoria *d.*1901 = Albert of Saxe-Coburg-Gotha

King Edward VII *d.*1910 = Alexandra of Oldenburg

King George V *d.*1935 = Mary of Teck

King Edward VIII *d.*1972 — King George VI *d.*1952 = Elizabeth Bowes-Lyon

Queen Elizabeth II = Philip of Greece (Oldenburg)

Prince Charles = Diana

CHAPTER 5

The Giddy Heights of Hohenzollern

Some 50 miles south of Stuttgart is the mountain of Hohenzollern rising 2,500 feet above sea level near Hechingen in the Schwabian Alb. On its slopes still stands the exotic nineteenth-century Teutonic fantasy of Hohenzollern Castle, a name which may have meant watch tower or high frontier. It lies roughly on the site of a much earlier castle built about 1050 by Burkhard I, the founder of this remarkable family. There was perhaps also an even earlier castle from the ninth century. Burkhard's castle was destroyed in a siege in 1423 and of its replacement built in 1454 nothing survived but the chapel, which was incorporated in the current monstrosity, a shrine to the ancestors of the Kaisers that was never lived in by the family until after 1918 when their meteoric career came finally to an end. Over the intervening centuries, they had hacked their way upwards to being counts, then electors of Brandenburg, then kings of Prussia and finally, in 1871, kaisers of a united Germany. In the process their ambition had probably caused more suffering even than that of the Romanovs.

As well as their domination first of Prussia, then all Germany and its subsequent empire, the family provided a branch dynasty for Romania and also one of the most influential queens of Great Britain, Caroline of Ansbach who was the brains behind George II and ancestress of all subsequent British royals.

The Move to Nürnberg

The rise of the Hohenzollern was like that of many other German dynasties, very gradual. Burkhard I, the founder of High Zolle, and his co-founder Wenzil were killed in 1061, it was over a hundred years before the family made their next advance and, as so often happened, it was the result of a marriage. Frederick III of High Zolle (*c.*1171-1204) married Sophia of Raabs, the heiress of the Burgrave (*Burggraf*, meaning Town Count) of Nürnberg, and in 1192 succeeded his father-in-law in that position, the master of a major imperial fortress, renumbering himself as Frederick I Burgrave of Nürnberg.

With the usual German preference for dividing up the inheritance between their sons, Frederick split his new possessions. His younger son Frederick had a short stint as Burgave and was given High Zolle, founding a family that was to remain in southern Germany and remain Catholic. The older son Conrad (*d.*1261) took over at Nürnberg in 1219 and founded a family that was to look northwards for promotion, to turn Protestant and ultimately win the biggest prize. Meanwhile, as guardians of an important imperial castle they occupied the massive five-sided Salian fortress the Funfecksturm, initially so intimidating the burgers of the city that they built an alternative castle, the Luginskindsturm, to keep them at bay.

Conrad became a major supporter of the Emperor Frederick II, Wonder of the World, and was so well thought of that he was entrusted with the guardianship of the emperor's son Henry. He also did solid work subjugating the local barons round Nürnberg who tended to attack merchants passing through their territories. In the course of this he, not surprisingly, picked up a few extra properties like Rangau and Pegnitz as well as part of Ansbach in 1254.

Meanwhile, another branch of the family had also done well, for one of Burkhard I's younger grandsons, another Burkhard, had won the countship of Hohenberg, a small castle east of Nürnberg. His grandson Albert, both a warrior and a well known singer of love songs, a *Minnesinger*, was a major supporter in the election of the controversial new Emperor Rudolf I of Habsburg, a candidate selected against the odds, in 1273, because he was old and expected to be weak (see p.34). It so happened that Rudolf had married Albert's sister Gertrude (*d.*1281) in 1245. Albert later won renown by dying in battle in 1298 fighting for Rudolf's son Albert of Habsburg.

The other member of the Hohenzollern family who played a major part in the election of Rudolf was Frederick III (*fl.*1262-97) Burgrave of Nürnberg and son of Conrad III. Thereafter Frederick played a key role in the battle of Durnkrut on the River March where he helped Rudolf defeat King Ottakar of Bohemia, the event which led to the Habsburgs taking over Austria.

Ironically, therefore, the Hohenzollerns gave their first leg-up to the Habsburgs, promoting their first taste of empire and helping them to conquer Austria. Yet six hundred years later they were to be responsible for their nemesis when the Hohenzollern won the German imperial crown at the expense of the Habsburgs in 1871. In the meantime, the Hohenzollerns were much more modest in their ambitions. Conveniently, in 1248 the lord of Kulmbach, with its great castle of Plassenburg, was murdered and left no sons. Since one of his younger sisters had married Frederick there was a subsequent scramble in which the Hohenzollern were able to add the towns of Bayreuth and Cadolzburg to their list of properties.

In the next generation Burgrave Frederick IV (1287-1332) bought neighbouring Ansbach in 1331 for 24,000 pounds of farthings just before his death. He had fought so bravely for the Emperor, Ludwig, at the battle of Mühldorf that he was known as the Saviour of the Empire. He even had the reputation for being considerate to the Jews. Then his son Johann II (1309-57), who had married the heiress of the bankrupt Counts of Orlamunde soon afterwards in 1340, bought Kulmbach and gave the Hohenzollerns the mighty castle of Plassenburg just north of Bayreuth, giving this branch of the family a significant fortress that was their own property and not just a tied residence like Nürnberg. Unfortunately, Johann was also the Burgrave during the onset of the Black Death, which severely reduced the population of Nürnberg, and he stood by when the survivors massacred the Jews of the city whom they blamed for the outbreak.

Frederick's grandson Frederick V (1333-98) did such a fine job for the Emperor Charles IV (Wenceslas of Bohemia) in defending the vital fortress of Nuremberg that he was promoted to be a sovereign Burgrave in 1363. However, as so often when a German dynasty began to get affluent, he chose to split his inheritance between two sons, Johann III taking Kulmbach and winning the Emperor's daughter Margaret as his bride whilst Frederick VI (1373-1440) was Burgrave of Nürnberg and held Ansbach.

ONWARD TO BERLIN

When Johann died leaving only a daughter his brother Frederick took over both parts of the inheritance and made his mark by fighting for the Emperor Sigismund, his brother-in-law (*fl.*1410-37). He was so rich that in 1411 he was able to lend the emperor 150,000 marks and was given custody of the border province of Brandenburg in return. Having moved north to his new acquisition as *Hauptman* he further extended his own and the emperor's authority in this area by wiping out the local Quitzo clan who were regarded, perhaps unfairly, as robber barons. After all, Brandenburg had been a Slavonic town conquered by the Germans in 983 and was then Slav again till 1150 after which it was Germanised. The town itself on the Havel River joined the Hanseatic league in 1314.

The ambitious Frederick shortly loaned even more money to the Emperor and because of this and his other services he was promoted again, this time to be Margrave (*Markgraf*, meaning Frontier Count) of Brandenburg and allowed to become one of the elite group who elected the Emperors. Thus he had to renumber himself and in his new role joined the Parakeet Society, the group aiming to undermine the dukes of Bavaria. Thus Frederick VI

Burgave of Nürnberg renumbered himself as the Elector Frederick I of Brandenburg, a position which he had effectively bought for himself. At about the same time he was invited by the council of the neighbouring small town of Berlin to become its protector. It was the start of a major new episode in the development of the family's fortunes.

In 1425, the Elector Frederick surprisingly abdicated and his three sons followed him as joint margraves in the peculiar way that German dynasties split up their possessions. The eldest son, Johann the Alchemist (1406-64), was incompetent and unaggressive, obsessed only by the desire for his court chemists to produce artificial gold, so he was persuaded to give up Brandenburg and concentrate on his hobby. The second brother Frederick II Eisenzahn, or Irontooth (1413-71), captured Berlin again with its neighbour Cölln and built the intimidating Stadtschloss on the Spree, home of the dynasty for the next 500 years. He also extracted the sizeable area of Pololis Neumark from the Teutonic Knights by demanding it as surety for a loan in 1454, then claiming it nine years later when the loan was not repaid. The third brother was known as Albert Achilles (1414-86) because of his reputation as a knight. He had made his name by conquering swathes of Pomerania and various prosperous but rebellious towns such as Cottbus, the textile centre east of Berlin and Krossen, now Krosno Ordzanskie in the Silesian part of Poland, where he doled out properties to his soldiers in lieu of wages and his daughter married the last Polish Duke of Krossen.

Albert's son the Elector Johann (1455-97), known as Cicero, arranged for his son to make a useful marriage to the heiress of Thuringia and added the Polish town of Zossen, south of Berlin, to the growing portfolio.

THE BENEFITS OF BEING PROTESTANT

As with so many German dynasties, the Hohenzollern's choice of religion was to be crucially important for their next moves up the ladder. Joachim I (1484-1535), known as Nestor, and the grandson of Albert Achilles, succeeded as head of the family in 1499 and married a Danish-German princess, Elizabeth of Oldenburg. He was a die-hard Catholic, and he walled her up because of her Lutheran tendencies and massacred many of his Protestant subjects in Bayreuth. Similarly, his brother the Archbishop of Mainz was one of Luther's most zealous opponents.

However, it was the conversion of one of the family to Protestantism that was to make possible the next great promotion of the Hohenzollern. Joachim's cousin Albert of Brandenburg (1490-1568) was in 1510 elected as the thirty-seventh Grandmaster (Hochmeister) of the Teutonic Knights,

1 The Schloss, Oldenburg

2 The original Habsburg Castle in Switzerland

3 Nassau Burg

4 Burg Hohenzollern

5 Veste Coburg

6 Sans Souci Palace, Potsdam

The Five Oldenburgs

Clockwise, from top-left:

7 King Kristian IV of Denmark and Norway

8 Queen Alexandra of Great Britain

9 King George I of Greece

10 Tsar Peter III of Russia

11 King Kristian VII of Denmark and Norway

Clockwise, from top-left:

12 The Emperor Charles V, a Habsburg

13 William the Silent of Nassau and Orange

14 William III of Orange

15 Kaiser Franz Josef of Austria, a Habsburg

16 Philip IV of Spain, a Habsburg

17 Henry the Lion, a Welf

18 *(left)* George II of Great Britain and Hanover, a Welf

19 *(centre)* Albrecht Duke of Prussia, a Hohenzollern

20 *(right)* Frederick the Great of Prussia, a Hohenzollern

21 Kaiser Wilhelm I, a Hohenzollern, with Bismarck at Versailles

22 *(above)* Queen Victoria and Prince Albert of Saxe-Coburg-Gotha

23 *(left)* King Ferdinand of Romania, a Hohenzollern

Clockwise, from above:

24 King Manuel of Portugal, a Saxe-Coburg

25 Tsar Ferdinand of Bulgaria, a Saxe-Coburg

26 King Karl XII of Sweden, a Wittelsbach

27 King Ludwig II of Bavaria, a Wittelsbach

28 King Leopold II of Belgium and the Congo, an Oldenburg

29 Prince Alexander of Bulgaria, a Battenberg

30 George V with his queen, Mary of Teck

31 *(above)* Catherine the Great of Russia, from Zerbst

32 *(left)* Tsarina Alexandra of Russia, from Hesse

the great crusading order which had been engaged for the previous two centuries in subduing and converting the alleged heathens of the Baltic coast. The original Prussians had, in fact, been a mixture of Polish and Lithuanian Slavs in the west and east of the area respectively, but their paganism had provided a useful excuse for spare German crusaders to give up their base in the Holy Land and band together to conquer them in 1226. The Teutonic Knights had founded the German city of Königsberg (now Kaliningrad in the Russian Republic) as their eastern capital and also built a massive brick castle at Marienburg, now Marbrok in Poland, with its luxurious palace for the grand master. From these bases, the Knights had ruled a considerable area from the Gulf of Finland down to the Polish border.

Theoretically at least, Albert was a good candidate to revive the fortunes of the knights, for not only had he been trained as a priest but, as a Hohenzollern, he was a member of one of the most influential families in Germany. However, by this time the Order was deeply unpopular, particularly with the Poles from whom they had suffered a heavy defeat back in 1410 at Tannenberg. They had lost their religious zeal and were guilty of exploitation and corruption. Albert became bogged down in a further war with the Poles in 1519 and as he grew progressively more disillusioned he found himself tempted by the ideas of the reformers. In 1522, on a trip to Wittenberg he fell under the spell of Martin Luther who made the tempting suggestion to the thirty-two-year-old celibate that he should abandon his vows and take a wife. To make this even more attractive Luther advised Albert to disband his monastic order, seize its treasure and turn Prussia into a Protestant province to be ruled by himself. To make this easier Luther would send some of his missionaries to convert the local inhabitants.

The next stage was far from straightforward for Albert faced the wrath of both the pope and the emperor, so initially he disguised his intentions and pretended to punish any of his own knights who strayed in the direction of Protestantism. So in one of the great confidence tricks of history, Albert, after careful preparation, declared his independence from the Order, laid hands on its treasure, turned himself into a duke and snatched East Prussia for his family. Then, like Luther, he repudiated his vows of celibacy and took a wife, Dorothea of Denmark. He had to hand out some of the money to assuage some of his less cooperative knights and he had to acknowledge his uncle the King of Poland as his overlord, but otherwise his coup was a complete success.

He also took it upon himself to liberate some of the serfs. For a long time the Prussians were to be regarded as little better than barbarians by other Germans, partly because of the level of intermarriage between

German settlers and the local Slavs, partly because of their remoteness from western Europe, and perhaps also because of the harsh climate and frequent state of war, which made the people more aggressive.

Meanwhile, Albert's fork-bearded cousin Joachim, the Elector of Brandenburg (1505-71), known as Hector, plucked up courage to come out as a Protestant as soon as his father died in 1555. Otherwise, he had a relatively quiet career except for adding the district of Ruppin west of Berlin, but his successors, particularly his great grandson, the Elector John Sigismund (1572-1619), were to reap huge political benefits from the change of faith, even though he nearly ruined everything by trying to make the reluctant Berlinners become Calvinists.

The main reward was Prussia, for the ex-monk Albert, its self-made duke, had no surviving children by his first wife so he was in his early fifties when his second wife gave birth to a son, Albert (1553-1618), who thus took over the duchy as a teenager. Unfortunately, Albert was unstable and, perhaps more importantly, failed to father any healthy sons, so on his death the duchy went to the husband of his eldest daughter Ann, none other than John Sigismund of Brandenburg who had married her with great prescience back in 1594. This marriage not only produced eight children but provided the main Hohenzollern dynasty with the hugely valuable accretion of East Prussia. But Ann had already proved her worth for she had also turned out to be the heiress of another eccentric and childless duke who died in 1609. Thus, after a brief war, half of his valuable duchy of Jülich-Cleves in the Rhineland was, in 1612, added to John Sigismund's growing portfolio. Ravensberg in Westphalia, with its great Sparrenberg Castle, came slightly later, in 1614, as did two towns east of Berlin, Beeskow on the Spree and Stockow, which had belonged to the King of Bohemia. Sadly, John Sigismund did not live long to enjoy his massively increased inheritance, but by his marriage he had been fruitful in every sense and he had laid the foundations for the future Brandenburg-Prussian state.

Berlin was at this time still a wooden town with a population of around 10,000, and the whole area of Brandenburg was relatively poor agricultural land with a thin scattering of people and no major seaports. So the addition of Prussia, with its fine city of Königsberg, made a big difference. Though there were large territorial gaps both between East Prussia and Brandenburg, and between both of them, Ansbach and Jülich-Cleves, the Hohenzollerns were now significantly more powerful and richer than they had ever been before. Yet John Sigismund had nearly endangered the whole edifice by trying to force his Lutheran subjects in Brandenburg to switch to Calvinism.

THE THIRTY YEARS' WAR

For the time being, the potential of this Hohenzollern conglomerate was wasted by the next elector George Wilhelm (1595-1640) who took over in 1619. He was a Calvinist like his father John Sigismund, but was violently disliked by his Lutheran mother Ann of Prussia who would have preferred her second son, a Lutheran, to have taken over. He had married Elizabeth, elder sister of the unfortunate Frederick of Bohemia, the man whose actions precipitated the Thirty Years' War, whereas his own sister had married the ultra-ambitious King Gustav Adolf of Sweden, who was to be one of the main participants. Though tall and impressive he was strong neither mentally nor physically and found himself squeezed between his own aggressively Lutheran subjects on one side and the bullying imperial Catholics on the other. Though his preference was to remain neutral he allowed himself to be sucked into the Thirty Years' War that split Germany viciously between Catholic and Protestant states without ever properly organising his army or defining his objectives. Despite being a Protestant himself, he left most of the decisions to his minister Schwarzenberg who was a Catholic. He allowed himself to be browbeaten into siding with the Swedes by his aggressive brother-in-law, so he fell out with the Emperor Ferdinand and suffered the consequences. His lands were devastated and large numbers of his subjects were killed by the armies on both sides or starved because the crops had been burned by passing armies, while he made himself safe in his remote Prussian base at Königsberg, hundreds of miles from the fighting. He died in his mid-forties.

George Wilhelm's only son, Frederick, the Great Elector (Grosser Kurfürst 1620-88), who succeeded at the age of twenty had learned the lessons from his father's dithering but was described, somewhat unkindly, by Carlyle as 'one of the stuffiest men in history'. Evacuated to Holland during the Thirty Years' War, he had studied at Leiden University and ostentatiously refused to join the pranks and minor orgies of his fellow students. Returning to Berlin in 1641 when the war was nearly over he found the city's population close to starving and set about encouraging the revival of agriculture in both Brandenburg and Prussia. To help build up commerce he showed himself a good Calvinist by encouraging the immigration of Dutch and French Huguenot craftsmen, particularly to towns like Kustrin and Krossen, which had lost many of their citizens due to war, famine and disease. It is estimated that the population of Brandenburg and Prussia had fallen as low as 600,000 by the end of the war and Frederick's policy meant that Huguenot immigrants increased this by a quarter. It also meant that the economy of his provinces grew rapidly and created a sound basis for his expansionist policies.

For the same reason he built a canal linking the River Elbe to the Oder and the Spree thus giving Berlin access to the Baltic and the North Sea. His other two ports, Memel and Königsberg, were in detached enclaves. Thus he could start to build a small navy to add to the standing army, which he had already substantially increased from an unreliable corps of perhaps 2,000 mercenaries to around 30,000 men picked from his own territories. He did this with the help of a subsidy from the French together with a cunning pact with his junkers by which they handed over cash in return for greater freedom of action, yet he later used the troops thus raised to cheat them out of their freedom. He soon also proved himself a skilful general who knew how to delegate to officers whom he trusted and also had a great understanding of the art of appearing suddenly where his enemies least expected him.

Meanwhile, he did surprisingly well out of the peace settlement of 1648 that finally ended the war. It was not due to any military muscle that Brandenburg-Prussia had displayed during the war but simply to the fact that it was staunchly Protestant and as such a useful buffer against the Empire. So East Pomerania, which had been occupied by the invading Swedes, was handed over to him as well as a useful clutch of Saxon cities, including Halberstadt, Minden and Kamin along with the promise of Magdeburg, the scene of the massacre of Protestants by Tilly, one of the worst atrocities of the war.

With his new army Frederick achieved two major victories, one in Warsaw in 1656 against the Poles, which meant that his Prussian duchy no longer came under the sovereignty of Poland, and the other in 1675 after a 150 mile forced march in fifteen days at Fehrbellin in Ruppin against the previously almost invincible Swedes who were thus discouraged in their attempts to interfere in his territories along the Baltic coast. As a result he acquired another two cities in east Pomerania, Butow (now Bytow) in 1675 and Lauenburg (now Lebork just west of Gdansk) in 1680.

Like most males in his family he was prone to sudden rages, apopleptic slamming of doors and constant rows with his children, of whom he had six with his first wife Louise of Orange and seven with his second. He had to suffer the death of his eldest surviving son, his favourite, Charles in battle when he was only nineteen and had to resign himself to handing over to his next son whom he, perhaps unfairly, regarded as a weakling.

The King in Prussia

So when the Great Elector died in 1688 it was his unpromising younger son Frederick III (1657-1713) who took over as Elector of Brandenburg and Duke of Prussia, but he proved to have unexpected strengths. Born in Königsberg he was far from the militaristic model his father would have liked, for a spinal injury in childhood had left him with a permanent limp, a perceived weakness for which he was prone to overcompensate. On his mother's side he was a cousin of William III of Orange and as she died when he was eleven he had to endure numerous quarrels with his unsympathetic father and his aggressive step-mother, Dorothea of Holstein-Glücksburg.

When he came to power in his early thirties he devoted himself to refurbishing Berlin as a cultural city to which he could attract scientists, musicians and philosophers like Leibniz. It was in this atmosphere that his half-brother Christian Ludwig (1677-1734) later invited Johann Sebastian Bach to Berlin and inspired the Brandenburg Concertos in 1721.

Despite his lack of military ambition, it was nevertheless Frederick who achieved by cunning the greatest single advancement for his dynasty since it first came to Brandenburg. In 1701, with admirable foresight, he chose to help the Emperor Leopold during the War of Spanish Succession and sent him a contingent of Prussian infantry. As his reward he asked for the apparently harmless honour of calling himself a king in his Prussian dominions, which were outside the borders of the Empire. He did not ask for the same title in Brandenburg since that would have upset the electoral pecking-order in Germany and drawn too much attention to his tinkering with titles. Thus, though in his capital at Berlin he remained a mere Margrave and Elector, he subtly moved himself up to the top of the European social scale just by juggling prepositions, for once he was known as king in Prussia it would be a very small step to become the King of Prussia, a step taken in due course by his famous grandson, Frederick II. Meanwhile, to emphasise his new status he had himself crowned at huge expense in Königsberg and renumbered himself as King Frederick I.

Having thus achieved his main ambition, without starting a war, he made the books balance and kept his troops busy by hiring them out to other rulers in need of a good army, the reason why his grandson called him 'the mercenary king'. Yet at the same time he was surreptitiously adding to the growing conglomerate of his dynastic holdings. Additions included Lingen on the Ems in 1702, his share of the spoils left by his cousin William of Orange; Quedlinburg, near Magdeburg, by purchase in 1689; Tecklenburg and Valangin, now in Switzerland in 1707, also by purchase; then Obergeldern, now in Holland, as a reward for help during the War of Spanish Succession.

The Hohenzollerns, also at this time, dabbled in the fashionable idea of an overseas empire, building their own slave-trading station at Friedrichsburg in Ghana in 1683, grabbing Arguin on the west coast of

Africa in 1685, Crab Island (or Caribik) in 1689 and Whydah in Togo in 1700. But they could not really compete with the great maritime powers of the age who had been collecting colonies for over a century already, so they did not make very profitable progress.

Frederick married three times and significantly it was his middle wife Sophia Charlotte, sister of George of Hanover, the future George II of Great Britain, who produced his only son, Frederick William.

Frederick William I (1688-1740), known as the Soldier King, or Soldatenkönig, succeeded in 1713 in his mid-twenties and was a totally different character. He had an almost ridiculous passion for drilling his troops, particularly his extra-tall guards regiments for which he scoured Europe looking for recruits of the right height. Nevertheless, he built on the foundations of Prussian military success that had been laid by his grandfather, so by hard training and rigorous reform of every aspect of administration his army became extremely efficient. He was also a hardworking and effective manager of all aspects of government, meticulous in detail and frugal to the point of meanness – no unnecessary candles – and he set an example by paying his own taxes. Despite the disadvantage of being king in only one of his provinces, and most of the component parts being separated from each other by a considerable mileage, he managed to encourage industry and, like his predecessors, used religious toleration as an attraction for skilled immigrants. The only extensions of territory during his reign were the useful port of Stettin (now Szetzin in Poland) where Catherine the Great of Russia was born in 1792 when her father was the Prussian general in command, and the rest of Pomerania.

On the cultural front Frederick William showed little interest and left the patronage of Bach to his uncle, but his wife Sophia Dorothea (she was also his cousin, for she was the daughter of his uncle George of Hanover) was less of a philistine and between them they organized the building of the Kronprinzpalais in Unter den Linden. They had fourteen children.

FREDERICK THE GREAT OR OLD FRITZ

Frederick William's contempt for the arts was just one of the many reasons why he had a long-running quarrel with his eldest surviving son Frederick (1712-86) who as a youth preferred practicing on his flute to army drill. It was also the usual ruthlessly oppressive training of royal princes by German dynasts that nearly always caused an adverse reaction. In addition, there may have been some kind of inkling of Frederick's ambivalent sexual orientation. There was evidence of an early crush on a pageboy, Peter Keith. As a cadet Frederick was guilty of minor derelictions of military drill that made his father apoplectic with rage. Frederick sulked and sometimes rebelled and things came to a head when he attempted to run away from Brandenburg to Britain where his uncle George II had just taken over as king and might have offered him asylum (though his own relationship with his eldest son was just as bad as Frederick William's).

In the event, Frederick was caught before he reached the border along with his close friend Lieutenant Catte and the old king ordered that the pair should be executed on charges of treason and desertion. Frederick was only spared thanks to the intervention of the Emperor Charles VI, an act of mercy that later proved very damaging for his own family. So Frederick was instead imprisoned at Küstrin, forced to watch while his friend Catte was beheaded and then made to return to his military duties. It took three years of perseverance before his father forgave him and at the same time he agreed reluctantly to an arranged marriage with Elizabeth of Brunswick-Wolfenbüttel, from one of the Welf branches like his mother.

Then followed six years spent mainly away from Berlin in his newly acquired castle of Rheinsberg where he could devote himself to music – he was by this time an excellent flautist; French literature – he wrote numerous poems in French himself and tended to discourage the use of German; science – he had a small laboratory; and philosophy – he had as a mentor Voltaire, the former mentor of Catherine the Great. He began to conceive of himself as a potential enlightened monarch. He virtually ignored his wife throughout this period, perhaps not so much because she was unattractive, for that made little difference, but because she shared none of his intellectual interests and appeared awkwardly immature – she was only three years younger than him.

Frederick was twenty-eight when his father died in 1740 and he at last took over. He now almost immediately embarked on his master plan to turn the kingdom of Prussia – he quickly dispensed with the 'in Prussia' formula – for the first time into a joined-up nation. The first step was to invade Silesia and snatch it from the Habsburg's first and only female head of state Maria Theresa, who was expected, as a woman, to be an easy target. In this he showed what was to become a characteristic disregard for treaties and convention: his standard tactic was to conduct a surprise attack, then talk about peace, then when it was least expected attack again. In the case of Silesia he was also motivated by the thought that his rival the Saxon King of Poland might try the same ploy, for he also wanted a joined-up kingdom. His excuse was like Hitler's many years later that though the population was mainly Slavic there was a large minority of German settlers.

Having won his first new province he offered peace to Austria and so, for the time being, got away with his unorthodox behaviour. Silesia not only gave him a better southern frontier but also a booming linen industry and rich metal ore deposits.

Frederick now waited four years before he made his second preemptive strike against the Habsburgs. This time he attacked Prague to force the Austrians to let him keep Silesia. As George II said of him, 'he is a bad friend, a bad ally, a bad relation and a bad neighbour… the most dangerous prince in Europe.' A decade later his sins began to catch up with him, for he had alienated nearly every other power in Europe, and in 1757 he was attacked on two fronts: France from the west and Austria from the east. Protracted fighting had resulted in his army being severely eroded by death and injury, yet he still tried to keep the initiative and defeated the French after one of his trademark surprise attacks at Rossbach. This he followed up with a similar defeat of the Austrians at Leuthen. It was this resilience that let him put the 'Great' after his name and at the same time gave him his popular nickname of Old Fritz.

His troubles, however, were far from over, for he was now faced with attack on a third front, this time from Russia, and he suffered a series of disastrous defeats that resulted in the Russians overrunning Prussia and even capturing Berlin. Frederick was said to have contemplated suicide and he was only saved from utter humiliation by the fact that the Russian generals had run out of ideas. Their mistress the Empress Elizabeth who disliked him died suddenly and was replaced by the German born Peter III (an Oldenburg – see p.27) who was one of his most ardent admirers and had married the daughter of a Prussian general (Sophia of Anhalt-Zerbst, aka Catherine the Great). So the death of Elizabeth was referred to as 'the miracle of the House of Brandenburg'.

By this time Frederick's army had been reduced to about a third of its original size for he had been utterly reckless with the lives of his soldiers and had come close to self-destruction. He was typically callous about the death in battle of two of his wife's brothers. Yet his steely determination revived, as did his lucky streak. In 1772, he gained a vital link in the chain to achieve a joined-up nation when his share in the first Partition of Poland gave him West Prussia, so Brandenburg was at last connected with East Prussia. The other key acquisition had been East Friesland, which was close to his existing properties of Lingen and Minden and gave him Emden, the mouth of the Ems River and his first direct access to the North Sea.

The result was that overall Frederick doubled the size of his kingdom and at the same time made it much more cohesive. He was thus in a position to put forward Prussia as a credible alternative to Austria for headship of the ethnic Germans and their multifarious princes and electors, so paving the way for German unification a century after his death. Approaching his mid-seventies when he died, he had led an austere life with little interest in women, except perhaps for his sister, but certainly passionate about literature, philosophy, music and architecture as well as the efficiency and expansion of his kingdom. There was no more quibbling about where he might use his royal title. In respect of his idea of enlightenment he did what suited him, as with his fashionable abolition of torture, but in other respects he was totally without principle. It is no coincidence that Hitler regarded him as a role model.

THE ANTICLIMAX

Since Frederick and his wife had produced no children he was succeeded in 1786 by his brother's son Frederick William II (1744-97), already in his mid-forties. Lazy and sensual he had been handsome as a young man but soon grew obese. He did not have his predecessor's skills in either war or civil administration. Learning the lessons of the French Revolution he embarked on a number of sensible reforms but spoiled the effect by his religious intolerance. In his late thirties he had joined the mystical Rosicrucian sect and made a fellow member, Johann Wöllner, his chief adviser – with disastrous consequences. He also neglected the formerly efficient Prussian army, so that after his death it was to prove ineffective against Napoleon. On the surface, in terms of building up the new nation-state, he did nearly as well during his relatively brief reign as Frederick, for without having to fight a war he gained two massive extra slices of Poland from the second and third partitions. However, all this came at considerable cost: South Prussia was only held from 1793-1815 and New East Prussia from 1795-1807. He did, however, in 1791, regain the two old Hohenzollern counties of Bayreuth and Ansbach for his now distant Hohenzollern cousins had run out of male heirs.

He had two wives, and the first, from Brunswick-Lüneburg, lasted four years before the union was dissolved and left him with a daughter Frederika who married the Prince of Orange; the second from Hesse-Darmstadt with whom he had a number of children including his first son, but whom he neglected in favour of his more sophisticated regular mistress Wilhelmina Enke, not to mention two other more casual mistresses. He reversed his predecessor's policy of discouraging the German language and patronized both Mozart and Beethoven, but his eccentric religious views and fiscal incompetence almost bankrupted the state. He was only in his mid-fifties when he died.

His son and successor Frederick William III (1770-1840) was even less effectual and took over at the age of twenty-seven just as the Napoleonic wars were about to start. He had fought as a colonel during the French revolutionary wars but was prone to depression and indecision. Initially he brought forward some liberal measures and reversed the policies of his father, but in the end he broke his promise to introduce a constitution.

Initially also, he opposed the idea of another war against France but was eventually goaded into it by his beautiful and high-spirited wife Louisa of Mecklenburg-Strelitz (1776-1810), the daughter of a field marshal who later used her persuasive charms on both Tsar Alexander I and Napoleon. Having thus missed the chance to join with Austria and Russia in the campaigns of 1805 he had to face Napoleon without their aid in 1806, and the once all-powerful Prussian army was crushed under his command by Napoleon at Jena-Auerstadt the following year. In the aftermath Napoleon captured Berlin and turned Prussia into a vassal state of his empire, even insisting that Prussian troops should join his ill-fated invasion of Russia. Frederick William meanwhile had fled to Memel in East Prussia and had to accept the humiliating treaty of Tilsit by which he lost half of his kingdom: all his lands west of the Elbe as well as the more recently acquired territories in Poland.

In the years of defeat and humiliation that followed it was Frederick William's feisty wife Louisa, described by Napoleon as 'the only man in Prussia', who did more than he did to inspire a resistance movement against the French conquerors. This saw the flourishing of patriotic poetry and a new heroic cult of a fatherland that had never previously existed, yet was to remain a growing German obsession for the 130 years. It also saw the restructuring of the Prussian army by able ministers like Scharnhorst and Gneisenau, which later had its repercussions. Initially the outcome was simply another series of defeats, such as Lützen and Bautzen, which had the by-product of giving Napoleon the confidence to attack Russia. In the end it was only the retreat from Moscow in 1812 that eventually gave Frederick William the courage to stand up to Napoleon, return to Berlin and join the Austrians in the campaign that climaxed with the victory of Leipzig the following year.

Despite ending up on the winning side, Frederick William did not do particularly well out of the Treaty of Vienna, for Prussia was treated as a junior power compared with the larger states of Russia and Austria. He lost most of his Polish territories apart from Posen to Russia, while Friesland was given to the Dutch. The old Hohenzollern estates of Ansbach and Bayreuth became part of Bavaria. Berg and Jülich were returned as was all of Pomerania, so at least Brandenburg stayed connected with East Prussia and there were modest gains in Saxony and Westphalia. But several of Napoleon's new German kingdoms, like Württemberg and Bavaria, were allowed to survive, which meant that Prussia was no longer unique.

Frederick William had lost his charismatic wife in 1810 but survived the war for a quarter of a century. As so often in the middle age of autocrats, liberal intentions gave way to extreme conservatism and he conveniently forgot all his old promises of reform, particularly of a constitution. He did allow the establishment of provincial assemblies or diets and he did endorse the Customs Union or Zollverein, which provided considerable encouragement for German industry. However, he ruthlessly suppressed the democratic movements that raised their heads in 1819 and 1830.

He and Louisa had ten children of whom three died in infancy. Of his three surviving sons two were to become kings of Prussia and one the first Kaiser. His daughter Charlotte married the future tsar Nicholas I of Russia and was thus, under her new name, the ancestress of the last three tsars.

Frederick William IV (1795-1861) was in his mid-forties when he took over in 1840 and seems to have inherited some of the indecisiveness of his father. He had trained in the normal Prussian way as a soldier and fought in the 1813 campaign without particular distinction. His main interests were intellectual and artistic: he was a gifted amateur architect and designer – the completion of Cologne cathedral was one of his pet projects. He patronized scientists, such as the chemist Bunsen and the naturalist von Humboldt. He loved romantic poetry and had his own mystical notion of a divinely ordained German Empire

Politically, like his father in middle age, he was extremely conservative and, also like his father, frustratingly promised a constitution with no intention of delivering. During the revolutionary turmoil of 1848 he hesitated over the use of troops to suppress the rioters, but instead rode boldly through the streets of Berlin wearing the national colours and appealing to his 'dear Berlinners'. At one point he was offered the crown of a united Germany but was persuaded to reject it by his ministers who thought the constitutional strings attached were too liberal.

Frederick William's marriage to the saintly Elizabeth of Bavaria was childless, so when in 1858 he suffered a severe stroke which left him partially brain-dead his brother William took over as regent for the last three years of his reign. His wife nursed him to the end before retiring to Charlottenburg and Stolzenfels.

THE NEW REICH

King William I (1797-1888) was only two years younger than his brother and thus took over the crown in his mid-sixties. He was to survive till he was over ninety despite numerous attempts to assassinate him, one very nearly successful. He was to complete a long and eventful reign that brought the Hohenzollern dynasty to such a peak that nemesis was almost certain to follow.

As the second son William had not received the education reserved for heirs to the throne but had instead been sent to join the army where he had proved himself a brave, if not exceptional, soldier serving under Blücher at Waterloo. Much more aggressive than his elder brother, he adopted a very different strategy in 1848, famously turning the guns on the rioting mobs, hence his nickname Kartatschenprinz, or Prince Grapeshot. He became so unpopular that he had to leave Berlin for a while and when he returned was involved in the suppression of democratic movements in various parts of Germany.

When he at last became king, William was faced with considerable pressure to reduce the powers of the monarchy and to accept a proper constitutional form of parliamentary government. However, he believed in a militaristic solution and chose the like-minded Otto von Bismarck as his chief minister. Between them they instigated a three-stage master plan for turning the kingdom of Prussia into a new German Empire. This was to involve three wars, spaced out at two-year intervals, and every effort was made by the wily Bismarck to provoke the other side into starting the wars first, so that international disapproval would be modified. The first war was against Denmark and followed a convenient appeal from the ethnically German population of Schleswig-Holstein who wanted to throw off the rule of the Copenhagen based Oldenburgs. Ironically the new Danish king was a German from Holstein (see p.29).

The second war, with its major Prussian victory against Austria at Sadowa, or Königratz, in 1866, paved the way for the Hohenzollerns to take over from the Habsburgs the role of overlords of the small German states. Hesse-Cassel, Nassau and Frankfurt were handed over to Prussia immediately along with Hanover, which was lost by the British and Queen Victoria because its king backed the wrong side.

Other German states, like Bavaria and Saxony, were allowed to keep their kings but were confederated to Prussia and lost control of their own foreign policy, so it was just a matter of time before there was total unification, especially as the chancellor of the new Confederacy was Bismarck.

An additional by-product of this victory was that the Hohenzollerns gained their second crown, for such was now their prestige that one of the junior princes from the Sigmaringen branch of the family, Karl (1839-1914), was elected the prince of Romania in 1866 and in 1881 became its first king as Carol I. His performance, as we shall see (p.114), was to be somewhat erratic.

The creation of a united German empire, the Kaiserreich followed the third of Bismarck's wars, which was against France in 1870 and, as usual, Bismarck made sure that his enemy was provoked into making the first move. His doctoring of the Ems telegram famously lured Napoleon III into adopting an aggressive posture from which he could not back down without humiliation. The French army was heavily defeated at Sedan, Napoleon lost his throne, the French had to pay a huge indemnity as surety for handing over Alsace Lorraine.

Thus at the age of seventy-four, in a ceremony at Versailles, William I at last became Kaiser Wilhelm I of Germany. He had throughout his life been relatively unassuming albeit rigidly conservative and Bismarck seems at times to have had little respect for his intelligence or that of his son Frederick. Nevertheless, they made an effective team and in their new roles were to last another seventeen years. During that period the new Germany began to snatch colonies for itself all over the world, for in this respect the Germans felt they had been left behind by the other states of Western Europe. By now there were only a limited number of potential colonies left untouched by the existing imperial powers. Thus in 1884 they seized the areas now known as Namibia and Botswana in southern Africa, as well as Togo, Cameroon, parts of northern Congo and of Nigeria and Chad further north. In 1885, they moved into the Pacific taking northern Papua New Guinea, the Bismarck Archipelago, the Marshall Islands. Then came a second tranche in Africa with what is now Tanzania and parts of Rwanda and Burundi, plus Witu on the coast of Kenya. It was the new Weltpolitik, a desperate last minute effort to turn Germany into a world power like Britain, France or Holland – a place in the sun.

The second Kaiser of the dynasty, King Frederick III of Prussia (1831-88), or Fritz, was one of the great might-have-beens of history. In the tradition of the Hohenzollerns he objected strongly to the policies of his father and, in turn, had his own ideas disapproved of by his more reactionary son, young Wilhelm. As crown prince he opposed Bismarck's repressive policies and as emperor he might have toned down Germany's imperial ambitions so that the holocaust of 1914-18 might have been less likely. He had, however, fought in Bismarck's wars and by the time of Sedan had been promoted to field marshal in charge of a major section of the battle, so he enjoyed the fruits of his father's strategy. He had married Victoria, the eldest daughter of Queen Victoria, and famously made her brother the future King Edward apopleptic in the post war euphoria, particularly after the defeat of Denmark, the home of Edward's wife Alexandra.

However, he was fifty-seven by the time he took over from his father and suffering from throat cancer, which killed him within a year.

ARMAGEDDON

The third and last Kaiser was Wilhelm II (1859-1941) who was only twenty-eight when he succeeded his father. His birth had been bungled by a confusion of doctors, some supplied to his mother by his over-anxious grandmother Queen Victoria, whose first grandchild he was. The result was that he had a deformed right arm, which made it very hard for him even to pretend to be a soldier and for Prussian dynasts there was no deeper humiliation than to be unfit for military service. His mother, in the Hanoverian-Saxe-Coburg tradition, was cold and irritable rather than sympathetic, so he trained desperately hard at the Kassel Gymnasium to win her approval and was an ultra-conscientious cadet and student at Bonn University, resting his useless right arm on his sword hilt as he inspected his troops, desperate to disguise his disability. He was, however, extremely intelligent, articulate and an able speaker, a point noted by President Theodore Roosevelt when they met in 1910. As a teenager he worshipped his war-hero father but the wily old Bismarck saw the ambitious youngster as a potential ally against what he saw as the excessively liberal tendencies of the father, so he encouraged his anti-parental rebellions and his delusions of grandeur.

By the time that Wilhelm became Kaiser the Chancellor Bismarck had been in effective charge for twenty-six years and had no intention of letting the young man interfere with his method of running affairs, especially not with Wilhelm's brand of populism. But having encouraged the young man to oppose his father's ideas, the chancellor found himself hoist by his own petard, for Wilhelm wanted to dictate policy, not just accept Bismarck's. In particular, Wilhelm wanted a much more aggressive foreign policy than Bismarck and they fell out over the possibility that a Hohenzollern would take over the throne of Spain. So the new Kaiser made the chancellor resign, famously 'dropping the pilot'.

As Wilhelm sought desperately for Germany's 'place in the sun' there was now a new flurry of colony acquisitions with Nauru, Marianne, Palau, the Carolines, Samoa and notably Kiautschou (Jiaozhou Bay) in Shandong on mainland China. What is more Wilhelm seemed to take great delight in annoying his grandmother in London, for example with his congratulatory telegram to Kruger in 1896 and his subsequent moral support for the Boers against the British three years later. At about the same time, after the passing of the first Navy Act in 1898, Admiral Tirpitz had the go-ahead to increase rapidly the size and quality of the German navy, in particular building what the British called Dreadnoughts. Tirpitz personally visited Kiautschou to assess its viability as a base for the German Pacific fleet, thus indicating the threat to British naval supremacy. To underline this threat the new Kaiser Wilhelm Kanal at Kiel was completed, which eased the passage of German naval ships from the Baltic to the North Sea and steps were taken almost immediately to widen it for the new larger battleships.

Meanwhile, as early as 1895 Wilhelm encouraged General Schlieffen to make the contingency plans for a preemptive strike against France that would involve a lightning attack through Belgium, knowing full well that Belgian neutrality had been guaranteed by Britain, so that such a move would almost certainly cause a general war. It was the kind of risky strategy that Bismarck had always taken care to avoid.

For the eighteen years between the fall of Bismarck and 1908 Wilhelm was in total charge and no minister dared disagree for fear of dismissal or one of the Kaiser's outbursts of apopleptic rage. His behaviour was so erratic that many contemporaries believed he was mentally unstable, and there may have been some truth in this for he suffered from growths and discharges in his inner ear that may well have contributed to his neurotic state. Nearly two decades of unshared decision-making and posing as the great Hun warrior, while chronically searching for his elusive self-esteem put undue stress on a temperament that was naturally febrile. Events like the Chinese crisis of 1900 and Moroccan crisis of 1905,when he was egged on by von Bulow and took unprovoked risks in antagonizing the other powers, must have caused him enormous stress, particularly if there was any question of him appearing to back down.

There are also suggestions that his sexual orientation at this time may have, at least temporarily, been ambivalent, for his relationship with von Eulenburg was notorious as was his selection of good looking younger men to be the new generals of his army. While he had apparently concerted with female prostitutes before his accession, he was monogamous thereafter with his wife Augusta, or Donna of Schleswig-Holstein (another Oldenburg), and they were to have seven children before her death in 1921. Things came to a head with the so-called 'Daily Telegraph Affair' in 1908, for it was about this time that Wilhelm appears to have suffered a nervous collapse. In the wake of Austria's annexation of Bosnia he had given a very intemperate interview to the paper, which caused offence particularly to the British ('you are mad, mad, mad as March hares') and Japanese, but also French and Russians at a time when the Balkans could well have erupted into open war. It severely damaged his credibility at home and abroad, shattered his confidence and caused something approaching a nervous breakdown. He was forty-nine.

Meanwhile, he had just bought an exotic new palace at Achilleion on the Greek island of Corfu where he could pose as the new Achilles and entertain diplomatic guests. He was so besotted with Greek dancing that he wrote and produced a ballet at the Berlin Opera in 1912 recycling the peasant dances of Corfu.

During the last ten years of his reign Wilhelm was much less active and after getting rid of von Bulow whom he blamed for his own extravagances, he delegated much more to his ministers, but his influence was still strong. From 1912, he appears to have been concentrating on Germany's readiness for war, perhaps he imagined just a defensive war, but nevertheless such preparations were tantamount to making war less avoidable. The Kiel Canal was due to reopen in 1914, so nothing could happen before then.

In the Sarajevo Crisis of August 1914 Wilhelm indulged in his characteristic inflammatory rantings, condemning the Habsburg regime for what he regarded as its weak handling of the Balkans problem. The Austrians were soft, the British and French behaved like Negroes and the Jews were guilty of the usual world conspiracy. Though it was none of his business, he demanded that the Austrians should punish the Serb nation because it was a Serb who had murdered Archduke Ferdinand.

Thus the irresponsible ravings of a half-psychotic middle-aged man, even though he was no longer a functioning autocrat, helped create the atmosphere that made the First World War almost inevitable. He egged on the rather more cautious but even prouder and older Kaiser Franz Joseph in Vienna to bluster like him against the Serbs, knowing that this would almost certainly provoke the third Kaiser or Czar, Nicholas II, whose genes were also almost 100 per cent German, to respond in favour of the Serbs. He also knew that if the Russians responded then the French would follow suit, and since the Schlieffen Plan was in place to take out the French after crushing Belgium, then the fourth Kaiser, George V, the head of the Saxe-Coburg dynasty based in London, would feel morally obliged to let the British join in as well.

So between them these four somewhat lackluster hereditary monarchs, with waning powers and an average age of fifty-eight, bore huge responsibility for the deaths of forty million people and the self-destruction of three out of the four dynasties. Wilhelm too late realized the potential enormity of the events he was helping precipitate and the famous 'Willy-Nicky letters' were his vain effort to halt the downward spiral. As the self-styled warlord (Kriegsherr) Wilhelm went to war, perhaps he had some reasonable expectation that he would be on the winning side, for while he could have foretold that most of the European powers would become involved he would have expected the Schlieffen Plan to be successful. Its implementation bore the cost of bringing the British into the war, but he could not have foreseen that the need to starve out Britain by means of his submarines sinking transatlantic merchant ships would then bring the wrath of the United States on his head.

Unlike many German fathers who had sons of the right age for military service, Wilhelm lost none of his sons in the war. Crown Prince Wilhelm, commanded the fifth army till he became disenchanted after Verdun and was nicknamed Clown Prince by the British. Later, he supported Hitler in the vain hope that he would bring him back as Kaiser. One of his sons was killed fighting in 1940 and he himself died in 1951 back near the old family home of Hohenzollern, for Brandenburg was by then in the Russian Zone of Germany. Prince Eitel was wounded on the Eastern Front but survived till 1942. Prince August became an obergruppenführer in the S.A. till he fell out with Goebbels. The nearest thing to genuine casualty amongst Wilhelm's sons was Prince Joachim who was half-offered a crown by the Irish at the time of the Easter Rising in 1916, but when that fell through he could not take demotion to the common herd and committed suicide in 1920.

Meanwhile, the strain of being, at least in theory, a warlord was proving too much for Wilhelm. By 1916, he was leaving most of the decisions to the dictatorial duumvirate of Hindenburg and Ludendorf. However, he seems to have taken it upon himself to preserve his navy from further damage after Jutland by keeping it in harbour, and he was also involved in the dangerous plot to smuggle Lenin back into Russia in 1917. He also still had some sense of humour left, for on hearing that George V had changed the family name to Windsor he is said to have quipped that he would enjoy a performance of Shakespeare's Merry Wives of Saxe-Coburg.

Kaiser Wilhelm was still only fifty-nine when his career as a warlord came to an end in 1918. Naturally, he blamed his defeat on the Jews but more fairly he must bear responsibility for the basic error of tackling enemies on more than one front at the same time, a fault which Bismarck would never have tolerated. As the end approached, President Wilson refused to negotiate any surrender by the Germans until he had abdicated. The Kaiserreich had only lasted forty-seven years. It had reached its greatest extent under Wilhelm but he had also presided over its destruction and the demise of a dynasty that had been royal for 317 years. He was exiled to a comfortable estate at Doorn in Holland and three years after his abdication his wife Donna died. He even acquired a second wife.

He was still at Doorn and into his eighties when Hitler's troops streamed past his estate on their way to achieve a more successful version of the Schlieffen Plan, conquering France, where Wilhelm had failed. Indirectly Wilhelm bore nearly as much responsibility for the Second World War as he had for the first. He had helped create the ambition for European conquest and left it frustratingly unfulfilled. His last grandson Wilhelm Karl died in 2007 and his latest theoretical heir was (Prince) George Frederick of Prussia (1976-) who attended Glenalmond boarding school in Scotland, did two years in the German army and took a degree in business.

ROMANIA

Meanwhile, Wilhelm's distant cousin Karl/Carol I of Romania (1839-1914) founder of the only other Hohenzollern royal dynasty had helped his relatively backward nation to industrialise and defend itself. Born in Sigmaringen north of Lake Constance, he was bearded, short and quite frail. The second son of the local Hohenzollern prince, he had trained at the Berlin artillery school and taken part in Prussia's war over Schleswig in 1864. It was partly some French blood on his side of the family that led to Napoleon III recommending him as potential prince, or Domnitor, for Romania. In that role he led the Romanian army during the Russo-Turkish war of 1877-8 that resulted in his country winning independence from the Ottoman Empire, so that he was able to assume the title of king in 1881.

In 1907, he brutally suppressed peasant rebellions in Moldavia and Wallachia, but in more liberal mode he built a bridge over the Danube and two universities. Like his distant cousin, he was an expansionist and won Dobruja in 1913. In 1914, by which time he was in his mid-seventies, he felt obliged to support his Hohenzollern cousin and side with the Triple Alliance, but luckily his parliament was opposed to the idea so in the end he chose wisely to keep Romania neutral during the first stages of the First World War.

In 1869, soon after taking over the princedom of Romania he had married the highly emotional German Princess Elizabeth of Wied who wrote novels under the pseudonym of Carmen Sylva, but sadly he was so obsessive about his dynastic role – according to her he wore his crown in his sleep – that she pined for normal company. Even the massive new castle he built for them at Peles was Germanically aggressive. They had a daughter who died in infancy and no other children, so when he died soon after the start of the war he was succeeded by his nephew Ferdinand.

King Ferdinand (1865-1927) had been born, like his uncle, in Sigmaringen and was a Catholic, for he had a Portuguese princess as his mother. Both his father and elder brother turned down the Romanian inheritance. He had a very well-connected wife, Marie, a grand daughter of Queen Victoria, daughter of Alfred Duke of Edinburgh and related to the Romanovs. With all these connections he wanted to reverse his predecessor's neutrality and to join the war against his neighbour Austria and Germany the country of his birth. By doing so he did his new allies no favours, for Romania was quickly overrun and the net result was that the promising Russian attacks of 1916 were outflanked by the Alliance's inroads into Romania. However, despite contributing little from a military point of view, Ferdinand was rewarded for choosing the winning side and by 1920 had substantially increased his kingdom with the addition of Bessarabia, Bukovina and Transylvania.

By the time that Ferdinand died in 1927, in his early sixties, his self-indulgent son and heir Carol (1893-1953) had already committed so many indiscretions that he had ruled himself out of the succession. Having unofficially married the exotic Zizi Lambrino when he was twenty, he divorced her for a respectable Greek (Oldenburg) princess, Helen (-1982), but after four years deserted her to go off with a mistress called Magda Lupescu, so in 1925 he renounced the throne.

Thus the succession went to Carol's nine-year-old son Michael, or Mihai (1921-), born at Foisor Castle in Sinaia, who became the nominal king with regents for the next three years.

Then, in 1930, Carol shamelessly reappeared in Romania and effectively deposed his own son, assuming dictatorial powers as Carol II for the next ten years. His reign was made difficult, however, by the rise of a pro-German Nazi party and when Carol tried to suppress it he was deposed. He escaped, allegedly, with a large cache of valuable paintings and other treasure so that he was able to live in comfort in Spain for another fifteen years, pausing only to marry his long-term mistress in Rio de Janiero.

Meanwhile, his son Mihai had been reinstated as a puppet king by the Nazi regime. However, at the age of twenty-three he showed considerable initiative in aiding the overthrow of the fascist dictator Antonescu, and in 1944 his new ministers declared war on Germany. Once again a Hohenzollern king of Romania had declared war on the fatherland and once again was on the winning side, but it did Mihai little good, for within two years of the victory there was a communist coup d'état and he was forced to abdicate a second time. He had a relatively productive exile compared with many ex-monarchs, for he became a commercial airline pilot. He had married a Bourbon-Parma and they had six daughters, one of whom he designated as his heir, for once dispensing with Salic Law.

CHAPTER 6

The Five Crowns of The House of Wettin

The small town of Wettin lies on the Saale River in Hosgau, Saxony, and is first heard of when a man called Dietrich or Theodoric became its count, shortly before dying around 982. About a century later the family acquired the more prosperous area of Meissen on the Elbe, eventually becoming Electors of Saxony and adding the later infamous Colditz to their list of properties. Their further promotion was gradual though they did provide two kings for Poland, but it was in the nineteenth century that their Saxe-Coburg descendants had an extraordinary flowering. They picked up the crown of Belgium in 1830, provided Queen Victoria with a mother and a husband, and then added the crowns of Portugal and Bulgaria before again subsiding into relative mediocrity, with Belgium as their one surviving throne apart from Britain.

From Meissen to Gotha

The upward path of the family, which eventually produced Prince Albert and a quartet of royal dynasties in the Victorian era, was extremely tortuous, even by the standards of German history. From the death of Dietrich of Wettin in 982 it took 100 years before his descendant Thimo of Wettin (1010-90) was promoted by the emperor Henry IV in 1089 to become *markgraf*, or margrave, of the frontier county of Meissen, an area rich in minerals that had then just recently been conquered from the Slavs and was close to the eastern borders of the Holy Roman Empire.

Thimo was followed by Count Conrad the Great (1097-1157) whose grandson, Count Dietrich the Oppressed of Meissen (1162-1221), had to wage a long war with his brother and their father after the usual acrimonious split of the inheritance. After disappearing for a while on pilgrimage to the Holy Land, he captured the city of Leipzig by trickery and pulled down its walls so that he could rule it from three new castles that he built for the purpose, but he was so unpopular there that the citizens began to plot his downfall. Soon afterwards he was poisoned by his own doctor.

In the next generation Count Heinrich/Henry III the Illustrious (1215-88) took part in the Teutonic Knights' crusade against the Old Prussians in 1237 and became famous as a model knight, poet and minnesinger who composed songs and put hymns to music. In a series of wars with Brandenburg he lost some towns but gained others and founded Fürstenberg. In 1263, he was rewarded by the Emperor Frederick II with the neighbouring county of Thuringia, for which he had a claim through his mother. The Emperor also offered his daughter as a bride for Henry's eldest son Albert.

Albrecht/Albert the Degenerate (1240-1314) was a huge disappointment to his father, for despite winning Princess Margaret of Sicily as his bride and having five children with her, he had a torrid affair and a second family with his mistress Kunigunde. Not only did he have quarrels with his own brothers but by creating two sets of opposing sons he caused an even worse than average war over his inheritance, which at the same time he had brought close to bankruptcy by his extravagance.

Friedrich I (1257-1323) the Brave or the Bitten (he had allegedly been bitten by his distraught mother when she heard about Kunigunde) was the eldest legitimate son who, after beating his father in battle, eventually succeeded to the remnants of the inheritance. As a result of his mother's royal blood he made claim to be the King of Jerusalem and Sicily, but despite a few campaigns in Italy was unable to turn this ambition into reality. He was followed as Margrave of Meissen and Landgrave of Thuringia by four more generations of Friedrichs. The first of these, Friedrich II the Serious (Ernshafte, 1310-49), was born in the Thuringian city of Gotha, later to play an important role in the family's history. His successor Friedrich III the Strict (1332-81), from the vast hilltop castle of Altenburg, married the heiress of Coburg, so the family now had two of the cities with which they were later to be famously associated. However, it was Friedrich IV the Belligerent (1370-1428) who achieved the next major advance in the family's fortunes, for in 1423 he played a major part in suppressing the Hussite heretics of Bohemia. As his reward the Emperor promoted him to the vacant title of Duke of Saxony and Prince Elector – the previous family had died out. He moved to his new capital of Wittenberg and renumbered himself as Duke Friedrich I.

As so often, when a German dynasty attained new levels of prosperity it resorted to the old Salian habit of subdividing itself. Thus Duke Friedrich II the Gentle (1412-64) in 1445 split the inheritance with three of his brothers, but all four of them kept the valuable mining rights in common. It was a classic recipe for strife. When one brother died and another was forced to become a bishop, Friedrich, as Elector of Saxony, had to wage a war with the remaining brother, William the Duke of Saxony, that lasted five years. This unfortunate pattern was to be repeated in subsequent generations.

Thus Friedrich's two sons further split the inheritance. They had earlier, in 1445, both been kidnapped in the famous Prinzenraub but managed to escape. They also combined to create a magnificent new six-storey palace for themselves, the Albrechtsburg, at Meissen. The elder Ernst (1441-86) became Elector of Saxony with his bases at Wittenberg and Colditz (acquired by the Wettin in 1404), whilst his brother Albert the Bold (1443-1500) took Meissen and Dresden where he made his home. Ernst gave his name to the Ernestine branch of the family, which later produced a number of royal dynasties, but sadly he died quite young after a fall from his horse at Colditz Castle by the River Mulde near Leipzig. His brother Albert had a distinguished career as an imperial general against Burgundy and Hungary, was a star in the tournaments and became Stadholder of the Netherlands for the Emperor Maximilian who unfortunately never paid him his considerable expenses.

As it turned out, the split between the Ernestine and Albertine lines of the Wettin was to last till 1918, for the Albertine branch produced electors from 1547 till the end of the Holy Roman Empire in 1806 and then resurrected themselves as kings of Saxony from 1806-1918. Meanwhile, they also produced two kings of Poland. The Ernestine branch, on the other hand, having lost the electorate in 1547 went on to subdivide itself into further painfully small units, one of which was to be Saxe-Coburg, which was to have such an extraordinary late flowering in the nineteenth century.

Just before Ernst's death there was another damaging division of the Wettin inheritance at a time when the neighbouring Hohenzollern in Brandenburg and Prussia were at last beginning to consolidate their powers. The internal family squabbles of the Wettin were further exacerbated when brothers and cousins took different sides in the religious divisions that followed the Reformation.

THE WARS OF RELIGION

Ernst's son, the new Elector of Saxony Friedrich III the Wise (1463-1525), who took over in 1486 was a devout Catholic who nevertheless favoured reform of the Church. So he decided to support the efforts of Martin Luther who in 1508 began teaching at the university of Wittenberg, Friedrich's electoral capital. Nine years later Luther nailed his famous Ninety Five Theses to the university church door and under Friedrich's protection the Reformed Church began to grow in strength with Wittenberg as its centre.

Despite all this, two years later, in 1519, the Pope put forward Friedrich as a candidate for the imperial throne against the Habsburg candidate Charles. Friedrich made little effort to follow up this opportunity and instead cast his electoral vote for the overwhelming favourite, who became Charles V. Even after that, when Friedrich was still sheltering Luther in his Wartburg Castle, the Pope perhaps underestimated the threat from Luther and awarded Friedrich the Golden Rose of Virtue. Unlike his protégée Luther, Friedrich chose not to marry, died a bachelor and was buried in the *schlosskirche* at Wittenberg.

He was succeeded as Elector by his brother, Johann the Steadfast (1468-1532), who also protected the infant Lutheran church. In due course in 1527, he turned it into the official church for Saxony with himself as its chief bishop, despite the fact that he had a wife and four children. He thus became the leader of the league of Protestant states, which now found itself at war with the emperor.

Johann's son and main heir Johann Friedrich I the Magnanimous (1503-54) inherited a state of war as well as the electorate of Saxony. Born in the family castle of Torgau on the Elbe, he was, like his predecessors, a champion of the Reformed Church and a fine scholar, but sadly he turned out to be the last of the Ernestine branch of the family to hold his high office in Germany. Yet significantly, before facing his nemesis he hived off to his youngest brother Johann Ernst a portion of his inheritance that was later to become so important for the dynasty, the little duchy of Saxe-Coburg.

His nemesis was his cousin Maurice (1521-53), grandson of Albert and head, therefore, of the Albertine branch of the family. He was a staunch Catholic and had a grudge against his Protestant cousin. Having gained the favour of the Emperor Charles V by serving in his army against the Turks in 1542 and the French two years later, he won the emperor's backing for an attack on his cousin.

In response, Johann Friedrich summoned his allies to join him at Schmalkalden, but their league was heavily defeated by the emperor at the Battle of Mühlberg in 1547. Johann Frederick was badly wounded and deposed as Elector of Saxony in favour of his cousin Maurice. Later, he was condemned to death and only avoided this sentence by surrendering his city of Wittenberg. He spent the next five years imprisoned in the cathedral city of Worms and when he was at last released he built himself a new palace at Weimar, which now replaced Wittenberg as the main base for the family's truncated version of the duchy of Saxony. There he patronized the great scholar Melanchthon and began the process that led soon afterwards to the foundation of Jena University. He died two years later.

Meanwhile, his ambitious cousin Maurice who had displaced him as Elector of Saxony and suffered taunts of being a Judas did not enjoy his new status for long. He had already alienated the Catholic establishment by dissolving the monasteries to fill his treasury, and then, in 1550, he fell out with his patron the emperor. Three years later he won a remarkable victory at Sievershausen but was fatally wounded and died soon afterwards at the age of thirty-two. A fine monument in Freiburg Cathedral marked his burial place.

THE WETTINS IN THE THIRTY YEARS' WAR

The next few generations of both wings of the Wettin dynasty were not particularly distinguished. On the Albertine side the new Elector August (1526-86) did a solid job of building up the Saxon state. He was followed by two innocuous electors, both called Christian, but then came Johann George (1585-1656), a bully and a drunkard who was known to indulge in seven hour feasts of beer and local produce, yet at the same time managed to sustain the role of a good father and faithful husband. Given the wealth of his territories, which covered the fertile plains of the Elbe and Mulde and contained the profitable merchant city of Leipzig, he could have stepped in to halt the drift towards a war that he did not want, but he lacked the commitment. He wisely turned down the dangerous throne of Bohemia in 1619 and then helped to drive out the man who accepted it, the Protestant champion Friedrich/Frederick of the Palatinate. Though himself a Protestant he sided with the Catholic Habsburgs during the early period of the Thirty Years' War but changed sides with disastrous consequences in 1631. His reputation was as the man who had betrayed the Protestants in 1620, the Swedes in 1635 and, later, the emperor in 1637. His territories were ravaged and he took to flight after the battle of Breitenfeld, only to suffer even more when he changed sides again in 1636. He lost this time to the Swedes at Wittstock and now had to watch while they ravaged Saxony. The devastation was so great that his barons forced him to reduce all his peasants back to the status of serfs.

His successor Johann Georg II (1613-80) had a much more peaceful period as Elector and did much to restore the prosperity of Saxony in the aftermath of the war. He beautified his capital at Dresden, which he turned into the leading musical city of Europe. It was at this point that the family produced one of its most formidable characters and its first crowned head, Friedrich August, who was to become King of Poland in 1697.

Meanwhile, the fortunes of the Ernestine branch of the family had been marked by much less drama as they continued to splinter the patrimony into smaller and smaller units. Johann Friedrich II (1529-95), son of the deposed elector, split the already dwindled inheritance with his brother Johann Wilhelm (1530-73) and himself moved to Gotha in the Thuringian Forest. He was briefly restored as Elector of Saxony in 1554 but fell out with the Emperor Maximilian II who then employed his jealous brother Johann Wilhelm to besiege him in Gotha. The younger brother defeated the older, made him a prisoner for the rest of his life and seized for himself the entire inheritance.

Next, however, it was the turn of Johann Wilhelm to fall out with the Emperor, for though a Protestant he took service with the French army to suppress the Huguenots, an act of treachery so far as the emperor was concerned and also for his own Protestant subjects. So this time his nephews were sent to depose him. He lost all his ill-gotten gains and reverted to being Duke of Saxe-Weimar. It was his nephew Johann Casimir who undertook the great rebuilding project at Coburg with its vast fortress of Veste Coburg and the superb extensions of Schloss Ehrenburg.

Thus the Ernestine branch of the House of Wettin became more splintered and less powerful than their cousins, the Albertine branch in Dresden. The subdivision of inheritances was set to continue with disastrous effect. At the beginning of the Thirty Years' War, Johann Ernst Duke of Saxe-Weimar was deposed by the emperor for disobedience and replaced by his brother, Wilhelm (1578-1662), who in turn became a fervent supporter of German freedoms and culture against the Habsburgs. He helped found the Fruitbearing Society and other patriotic groups but was captured at the battle of Stadtlohn in 1623 along with his brother, Bernard, who was the joint Duke of Saxe-Weimar.

Subsequently, he served in the Swedish invading force under Gustav Adolf and rose to the rank of general. Bernard, who was the youngest of ten brothers, also rose in the Swedish army and famously took charge after Gustav Adolf was killed at Lützen, so that his brave defiance saved the day. Later, he conquered Alsace and tried to create a new dukedom for himself there but died before he could get Richelieu's permission. As in Saxony, there was considerable devastation caused by the war, and in 1635, the starving citizens of Coburg were said to be resorting to cannibalism to survive.

THE GOLDEN AGE OF WEIMAR

Duke Ernst the Pious of Saxe-Coburg (1601-75) managed to marry the heiress of his Saxe-Altenburg cousins in 1672 thus reuniting three of the previously splintered branches of the family, but his son, Duke Friedrich, had to share the minuscule duchy and its limited income with six brothers.

His son, Duke Friedrich II (1672-1732) of Saxe-Gotha-Altenburg, also made life difficult by having nineteen children but, amazingly, the eighteenth of this brood, Augusta (1719-72), born in Gotha, was chosen at the age of sixteen by King George II of Great Britain to be the wife of his eldest son, Frederick Prince of Wales. Despite a twelve-year age gap, she seems to have been a happy enough wife of this otherwise rebellious and discontented Prince of Wales who was loathed by his own parents (see p.76) and believed by them incapable of fathering a child. He proved them wrong, producing both the future King George III and eight other children before dying prematurely after a sweaty cricket match. Augusta was thus never a queen, but was at least the ancestress of all subsequent British royals and survived to become a founding patron of Kew Gardens.

Meanwhile, the youngest of Duke Friedrich I's six brothers, Johann Ernst (1658-1729), had added somewhat to his small share of the duchy when the intervening brothers died without children, but had to divide it between four sons of his own. It was his own fourth son, Franz Josias (1695-1764), who carried on this over-fertile but ill-endowed family, and he had to serve in the Imperial Army to earn his living. The financial difficulties of a petty duchy with a vast palace and an embarrassingly extended ducal family continued with his son Ernst. Friedrich (1724-1800), Duke of Saxe-Coburg-Saalfeld, who moved to Coburg was so deeply in debt that the Emperor Joseph II made him pay it off in installments.

Meanwhile, in a similar way the dukedoms of Saxe-Weimar and Saxe-Eisenach had been reunited in 1748, which made possible the great flowering of culture in Weimar under Grand Duke Karl August/Charles Augustus (1757-1828) who became the patron of both Goethe and Schiller. A hard drinker and reckless sportsman, he encouraged the liberal intellectuals of Jena University and, to the horror of right-wing contemporaries, advocated constitutional government for what might have become a united Germany. Some of this enlightenment spread also to Saxe-Coburg, for the next duke of Saxe-Coburg-Saalfeld Franz Friedrich (1750-1806) was a lover of books, and he produced a clutch of extraordinarily gifted and ambitious children who from fairly humble origins were totally to transform the fortunes of the family. His grandchildren were to include two kings and an empress.

THE POLISH INTERLUDE

Meanwhile, the Albertine branch of the Wettin, the Electors of Saxony in their exquisite capital at Dresden, were reaching new heights. In 1697, Friedrich August (1670-1733), who had taken over as elector from his brother four years earlier, was elected as the new King of Poland. There, on account of his considerable physical presence, he was known as Augustus II the Strong. He already had a reputation as a general having served in the wars against the Turks and the French. All that the crown of Poland cost him was conversion from Protestant to Roman Catholic.

Apart from a gap of five years from 1704-9 he was king of the Poles for the next thirty-six years, during which he beautified his new capital at Warsaw and his old one at Dresden. The gap after 1704 was his own fault, as he had attempted to conquer Swedish Livonia in 1699 and was thoroughly out-generaled by the brilliant King Karl XII (Charles XII, another Germanic export – see p.142) of Sweden. It was only when his ally Tsar Peter of Russia defeated the Swedes for him that Augustus was able to get back his kingdom.

He was notorious for two other facets of his character: he was a prodigious womanizer and was estimated to have fathered at least 365 bastards, many of them acknowledged, including the brilliant Maurice Saxe (1696-1750), born in Goslar, who became one of the finest generals of his generation, was made a marshal of France and, amongst other victories, defeated the Duke of Cumberland at Fontenoy in 1745.

The other aspect of Augustus's excessive appetites was his greed for gold, so that he immured an alchemist called Böttger in one of his castles to force him to find the secret of making gold. Instead, Böttger achieved something more sensible, for by experimenting with very high temperatures he worked out the secret for making porcelain for the first time in Europe and thus made possible the founding of a new industry that made Meissen and Dresden famous.

Augustus made great efforts to change the constitution of Poland so that future kings would be hereditary instead of elected, and though he failed he did enough to make sure that his only legitimate son was allowed to succeed him. This was Augustus II the Corpulent (1696-1763) who thus in 1733 became King of Poland, Elector of Saxony and Grand Duke of Lithuania. He did little to justify his election, for he only spent three years out of his thirty year reign in Poland itself, building a pair of unnecessary palaces in Warsaw, both of which were destroyed in 1944. While he spent his time hunting, going to the opera and collecting miniatures, he left the difficult task of governing Poland in the hands of Count Brühl who mismanaged affairs to such an extent that when Augustus died there was little chance of the Wettin dynasty keeping the crown. Instead, there was a coup, aided by Russian troops, in favour of one of Catherine the Great's ex-lovers. This was just a sad prelude to the destruction of the Polish nation and the division of the spoils between its three powerful neighbours, Russia, Austria and Prussia. This disaster owed a lot to the idleness of Augustus the Corpulent and condemned the Poles to misery for nearly two centuries.

With his Habsburg wife Augustus II had fifteen children and his son, the crippled Friedrich Christian, succeeded as Elector of Saxony in 1763 but then almost immediately died. His own son Friedrich August (1750-1827) succeeded him and was the last Elector, for the empire was crushed by Napoleon in 1806. To compensate he was made Duke of Warsaw, and when Napoleon fell, the great powers let him return to Dresden as King of Saxony. He was succeeded by his brother, Anton, and the family produced further kings of Saxony whose powers became increasingly meaningless until they were finally abolished in 1918. Thus the Albertine branch of the Wettin dynasty at last came to an end.

THE BIRTH OF BELGIUM

Meanwhile, the Ernestine branch, which had since 1547 been the poor relation, at last came into its own again. The bibliophile Franz Friedrich, Duke of Saxe-Coburg-Saalfeld, produced ten children, far too many to be able to live off a tiny duchy with big overheads. Even the eldest son, Ernst Anton (1784-1844), had to go and earn his keep as a general in the Prussian army; he fought against Napoleon at both Lützen and Leipzig, but is best known as the father of his younger son prince Albert, the consort of Queen Victoria and ancestor of all subsequent British royals. It was probably in reaction to Ernst Anton's callous womanizing that Albert developed his own almost puritanical streak of morality.

In the meantime, it was Franz Friedrich's second son, Leopold (1790-1865), who by sheer force of personality lifted the House of Wettin to a new level. He had served in the Russian army in his youth and he too fought at both Lützen and Leipzig. It did him no harm that one of his sisters, Juliane, had married the Tsar's brother. At the age of twenty-six he persuaded Charlotte (see p.79) the daughter of the Prince of Wales and heiress to the British throne to marry him despite opposition from her father. In all probability he would have become Prince Consort of Great Britain on the death of George IV in 1830 had his new wife not tragically died in childbirth. However, he did not stop coming to London and masterminded the engagement of his widowed sister Victoria to Edward, Duke of Kent, which resulted in the birth of their daughter, the future Queen Victoria in 1819.

In 1830, Leopold was at last offered a crown, that of newly liberated Greece, which had won its independence from the Turks, but he decided the situation there was insufficiently stable and held out for something better.

This materialized less than a year later when Belgium won its independence from Holland and this time he accepted the offer of the throne. He was forty and for the next twenty-five years he was a conscientious constitutional monarch, successfully establishing a new Saxe-Coburg dynasty that lasted into the twenty-first century. By liberal policies and tact he ensured a much more peaceful transition of the revolutionary ferment of 1848 to which his father-in-law, Louis Philippe of France, succumbed. Sadly his second official marriage to the French king's daughter was nearly as short as his first, for she was only thirty-eight when she died.

Leopold also continued his matchmaking activities and by arranging the marriage of his niece Victoria to his nephew Albert he effectively organized a new Saxe-Coburg dynasty for the British.

His half-French son, Leopold II (1835-1909), born in Brussels, took over at the age of thirty and proved much more aggressive. He devoted considerable energy to the development of Belgian trade and industry, competing with the other European powers to grab some of the remaining uncolonised areas of Africa. In particular, he turned the Congo into his personal fief as its self-appointed king from 1885, having employed the explorer Stanley to prospect the huge area on his behalf. He then ruthlessly exploited both its vast mineral resources and native work force for the benefit of himself and Belgium, but not of the Congo where some of the ethnic squabbles that he encouraged for his own purposes have caused problems ever since and his actions came close to genocide. Using a private army he created conditions of virtual slavery that caused an international scandal, particularly with the exposure in 1904 by Roger Casement of the cruel treatment of rubber collectors. He spent large sums strengthening the defenses of Belgium in response to the growing threat from Germany and united his two kingdoms of Belgium and Congo just before his death. He also spent some of his massive profits on grandiose building projects including additions to his palace at Laeken and his Villa des Cedres on the Riviera.

He had a Habsburg wife who produced three daughters and a son, who sadly died after falling into a pond at the age of ten, but had another two sons with a favourite prostitute whom he married unofficially five days before his death. He was also rumoured to have been a client of a sado-masochistic brothel in London.

He was succeeded by his nephew Albert I (1875-1934), a much more popular figure and a devoted Catholic who immediately set about reforms in the Congo. He led the heroic defense of the Belgians against the German invasion of 1914 and the victorious army which re-entered Brussels in 1918. Ironically, his mother was a Hohenzollern and his wife a Bavarian Wittelsbach. The royal couple were utterly devoted to each other and made themselves popular by adopting an unpretentious lifestyle; they even let their thirteen year old son Leopold serve in the army as a private. Though Albert was a skilled rock climber, he was killed tragically in a climbing accident in the Ardennes in 1934.

Albert's son and successor, Leopold III (1901-83), was less heroic and less popular. Though as a teenager he had fought in the ranks against the Germans, his own genes were over 80 per cent German, but the reasons for his unpopularity were different. He had married an exceptionally beautiful and charismatic Swedish princess, Astrid, who was much more outgoing than himself. A year after his accession he lost control of their car whilst driving in Switzerland, so that she and their unborn fourth child were both killed. He was blamed and later made things worse by taking a second wife. He also failed in comparison with his father, for he personally capitulated with the Belgian army to Hitler in 1940 and spent the rest of the war under house arrest at his Laeken Palace. At length, in 1951, he was persuaded to abdicate in favour of his elder son, the somewhat colourless King Baudoin (1930-93), who died childless and was succeeded by his brother Albert II (1934-). His heir Prince Philippe (1960-) has degrees from Oxford and Stanford, has been a fighter pilot and commando.

THE LONDON SAXE-COBURGS

As we have seen, Leopold I of Belgium was the moving force behind two marriages which transformed the Hanoverian dynasty of Great Britain. The first was between his sister Victoria, an impoverished widow, and the middle-aged reprobate Edward Duke of Kent, one of the younger sons of George III who was belatedly called upon to do his duty as a procreator when his elder brothers all failed. Two decades later Leopold masterminded the second wedding, for by this time his sister's daughter, Victoria, had succeeded to the British throne and he introduced her to her Saxe-Coburg cousin, Albert, the second son of his brother Ernst Anton. The Hanoverian dynasty therefore became doubly Saxe-Coburg and was officially Saxe-Coburg from 1901 till the name was dropped in favour of Windsor in 1917 for public relations reasons.

THE PORTUGUESE CONNECTION

We now have to backtrack to the bibliophile Franz Friedrich of Saxe-Coburg-Saalfeld and his fourth child, the younger brother of Leopold of Belgium. This was Ferdinand (1785-1831) who made a fine career for himself by marrying one of the richest heiresses in Europe, Maria Antonia Kohary, a Hungarian Catholic who was due to inherit the estates of Cabrad and Sitno in what is now Slovakia. Ferdinand, understandably in the circumstances, converted to Catholicism and in a situation where vacancies for kings were now cropping up quite regularly in Europe there was potential in being a Catholic. Thus the couple's son Ferdinand (1816-85) was an acceptable husband for the heiress of Portugal, Maria II. They married in 1836 and he was made king consort a year later when they produced a son. Thus he created a new Saxe-Coburg dynasty in Portugal that lasted for nearly seventy-five years and ruled a substantial empire as well as Portugal itself. Ferdinand outlived his wife and later somewhat demeaned his reputation by marrying an opera singer called Eilsa Hensler.

Ferdinand's son, Pedro V the Hopeful (1837-61), succeeded his mother in 1853 as first of the Wettin Braganza dynasty or Saxe-Coburgo-Gotha e Braganca. He was a liberal, modernising king but sadly died in a cholera epidemic when he was still in his mid-twenties. He had married a Hohenzollern from Sigmaringen but they had no family.

He was succeeded, therefore, in 1861 by this brother, Luis the Popular (1838-89), a poet and passionate oceanographer who founded the world's first major aquarium in Lisbon. In 1870, he was one of the German candidates for the crown of Spain in the crisis that gave Bismarck his excuse to attack the French. He had an Italian princess for his wife who produced the requisite heirs, but he also had an illegitimate son.

Luis's son Carlos I the Diplomat (1863-1908), or the Martyr, was intelligent but so self-indulgent and insensitive to the need for change that he takes the blame for the self-destruction of his dynasty. Though married to a French princess, he indulged in extra-marital affairs and personal extravagance as well as presiding over governments that twice in his reign had to declare Portugal bankrupt. He also made himself unpopular by accepting British plans to limit the expansion of Portugal's considerable empire in Africa. He was assassinated by republican marksmen in the streets of Lisbon, and his eldest son was wounded but died soon afterwards. Thus it was his second son, Manuel (1889-1932), who took over at the age of nineteen, without having received any relevant training. The credibility of the monarchy had already been severely eroded by his father and he stood little chance of success. After two years he was ousted in a military coup in 1910 and lived for most of his remaining years in England. He had a Hohenzollern wife but no children.

THE SAXE-COBURG TSARS OF BULGARIA

Meanwhile, the Kohary branch of the ubiquitous Saxe-Coburgs had another success. The nephew of Ferdinand of Portugal, another Ferdinand (1861-1948), known to his friends as 'Foxy', had been born in Vienna and served in the Austrian army. Despite early signs of eccentricity and uncertain sexuality, his Kohary money, his blend of Saxe-Coburg and Bourbon genes plus a very tenuous genetic connection with the medieval tsars of Bulgaria were enough for him to be, in 1887, a candidate for the revived throne of Bulgaria, a newly half-liberated nation that was still technically part of the Turkish Empire. The previous incumbent, another German, Alexander of Battenberg, had been deposed by a military coup, so there was some reluctance from some of the candidates better qualified than Ferdinand. Most of his relations, including Queen Victoria, thought him totally unsuited to the appointment, 'lazy and effeminate', but he was to display unexpected competence and ambition once the opportunity presented itself. Equally, he appeared painfully obsessive about his new status and was known to sulk if other monarchs were given any form of precedence over him, whether it was the order in processions or the positioning of his private railway carriage.

As the decline of the Turkish Empire continued, Ferdinand was able, by 1908, to declare his country's independence, proclaimed at the St Forty Martyrs Church, Turnovo. He was also able to upgrade his title from prince to tsar. He took part with some success in the Balkan War of 1912, proclaimed as a crusade against Islam. As a result, he gained part of Macedonia, only to lose it again in the Second Balkan War of 1913 when his previous allies turned against him. In the First World War, he was so incensed by his former allies that he allied himself with the Germans, Turks and Austrians, with none of whom he had any real sympathy. However, this gave him the confidence to undertake rash invasions first of Serbia, so that he could regain Macedonia, and then of Romania when it switched to the Allied side in 1916. Towards the end of the war his army was badly defeated by the Allied army in Greece, and to save his dynasty he abdicated in October 1918 in favour of his son, Boris, who then immediately announced Bulgaria's surrender.

Ferdinand lived for another thirty years, which he split between Coburg and Capri, where his sexual orientation became more obvious. Amiably bisexual, he had married an Italian Bourbon princess and produced four children but when she died he made no effort to replace her. Meanwhile, Tsar Ferdinand's son, Boris III (1894-1943), had succeeded at the age of twenty-four and almost immediately had to preside over the surrender of his country to the Allies. This meant once again the loss of Macedonia and

THE HOUSE OF WETTIN AND SAXE-COBURG

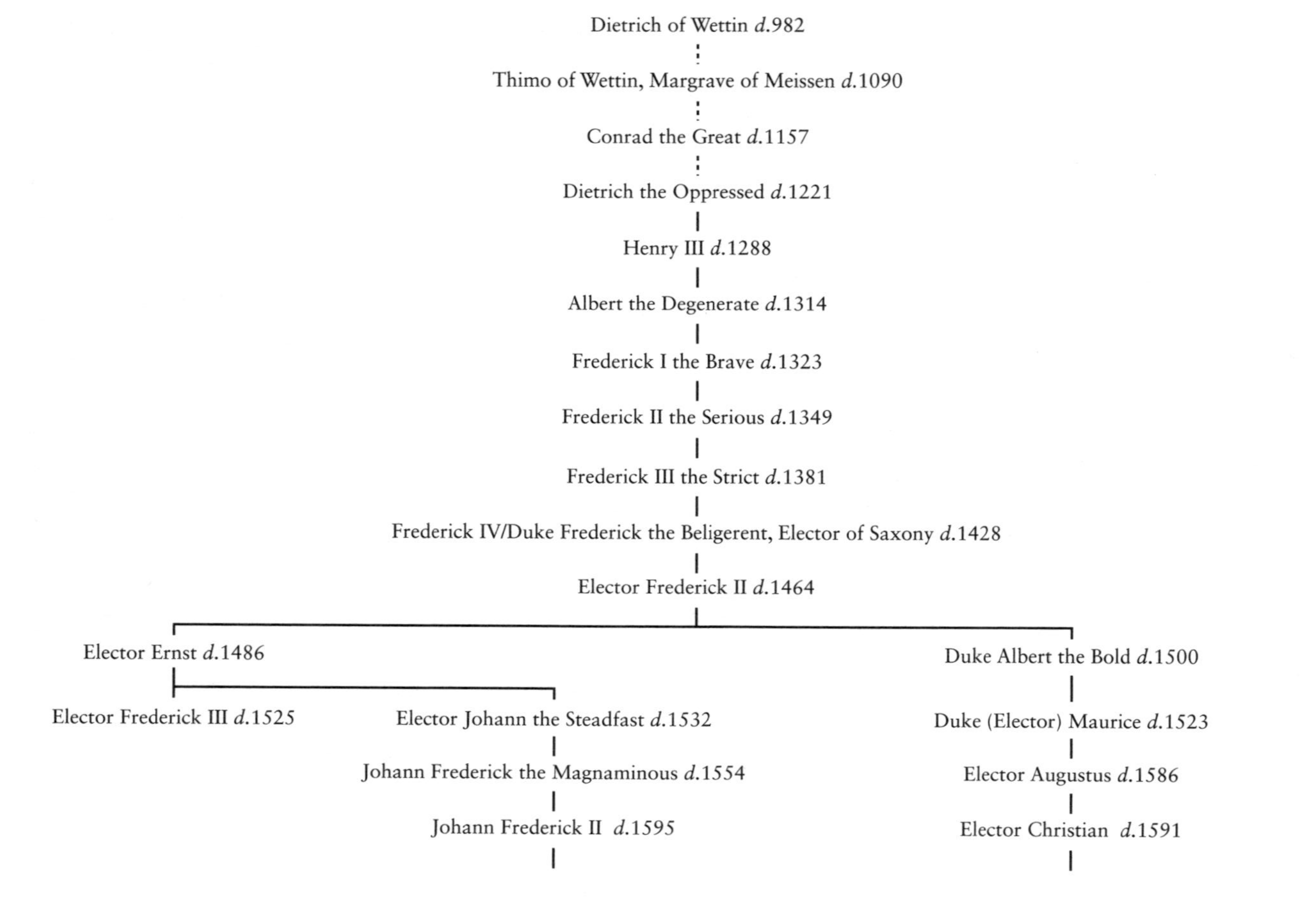

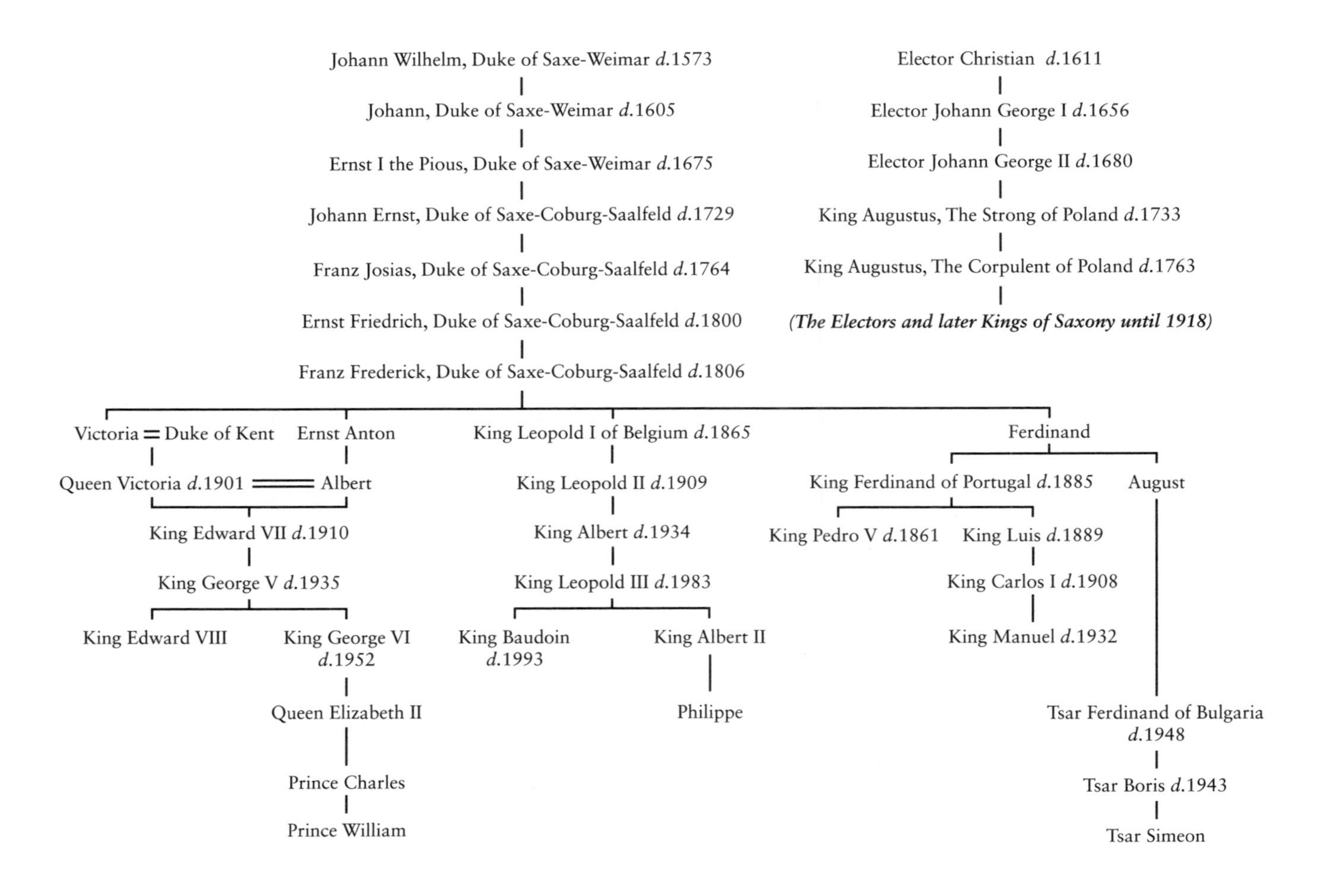
Johann Wilhelm, Duke of Saxe-Weimar d.1573
Johann, Duke of Saxe-Weimar d.1605
Ernst I the Pious, Duke of Saxe-Weimar d.1675
Johann Ernst, Duke of Saxe-Coburg-Saalfeld d.1729
Franz Josias, Duke of Saxe-Coburg-Saalfeld d.1764
Ernst Friedrich, Duke of Saxe-Coburg-Saalfeld d.1800
Franz Frederick, Duke of Saxe-Coburg-Saalfeld d.1806
Elector Christian d.1611
Elector Johann George I d.1656
Elector Johann George II d.1680
King Augustus, The Strong of Poland d.1733
King Augustus, The Corpulent of Poland d.1763
(The Electors and later Kings of Saxony until 1918)
Victoria = Duke of Kent
Ernst Anton
King Leopold I of Belgium d.1865
Ferdinand
Queen Victoria d.1901 = Albert
King Edward VII d.1910
King George V d.1935
King Edward VIII
King George VI d.1952
Queen Elizabeth II
Prince Charles
Prince William
King Leopold II d.1909
King Albert d.1934
King Leopold III d.1983
King Baudoin d.1993
King Albert II
Philippe
King Ferdinand of Portugal d.1885
August
King Pedro V d.1861
King Luis d.1889
King Carlos I d.1908
King Manuel d.1932
Tsar Ferdinand of Bulgaria d.1948
Tsar Boris d.1943
Tsar Simeon

the payment of crushing indemnities, which severely weakened an already strained economy. His difficulties continued, for he was exposed to pressure from both extreme right and extreme left parties, so that at times he was little better than a puppet. In the late 1930s, the right-wingers came to dominate and this put him in a particularly difficult position when Hitler precipitated the Germans once more into war in 1939. He irritated Hitler by trying to remain neutral but was eventually pushed into declaring war with the usual bait of recovering Macedonia. He annoyed Hitler again by bravely refusing to deport Bulgaria's 50,000 Jews and then even more by refusing to join in the attack on Russia in 1943. Thus, when he died suddenly, perhaps of a heart attack, at the age of forty-nine shortly after returning from a meeting with Hitler in East Prussia there were suspicions that he had been murdered, but here was no solid evidence to prove it. Like his father, he had married an Italian princess and had two children.

The third and last of the Bulgarian Saxe-Coburgs was Boris's young son, Simeon II (1937-), who became tsar at the age of six with a regency council. His brief reign coincided with the last stages of the Second World War, the bombing of Sofia by the allies and the invasion of Bulgaria by the Russians. As in other east European countries, this led to a Communist coup and the country soon afterwards becoming a Soviet satellite. Thus, after only three years, Simeon was deposed and went into exile, though significantly he never abdicated and there was always the possibility that his dormant tsardom might be resurrected.

Astonishingly, after fifty years this very nearly happened, for after the fall of Communism in Bulgaria in 1996 Simeon was allowed to return and found himself remarkably popular. Having served in the United States Army and then enjoyed a successful business career in Spain, he was a good administrator and had useful contacts in the west. In the end, however, instead of resuming the throne he was elected by a landslide majority as the prime minister of Bulgaria in 2001 and served competently for five years. With the exception of Cambodia, there is no other example of an ex-monarch returning to power as a democratically elected prime minister. Thereafter he served for a while also as opposition leader and retired to the royal country estate of Vrana Palace near Sofia where his father's heart had been buried.

CHAPTER 7

THE EXTRAORDINARY HOUSE OF WITTELSBACH

Otto Count of Dachau and Scheyern acquired Wittelsbach and built a castle there in 1115 from which his successors took their name. The castle, which was later destroyed, stood by the River Paar near Aichach in Bavaria just north-east of Augsburg and to the north of Dachau and Munich.

The Wittelsbachs had a less controlled and more erratic progress to royal status than the other dynasties we have looked at so far. They produced two Holy Roman Emperors, a king of Denmark, one luckless king of Bohemia, a fairly incompetent king of Greece, a brilliant but perhaps overambitious series of Swedish kings and some mad kings of Bavaria, yet one of them, by marrying the grand daughter of Mary Queen of Scots that created the link which brought the House of Hanover to London and was thus the ancestor of all British royalty since George I. They also produced some attractively maverick characters like Prince Rupert of the Rhine.

THE ROAD TO HEIDELBERG

Wittelsbach Castle was held by the counts of Dachau, including Otto IV (*d.*1135) and his son Otto V (1117-83). This Otto was made Count Palatine of Bavaria after he had proved himself one of the most able knights of the Emperor Frederick I by saving the day at Verona and after the fall from grace of the previous incumbent Henry the Lion (see p.66). Otto V renumbered himself as Otto I Duke of Bavaria and died during a trip to Pfullendorf. Wittelsbach Castle was destroyed in 1209 and never rebuilt, but the family who took their name from it were to be the rulers of Bavaria for the next 709 years until their fall in 1918. Their main base was Kelheim on the Danube, where their castle is now a meagre ruin.

Otto's son, Ludwig I (1173-1231), the next Duke of Bavaria, supported the Welf candidate as emperor, Otto IV, and as his reward the duchy of Bavaria was confirmed as the hereditary right of his descendants. However, he deserted the Emperor Otto soon afterwards and as his reward from the replacement emperor, Frederick II, he was also made Count Palatine of the Rhine in 1214. The Palatinate, or Kurpfalz, a historic area of the Holy Roman Empire, embraced the east bank of the Rhine and the cities of Heidelberg and Mannheim. This too was a title the family were to retain till 1918 and their claim was strengthened when Ludwig's son, Otto, married the heiress of the previous incumbent.

Meanwhile, Ludwig strengthened his knightly credentials by joining the 5th Crusade and was unlucky to become a prisoner of war in Egypt. Ten years after his return he was mysteriously murdered at Kelheim and buried in the family vault at Scheyern Abbey. The murder was never explained, as the culprit was killed immediately afterwards. His son, Otto, consolidated the family's grip on the Palatinate particularly after he had married its heiress, Agnes, and he adopted the iconic lion as the symbol for both Bavaria and the Palatinate.

Thereafter, as with so many German dynasties, the reluctance of the Salic Law to adopt primogeniture let to a splintering of the fast growing inheritance. The brothers Ludwig (1229-94) and Heinrich split the lands between them and continued to quarrel about it for most of their lives. Then Ludwig's son, Rudolf (1274-1317), went to war with his younger brother, Ludwig (1282-1347), and this lasted till 1313.

The following year, Ludwig decided to oppose the efforts of his mother's Habsburg relations to make the empire hereditary to their family, and he set himself up as an alternative King of Germany, calling himself Ludwig IV. He won the battle of Gamelsdorf against the Habsburgs and had to depose Pope John XXII before he could be crowned as emperor in Rome in 1328. In the course of his diplomacy he gave Switzerland its independence from the Habsburgs and backed the Teutonic Knights in their conquest of Lithuania. In the end he died of a stroke during a bear hunt. He had numerous sons but none of them attempted seriously to succeed him as emperor, but instead splintered the family estate into Upper and Lower Bavaria, the Palatinate and Brandenburg.

There were thus five simultaneous Dukes of Bavaria and the eldest, Ludwig V, had been given Brandenburg by his father in 1323. He might have been a candidate for the crown had he not contracted a bigamous marriage with the heiress of Tyrol, so once he was excommunicated his chance had gone. He also faced many difficulties from the locals in Brandenburg and passed it on to two of his ambitious half-brothers, neither of whom had any male heirs. So the Wittelsbach tenure of Brandenburg ended after forty-four years.

This generation was followed by three Ruperts or Ruprechts: Rupert I the Red (1309-90), who founded Heidelberg University; Rupert II (1325-98), who banished Jews and prostitutes from his realms; and Rupert III (1352-1410), who joined in the deposition of King Wenceslas in 1400 and himself claimed the crown of Germany in his stead a year later. He was crowned at Cologne and built Heidelberg Castle but died suddenly at his other clifftop castle of Landskron near Oppenheim.

THE FIRST SCANDINAVIAN INTERLUDE

After Rupert's death there followed another of those damaging divisions of the patrimony. Ludwig III (1378-1436) was followed as Count Palatine by a son of the same name, Ludwig IV (1424-49), who died at the age of twenty-five and though he had a son, Philip, he was succeeded by his brother, Friedrich I (1425-76), best known for the fact that, against the unwritten rules of the dynasty, he married his long term mistress Klara Tott, a commoner, so neither of their children were moved to succeed him.

One of Rupert's other sons, Johann (1383-1443), became Duke of Pfalz or Upper Palatinate, and had his capital at Neumarkt with an additional new fortress at Sulzbach. As usual, he fell out with his brothers over their respective shares of Bavaria and was a leading member of the Parakeet Society formed to attack their bad tempered Wittelsbach cousin, Duke Ludwig VII of Bavaria. However, his main interests were further to the north, for he married Catharina, the sister of Eric of Pomerania, King of Denmark, and herself one of a very small number of descendants from both Kings Waldemar IV of Denmark and Magnus II of Sweden. He thus spent much time in Copenhagen dabbling in Danish politics, and when Eric of Pomerania was deposed in 1439 by the Danish and Swedish nobles he was in a good position to put forward his son, Christopher, the former king's nephew, as his successor.

To the Danes the main attraction of Christopher, or Kristoffer, III (1416-48), a young man of twenty-three, born at Pfalz Neumarkt, was the belief that he was a malleable character who would easily be manipulated by the quarrelsome nobles. However, Denmark was threatened with a series of peasant revolts and when the nobles tried to suppress them they were surprisingly outwitted by the peasants, so Kristoffer was unexpectedly able to demonstrate his abilities as a leader, succeeding where they had failed.

The result was the drastic suppression of the Danish peasants who were reduced to the status of serfs. Following this success, Kristoffer was also elected King of Sweden in 1441 and Norway in 1443, the year his father died. In Denmark his castle at Roskilde was destroyed by fire so he moved to Copenhagen, which thereafter became the official capital and whose development was thus accelerated. In Sweden he was much less popular, as there was an agricultural crisis and he had the flour mixed with tree bark to make up the short-fall, hence his nickname there of King Bark.

Before he could start a dynasty he died at the age of only thirty-two, the last living descendant of Valdemar IV, so, as we have seen, the three crowns next went to the Count of Oldenburg, as did his grieving widow, Dorothea (see p.19)

THE RELIGIOUS WARS

Philip, known as the Upright, or Aufrichitige (1448-1508), eventually took over from his uncle as Elector Palatine but lost a war against his Bavarian cousins in 1504. Ludwig V (1478-1524) voted for Charles V as emperor and became involved in the war against the rebellious peasants of 1525. He had no children so his brother Frederick II (1482-1556) took over and, having served in the Habsburg army under Ferdinand I, was the first of the family to swing towards Protestantism, so that he was outlawed by Charles V. He too left no direct heirs and was replaced by his nephew Otto Heinrich (1502-59), who took the state close to bankruptcy by his extravagant patronage of the arts and was the third count in a row to leave no surviving children.

Since the main line had now run out of male heirs, the succession went to one of the Wittelsbach offshoots, the Dukes of Simmern. Thus Frederick III the Pious (1516-76) took over in 1559 having undergone a dramatic conversion to Calvinism, so he devoted his life to spreading the word. He even sent help to the Huguenots and displayed his fanaticism by executing the scholar Johannes Sylvanus for arguing about the Trinity.

Despite this, Frederick never managed to convert his own son and heir to Calvinism, so when Ludwig VI (1539-83), a dedicated Lutheran, took over he purged all the Calvinist clerics from their posts. Sadly, he died soon afterwards and, since his five eldest sons had all died, it was Frederick IV (1574-1610), known later as the Upright, or *Der Aufrichtige*, who took over at the age of nine. He, surprisingly, had been brought up not a Lutheran but a Calvinist like his grandfather and in 1608 became the leader of the Protestant Alliance, but died at the age of only thirty-six. Nevertheless, his Calvinist credentials were to have huge importance for the future of Europe.

The next Elector Palatine was a major figure in European history, mainly for all the wrong reasons. Frederick V (1596-1632) was another Calvinist, an intellectual and champion of Protestantism. Born at the *Jagdschloss*, or hunting lodge, of Deinschwang near Amberg, he was superficially charismatic but moody, sensitive and lacking real confidence. Nevertheless, he was prominent enough to be chosen as a potential bridegroom for Elizabeth, the daughter of King James VI of Scotland and I of Great

Britain, in 1613, a red-haired feisty beauty of whom her grandmother Mary Queen of Scots would have been proud. It was thus because of him that the royal Stuart genes were passed via his daughter, Sophia, to the House of Hanover and he is the ancestor of all British monarchs since George I. He was also prominent enough seven years later to be offered the crown of Bohemia whose Catholic king, Wenceslas, had been deposed in a Protestant coup. This event so shocked the Habsburg emperor that he instigated an immediate attack and the new King Frederick, known because of his short reign as 'The Winter King', was heavily defeated at the Battle of the White Mountain four days after first wearing the crown of St Wenceslas. Three years later the emperor and a majority of his fellow electors voted that he should lose his electoral status and his princedom.

Frederick and Elizabeth went into exile in the Hague and three of their sons took part in the English Civil War on the side of their cousin Charles I. The eldest Charles Luis, or Karl Ludwig (1617-80), was the least popular in England, partly because he resented the British failure to help him regain his inheritance, and did not last long. In the end he only managed to return to his by the then devastated Palatinate when the Thirty Years' War came to an end, by which time his father was long dead and his uncle King Charles I had been executed. His brother, Prince Rupert (1617-82) was more charismatic and a brilliant, if sometimes impetuous, cavalry commander who was one of the leading Royalist generals. Later, after a short spell as a privateer, he served as a successful admiral and became something of an inventor and an accomplished artist as well as being the founding governor of the Hudson's Bay Company in Canada. He lived near Drury Lane with his actress mistress Peg Hughes and died a bachelor in Windsor.

The third brother, Maurice (1620-52), was also an able leader of cavalry who won a number of Civil War battles, including Roundway Down in 1643, before falling out with King Charles. Subsequently, he served as a vice admiral in the navy but was drowned when his flagship, HMS *Defiance*, was struck by a hurricane in the West Indies.

MEANWHILE, BACK IN BAVARIA

As we have seen, the legacy of the Emperor Ludwig IV was a huge splintering of the Wittelsbach estates and, in particular, a deep divide between the Palatine and Bavarian branches of the family, which was to be exacerbated by the Reformation when the two branches of the family chose different sides. Heinrich XIII of Bavaria (1235-90) had married a Hungarian and introduced an eastwards orientation to the family that persisted as they alternated between marrying Habsburgs and treating them as their greatest rivals and enemies. One of his sons, Otto III (1261-1312), became, briefly, a king of Hungary for two years (1305-7) as Bela V. Yet even within the Bavarian inheritance there were endless subdivisions of the estates amongst groups of brothers, which frequently weakened the overall dynasty. Heinrich's other son, Stephen I (1271-1310), born in Landshut, had to share the inheritance with two brothers, and in the next generation, Heinrich XIV (1305-39) waged war against his own brother, Otto IV, before dying of leprosy. His young son Johann I (1329-40) took over but died whilst still a child. So Bavaria briefly went back to the Emperor Ludwig IV who passed it on to his son Stephen II (1319-75), but he had such a prolonged quarrel with his five brothers over their disputed shares that the Wittelsbachs were, in 1367, deprived of Brandenburg, a prize that instead went to the Hohenzollern.

There was another war between three Wittelsbach brothers in 1395 and rival camps developed at Ingolstadt, Dachau, Landshut and Strauburg. Occasionally, the monotonously acrimonious subdividing was repaired when one of the branches became extinct, so that the remaining brothers or cousins fought for the residue, as when Duke Ernst (1373-1438) grabbed back Strauburg. He was so obsessed with the family line that when his son, Albert III (1401-60), married a commoner called Agnes he arranged for her to be accused of witchcraft and tossed into the Danube. Albert eventually forgave him and took advantage when his cousin at Bavaria-Ingolstadt died without direct heirs. Perhaps wisely, he turned down an offer of the toxic crown of Bohemia.

Albert IV the Wise (1447-1508) made a valiant attempt to introduce primogeniture to stop the endless splintering but when in 1503 he came to reunite the branches of Landshut and Dachau he had to fight a war with his even more distant relatives from the Palatinate.

It was whilst Wilhelm IV (1493-1550) was duke that the big religious divide between the Protestant Wittelsbachs of the Palatinate and the Catholics of Bavaria first became evident. Along with his brother Ludwig, who was trying for the crown of Bohemia, he banned all Lutheran preachers and ruthlessly suppressed the peasantry. Memorably, in 1516 he also set the purity standards for the production of Bavarian beer, which were to be in force till the EEC insisted on change in 1986.

Albert V (1528-79), brought up in Ingolstadt, was also a staunch Catholic, and over the next two centuries the Bavarian Wittelsbachs were to provide all the archbishops of Cologne and several cardinals. Albert himself was a dilettante art collector who nevertheless took time to repress any Protestants found in his territory. His successor, Wilhelm (V (1548-1626), was even more fanatical: operating from his fortress of Trausnitz in Landshut, he spent lavishly on sending missionaries abroad, built the Michaelskirche in Munich and eventually abdicated at the age of forty-nine to become a monk. Some years later he was to regret it, for his son cut back his allowances drastically and pursued policies with which he disagreed.

His arrogant successor Maximilian I the Great (1573-1651), who took over in 1597, was tall and adenoidal with a squeaky voice but patient, intelligent and efficient. Prim in his morals, he instituted the death penalty for adultery, tortured witches, made dancing illegal for the peasants and forbad carriages except for the very old so that his subjects would practice their horsemanship. By working his tax collectors hard and saving money on everything except his army he turned Bavaria into a rich, powerful and paternalistically benevolent state. A dedicated Jesuit, brought up in Munich, he would tolerate no heresy and helped form the Catholic League, besieging the Protestant enclave of Donauworth in 1607. He could have stood for election to the imperial throne instead of the fanatical Ferdinand of Habsburg, but he held back. Thus though he was one of the few princes capable of preventing the Habsburgs from starting the disastrous Thirty Years' War he joined the Catholic/Imperial side at an early stage and with 25,000 troops and his favourite general Count Tilly he took a major part in the defeat of his distant cousin Frederick King of Bohemia at the Battle of the White Mountain in 1620.

His reward was to win the position of elector from his beaten rival and also control of upper Austria, but he was ambitious for even more. Too late he realised that his religious prejudices and hesitation in 1619 had led to him increasing the power of the Habsburgs at the expense of himself and his fellow princes. His first wife died without producing children and he was so anxious to keep the line going that he married his own niece, his sister's Habsburg daughter, who luckily produced two sons. Meanwhile, he had to put down a bloody peasant revolt in Austria and his devious attempts to play both sides off against each other ended in disaster. A secret treaty with the French did him little good and Bavaria was devastated by the Swedes, his people close to starvation. In 1631 he was responsible for the massacre at Magdeburg and he was driven out of his own capital, Munich. He recovered and in old age had still not lost his ruthless will, for in 1650 he used his artillery to gun down the mutineers in his own army.

His successor, Ferdinand Maria (1636-79), also had the opportunity to stand for election as emperor but likewise rejected it to avoid trouble with the Habsburgs. He even tried to found a Bavarian colony beside New York but contented himself instead with starting the ostentatious Nymphenburg Palace in Munich. Duke Maximilian II (1662-1726) was extremely ambitious and a successful soldier who helped the Habsburgs to save Vienna from capture by the Turks and was the general who captured Belgrade from them. He was appointed governor of the Spanish Netherlands and fancied the crown of Holland or Poland but missed out on both. At least he managed to collect a large quantity of Dutch masters.

His son, Joseph Ferdinand (1692-99), came even closer to a crown for the great powers had all agreed that he would be the ideal compromise candidate for the throne of Spain, since neither a Habsburg nor a Bourbon was acceptable. Yet the year before he would, in theory, have assumed this role, he died at he age of seven. The result was that Louis XIV decided to risk war and have his grandson take over Spain, whatever the consequences. Maximilian had by this time set his sights on becoming emperor, so he chose the French side against the Habsburgs in the war that followed in 1701. The result was catastrophic for his branch of the dynasty. When the French and Bavarians were defeated by Marlborough at Blenheim he lost even Bavaria, which passed to his now very distant cousins, the Wittelsbachs of the Palatinate. His family was imprisoned until 1715, after which he spent his final decade extending the Nymphenburg Palace and starting a new one, the Schleissheim.

THE SECOND SCANDINAVIAN INTERLUDE

One of the many subdivisions of the original Wittelsbach family inheritance had been created by Rupert II at Simmern-Zweibrücken, near Saarbrücke and west of Heidelberg. Here Rupert's son, Stefan (1385-1459), became the first count palatine and further sub-divided the duchy for his own sons. A few generations later, in 1613, Johann Casimir (1585-1652), Count Palatine of Zweibrücken-Kleeburg, married Katerina, the daughter of King Karl IX Vasa of Sweden. She was also the half-sister of King Gustav Adolf, the iconic leader of Sweden, who had played such a dramatic part in the Thirty Years' War.

The death of Gustav Adolf in battle in 1632 left only his daughter Kristina (1626-89), aged six, to succeed him. Johann Casimir and Katerina meanwhile had a son, Karl Gustav (1622-60), who was at this point ten and was thus the half first cousin to Kristina. It was not surprising, therefore, that the chief minister, Oxenstierna, and others should consider the possibility of the two marrying so that Queen Kristina would have a man at her side who was also her half first cousin. An understanding was reached but for the time being Gustav Adolf's widow was having none of it and exiled Johann Casimir and his family from the court.

Kristina, however, grew to be beautiful, well educated and complicated. She had been brought up as if she was the king's son, often wore male clothing and received the title King. She had early on been subjected to the neuroses of her Hohenzollern mother who may well have put her off the idea of marriage with her horrific accounts of her own child-bearing experiences, but there is no clear evidence of Kristina's sexual orientation except her strange correspondence with her guru Cardinal Azzolino and her intense friendships with women such as Ebba Sparre. However, at the age of twenty-three she decided that she had no desire to marry Karl Gustav, who by this time was commander-in-chief of the Swedish army in Germany during the final years of the war. To mollify him for being jilted she named him as her successor, a sign also that she was not interested in marrying any of her other potential suitors. At the same time she seems to have sought solace from her personal problems by converting to Catholicism.

For the next five years, Kristina ruled Sweden on her own, but her Catholicism, her eccentricities and her extravagance all led to her increasing unpopularity. Perhaps sensing this or perhaps just frustrated by her ambivalent roles and by the restraints put upon her, she decided to abdicate in 1654 so that Karl Gustav could take over. She was to live another thirty-five years in exile and caused scandal by riding round Europe dressed as a man. She made various later efforts to win back a crown. Her effort to win Naples in 1657 ended when she had her equerry executed for thwarting her plans, then she made an ineffective effort to win back Sweden in 1660 and finally a last gasp attempt to seize Poland in 1667.

Her ex-fiancé King Karl X Gustav was thirty-two when he was, unexpectedly, crowned by his predecessor at Uppsala Castle as the first Wittelsbach king of Sweden. He had also just recently succeeded his father as Count Palatine of Zweibrücken-Kleeburg in Germany. Having already proved himself a competent and ambitious general, he was anxious to emulate his famous uncle, Gustav Adolf, and to expand the Swedish empire. So almost immediately he made an unprovoked attack on Poland with an army of 50,000 and a large fleet. He captured both Krakow and Warsaw after a horrendous three-day battle, then deposed the Polish king, but failed in his main effort to conquer Prussia. He was then the subject of a counter-attack both from the Poles and the Hohenzollerns in Brandenburg whose Prussian duchy he had threatened.

As he faced war on two fronts he had to buy the forbearance of Brandenburg by letting them have Prussia as a sovereign state, so that he thus unwittingly paved the way for the Hohenzollerns to grab the title of kings in Prussia.

His next exploit was a lightning attack on Denmark during which he captured Bremen and Jutland in 1657. He followed this up with a remarkable surprise attack across the frozen sea to Fünen and then with an even riskier ice-crossing to invade Zealand. However, yet again his empire-building was thwarted by the intervention of a third party, this time the Dutch who did not want Sweden to control the Baltic trade and therefore sent their fleet to help the Danes. Just at this vital moment Karl Gustav, his body and mind perhaps overstretched by the responsibility of such constant warfare and the strain of taking such huge risks, had a stroke at Göteborg and died suddenly aged only thirty-seven, leaving a son of four.

His wife was Hedwig Leonora, one of the ubiquitous Oldenburgs from Holstein-Gottorp, who played a major role in several regencies that followed his death. She had produced his only legitimate son, Karl XI (1655-97) of Sweden, who also took over as Count of Zweibrücken, but he had also had another son by his mistress Brita Allerts.

Despite an unorthodox education, manipulated by his mother and a reputation for being interested in nothing but bear hunts, Karl XI turned out a precociously brilliant general-like his father and grand uncle Gustav Adolf. In 1676, at the age of only twenty-one, his personal gallantry helped achieve a remarkable victory over the Danes at Lund. He led the Swedish army to a series of very bloody victories over the Danes until he was pressed to stop the war by Louis XIV of France. Besides, the Swedish economy was reeling under the burden of his expensive campaigns and he could not afford mercenaries, so he resorted to the forcible conscription of peasants, which was extremely unpopular. As a peace offering he married the beautiful Danish Princess Ulrika Eleonora, yet another Oldenburg. Thereafter he devoted the rest of his reign to very sensible improvements in administration and finance. At the same time he eliminated the interference of the Swedish nobles in his government and turned himself into an absolute ruler. Sadly, his wife died at the age of only thirty-seven and Karl, who seems to have been genuinely heart-broken, followed her four years later at the age of forty-one. Of their three surviving children two, a son and a daughter, became subsequent rulers of Sweden, while the younger daughter Sophia married the Duke of Holstein-Gottorp, another Oldenburg, and was thus the grandmother of Tsar Peter III of Russia. Meanwhile, Karl's manipulative mother once more stepped in as regent.

Karl XII (1682-1718), known as the 'Swedish Thunderbolt', took over the crown of Sweden at the age of fifteen, and was the last and most spectacular of the Wittelsbach kings of Sweden. The Swedish empire was at its peak, including at this time Finland, Estonia, Livonia, Zweibrücken and other small areas of Germany. This was not enough to satisfy Karl and, like his two Wittelsbach predecessors, he was ambitious to make it even bigger by attacking his neighbours. Like them, he was also a brilliantly precocious general but, like his grandfather in particular, prone to taking unnecessary risks. At times his over-confidence achieved spectacular success, and at others he was to put at risk the whole edifice of the Swedish Empire. Immune to the charms of both alcohol and women, he was famous for his high pain threshold and his total lack of emotion. Like his predecessors, he took huge risks with his army that often but not always came off, and he also seemed to enjoy risking his own life, as with his penchant for wrestling with bears. Yet he was also fascinated, like his great rival Peter of Russia, with scientific innovation and the use of mathematics to solve military problems.

To start with it all went well for him. At he age of eighteen he thwarted an invasion of his territories by the Danes and Saxons in 1700, the beginning of the Great Northern War. He then counterattacked and with some British naval help defeated his Oldenburg rival, Frederik IV of Denmark. Then, by forced marches, he headed into Estonia and saved his base at Narva from a Russian siege by a spectacular victory over Peter the Great in foul winter conditions, against a bigger force. He followed this up with two bloody victories over Augustus the Strong, the Saxon King of Poland, whom he subsequently deposed in 1704. By this time he dominated the Baltic and appeared invincible, but in 1707, he made the same error of judgment that was later to bring nemesis to both Napoleon and Hitler: he invaded Russia, fatally underestimating the huge distances involved and the dangers of the climate. Like these two, he initially enjoyed success on the way to Moscow, coming close to capturing the tsar at Grodno, but Peter had been working hard on his army and navy in the seven years since Narva. He had also had time to build a new fortified city east of Narva, which he named St Petersburg. He avoided pitched battle with Karl until the Swedes had been weakened by a foul Russian winter, then pounced on Karl at Poltava in 1709. By this time Karl's army had lost a third of its men from casualties and illness and Karl himself was in a poor state due to previous injuries. It was a devastating defeat followed by the surrender of the Swedish army and the flight of King Karl.

Karl sought help from the Turks in Istanbul and for some time was subsidised by the Sultan whilst he tried to promote a Turkish attack on Russia, but he was eventually imprisoned by them as a trouble-maker. With his usual resilience he managed to escape and reputedly rode 1,250 miles across Europe in fifteen days. At this point he had been away from Sweden for fifteen years. Undeterred by his experiences he now launched an attack on Norway, which was to be followed up by an invasion of Scotland in support of James Stuart, the Old Pretender. Despite the fact that he seemed to have lost touch with reality, it all began well enough, but by 1718, he was getting bogged down and his campaign was having a severe effect on the Swedish economy. He died from a bullet wound at the siege of Frederiksten and even the fact that some people suspected, probably incorrectly, that he was shot by one of his own people and not a Norwegian sniper, reflects the unpopularity of his incessant warmongering. He was thirty-six.

Karl died without marrying, so his younger sister, Ulrika Eleonora (1688-1741), took over as the elected ruler of Sweden, while by Salic Law the title Count of Zweibrücken had to go to her male cousin, Gustav Leopold (1670-1731).

The new queen had recently married Prince Frederick of Hesse-Kassel (1675-1751), and the Swedes had suffered so much from a series of militaristic and extravagant kings that they passed a new constitution that severely reduced the powers of the monarchy. Queen Ulrika Eleonora was so shocked that she abdicated in favour of her husband who, in turn, found his new role so frustrating that he devoted his reign to philandering and hunting. The sadly neglected Ulrika died of smallpox ten years before him and, as they had no children, this was the end of the Palatine Wittelsbach dynasty of Sweden. Needless to say, they were replaced by another German dynasty, the Oldenburgs (see p.26).

MEANWHILE, BACK IN THE PALATINATE

In 1680, the uncharismatic brother of Prince Rupert, Elector Karl Ludwig, who had been restored in 1648, was succeeded in the Palatinate by his son, Karl II (1651-85), another Calvinist, but despite marrying an Oldenburg he died young and left no children nor any other close male heir, so the succession reverted to a branch of the Wittelsbachs that was still Catholic and based in Neuburg on the Danube. This caused such a row that it provided the voracious Louis XIV with an excuse for a brutal French invasion of the Palatinate in 1688; he, of course, was still obsessed with the idea of a Rhine frontier and Karl II's sister had married his brother, the Duke of Orleans, so they had a vague claim to the inheritance. This French attack caused outrage, particularly in London, so it soon turned into a full-scale European war that lasted nine years and embraced the whole power struggle between William of Orange and ex-king James II of Great Britain supported by Louis XIV.

The new Elector Philip Wilhelm of Neuburg (1615-90) is mainly remembered for being the father of seventeen children, including three daughters who made glittering marriages: one as Queen of Spain, a second as Queen of Portugal and a third as a Habsburg empress. He also had two sons who succeeded him. The first, Johann Wilhelm (1658-1716), chose Düsseldorf as his capital and ran a lavish court at Bensberg in Jülich-Berg where he built a new palace and amassed a huge collection of Rubens, which is now in Munich. Despite having two wives, he had no surviving children.

His brother, Karl Philip (1661-1742), found the Protestant atmosphere offensive and moved his capital to Mannheim where he built a huge Baroque palace for himself. There he spent vast sums on an orchestra that was much admired by the Mozarts. He had three wives and at least half a dozen children but he outlived them all, so having had too many heirs in the previous generation in this one there were now none and the house of Neuburg came to an end. Thus the inheritance shifted to yet another minor branch of the Wittelsbachs, the counts of Zweibrücken-Sulzbach.

This meant spectacular promotion for the eighteen-year-old new Elector Palatine Karl Theodor (1724-99), born in Brussels to a very minor branch of the family. It had been a huge surprise for him even to become Count of Sulzbach, but there was more to come for, as we shall see, in his fifties he was also to inherit Bavaria, thus bringing back under one roof two of the major branches of the Wittelsbachs.

MEANWHILE, BACK IN BAVARIA

When the ambitious Maximilian II, Duke of Bavaria, died in 1726 his equally ambitious younger son, Charles Albert (1697-1745), took over, while an even younger son, Clemens August, became Prince Archbishop of Cologne. Charles Albert's lust for promotion was fuelled by two factors: he had married the daughter of the Emperor Joseph I who had produced no sons and whose brother, the next Emperor Charles, had likewise failed to produce male heirs. So as the ailing Emperor Charles sought to safeguard the Habsburg inheritance by ring-fencing his daughter Maria Theresa with protectors, Charles Albert saw an opportunity to succeed where his father had failed. Thus almost as soon as the Emperor Charles died in 1740 Charles Albert invaded Austria, with some help from the French, and claimed the crown of the Holy Roman Empire.

Unfortunately, he allowed himself to be diverted from a final onslaught on the Habsburgs in Vienna and instead took Prague and the crown of Bohemia. His brother, the Archbishop Clemens August, was far from wholehearted in his support but nevertheless crowned him in Frankfurt, the second member of the Wittelsbach family to be an emperor.

However, the mistakes had already been made. Maria Theresa still held Vienna and refused to take an initial defeat lying down. She counterattacked by invading Bohemia and Bavaria, so that Charles Albert came close to losing everything and only survived in Munich because Frederick of Prussia had also decided to attack the Habsburgs. By this time the Emperor Charles was suffering severely from gout and died soon afterwards in his late forties.

His son and successor in Bavaria, Maximilian III Joseph (1727-77), not only appreciated the great danger of taking on the Habsburgs but on his mother's side was a cousin of Maria Theresa, so he quickly made peace and devoted the rest of his reign to non-military matters. Among his achievements were the founding of the Nymphenburg porcelain factory and the Bavarian Academy of Sciences. Generally, his approach was progressive, and in 1770, he even sold the crown jewels so that he could buy corn for his people during the famine of that year. The Rococo extravagances of the Catholic Church were restricted and he banned the Oberammergau Passion Play, which had first been performed in 1634 as thanksgiving for survival from the plague. Despite the fact that he had a good musical ear, he failed to offer a post to Mozart, apparently because of shortage of cash.

Maximilian had married a Saxon princess but they had no family, so when he died of smallpox aged fifty the junior branch of the Wittelsbachs became extinct and most of the senior branch had also become extinct apart from the small dukedoms of Sulzbach and Zweibrücken-Birkenfeld. So, due to a remarkably high number of line-failures, Karl Theodor of Sulzbach (1724-99) extraordinarily achieved his fourth massive inheritance. Born in Brussels and made Margrave of Bergen op Zoom, he had become Count of Sulzbach in 1733, then nine years later took over as Elector Palatine and Duke of Jülich and Berg on the extinction of the main branch of the family and finally, thirty-five years later, took over the Electorship of Bavaria when the second main branch of the family also died out. It was one of the most remarkable reconnections of a splintered dynasty in German history.

Despite moving to Munich in 1777, Karl Theodor did not care much for Bavarians nor they for him and he tried hard to swap his new dukedom for the rest of Holland. This was so unpopular that it caused the War of Bavarian Succession, otherwise known as the Potato War (Kartoffelkrieg) because the two sides spent so much time manoeuvering round their food supplies that they hardly did any fighting. Like his predecessor, he turned down Mozart for a post in his orchestra in Mannheim despite the fact that he continued building one of the largest palaces in Europe there and that he patronized Schiller. He added the magnificent Schwetzingen Palace as a country place midway between Mannheim and Heidelberg, and Benrath Palace near Düsseldorf. Despite two wives and two mistresses, he only had one legitimate child who died soon after birth, so just as his rise to eminence had been caused by the extinction of three senior branches of the family he was the last of a fourth line, the Sulzbachs, and responsible for its extinction too.

Thus Karl Theodore's triple inheritance now went to the other minor surviving branch of the Wittelsbachs at Zweibrücken, close to the French border. So Maximilian Joseph (1756-1825) became the new Prince Elector of Bavaria and the Palatinate in 1799. Maximilian, who had not expected such elevation, had made his career in the French Army and after twenty years had risen to the rank of major general when the French Revolution persuaded him that he should change to the Austrian Army. About this time he inherited the little family dukedom of Zweibrücken and showed himself a progressive thinker, even preferring Napoleon, whom he greatly admired, to his ethnically closer neighbours in Prussia. So when Napoleon conquered Prussia he won his reward and was made King Maximilian I of Bavaria in 1805. Then when Napoleon began to look doomed in 1813 Maximilian changed sides in return for the allies allowing him to remain King of Bavaria. Thereafter he maintained his fairly liberal stance, granting a constitution and a new legal code and even trying to create a united Germany under Bavarian leadership, but he was too left wing for the Prussians. With his relatively humble origins, he liked to wear simple clothes and stroll along the streets for a chat.

His son, King Ludwig I (1786-1868), who took over the crown in 1825 is perhaps best remembered for his eccentricities, in particular the scandals associated with his two notorious mistresses Lola Montez (an Irish-born dancer who had previous affairs with Franz Liszt and possibly Alexandre Dumas) and Lady Jane Digby (the promiscuous, twice-divorced daughter of one of Nelson's admirals). He inaugurated the first Oktoberfest in Munich for his wedding and rebuilt a number of monasteries. He was a surprising advocate of Greek independence. Yet he also built the first railway line in Germany and the Main to Danube Canal. By 1848, the year of revolutions, his extravagances, particularly the unpopularity of the temperamental Montez, were catching up with him and he abdicated in his early sixties rather than adapt to change. Ludwig passed the crown on to his almost equally eccentric eldest son Maximilian II, but meanwhile we divert to the career of his younger son, Otto.

THE GREEK INTERLUDE

Mainly thanks to Ludwig I's romantic support of the Greek War of Independence but also to a minuscule inheritance of Greek imperial genes from the Comnenos dynasty via Duke Johann II of Bavaria, Ludwig's younger son, Otto (1815-67), was recommended by the great powers as the new king of Greece in 1832. He was seventeen and headed for Greece in a British warship with a council of Bavarian bureaucrats to wield the real power. He was hampered by the restriction that he should not let the Greeks take over any more technically Greek enclaves from Turkey and that he must tax the Greeks heavily so that the large loans from Rothschilds could be repaid. When he came of age he dismissed what the Greeks had called the Bavarocrats and tried to govern as an absolute monarch but, though well intentioned, he did not quite have the ability to carry it off.

Despite good progress building schools and hospitals, Otto failed to win much loyalty. In 1841, the Great Powers stopped him from invading Crete, which was still in Turkish hands and a popular cause amongst his people. Thus his puppet status was obvious to all and his credibility severely damaged. In 1843, he was forced during a military coup to grant a constitution. Then, in 1850, he was humiliated by the British naval blockade during Palmerston's period of gunboat diplomacy – the notorious Don Pacifico incident. The same thing happened in 1853 when the British would not let the Greeks attack the Turks, since it would have helped the Russians to capture Constantinople. Then there was an attempt to murder his German-born wife, which deeply shocked him even though he had been far from faithful, for he had taken over his father's ex-mistress, Jane Digby, who was by this time in her mid-forties and with a long string of other affairs both behind and ahead of her.

Finally, in 1862, came another military coup and he was deposed. He spent his last five years back in Bavaria and remarkably donated most of his money to his former kingdom when it tried to capture Crete in 1866. He was replaced in Greece by an Oldenburg (see p.31).

THE LAST KINGS OF BAVARIA

Maximilian II (1811-65) took over on his father's abdication in 1848 and adopted a more liberal approach as dictated by the mood of revolution that had swept Europe. Like his predecessors, he was at least mildly eccentric, something of an academic and a romantic who was hugely impressed by Hans Andersen and loved long distance hikes. He had his castle at Starnberg in the Five Lakes district south of Munich and built the golden yellow Schloss Hohenschwangau by the Swan Lake of Füssen. Though he married a Hohenzollern princess, he was anti-Prussian and opposed German unification, but died before it became a reality.

His elder son, the enigmatic Ludwig II (1845-86), exaggerated the eccentricities of both his father and grandfather. Having sided with the Habsburgs against Bismarck in 1866 he changed from the losing side to the winners in return for keeping his kingdom, albeit under the hegemony of a united Germany in 1871. Though extremely friendly with his cousin

Elizabeth (later the wife of the Emperor Franz Joseph) and engaged to her for a while, he was almost certainly a religiously inhibited homosexual and reneged on his engagement. Various male friendships are mentioned but there is no evidence other than of platonic affairs. Famously, at the age of eighteen he had been so impressed by Wagner's *Lohengrin* that he invited the middle-aged composer to come to Munich and provided the new Festspielhaus at Bayreuth with additional patronage, which resulted, in 1876, in the otherwise almost totally impracticable production of *The Ring*. Meanwhile, he was using his own money and bankrupting the dynasty, but not the Bavarians, by building three massive new castles: Neuschwanstein above the Poellat Gorge, Linderhof in the Ammer valley and Herenschiemsee, a miniature Versailles, all of which greatly reduced unemployment and used cutting edge technology. He also avoided wars, so this added to his popularity.

In retrospect, it is impossible to judge whether the doctors were right to declare Ludwig insane in 1886, three years after Wagner's death. It has been argued that overuse of chloroform or opium smoking to dull his incessant toothache may have contributed to his symptoms of paranoia. Certainly he was a megalomaniac. When threatened with imprisonment he resisted arrest and was soon afterwards found dead in shallow water. No obvious signs of death were recorded and there was no water in his lungs, so he did not drown. He may have had a heart attack or he may have been murdered. He was forty-one.

Naturally, Ludwig had produced no direct heir, so his crown now went to his younger brother, Otto (1848-1916). He had managed to serve for a time in the Bavarian army from 1863 when he was a teenager but by the time of his accession, when he was in his late thirties, he had already been diagnosed as medically insane and this was declared publicly in 1878. He spent virtually his entire reign as a prisoner in the Schloss Fürstenried, while his uncle, Liutpold (1821-1912), the brother of both Ludwig I and Otto of Greece, ruled in his stead.

This farce continued till Liutpold died and his son Ludwig (1845-1921) grew impatient. Ludwig had been in line to succeed his uncle Otto on the throne of Greece but had renounced his rights there. Still the understudy in his late sixties, he had fought in the Austro-Prussian war of 1866 but later changed his allegiance to Kaiser Wilhelm II, a move far from popular with his own people. Thus as the hardships of the First World War made him look even more out of touch there was a revolution in Bavaria on 7 November 1918 and he was deposed, the last of the royal Wittelsbachs, though he left thirteen children to claim long-forgotten titles, including even the Stuart inheritance in Britain.

CHAPTER 8
THE MARSHES OF MECKLENBURG

The house of Mecklenburg originated in the castle of Micklinburg between Schwerin and Wismar, a largely infertile stretch of land dotted with marshy lakes, peat bogs and forest south of the Baltic Sea and west of Berlin. It was founded by Niklot (*d.*1160), a Wendish or Obotrite leader, in an area that was ethnically Slavonic rather than German until it was conquered by Henry the Lion who founded the new town of Schwerin in 1160. In subsequent years the area was prone to invasion by Danes and Swedes, so a number of the heads of the family had married Scandinavian princesses rather than Germans. This resulted in some serious opportunities for advancement but mostly they came to nothing. Erik of Pomerania (1381-1459) from Mecklenburg-Schwerin was elected King of Denmark at the age of fifteen but deposed only four years later. Sophie of Mecklenburg-Schwerin was the mother of King Kristian IV.

The allegiance of the Mecklenburg families to Scandinavia during the Thirty Years' War led to them being deprived of their lands for five years.

As the centuries went by, the family estates were subdivided in the usual way, and one of the new branches created in 1701 was the midget state of Mecklenburg-Strelitz, which produced some remarkable characters. The capital of the new duchy was Neustrelitz, founded in 1732, with geometric streets surrounding the ducal palace after the previous town had burned down. Thanks mainly to their earlier marriages to Scandinavian royalty, they began to put themselves forward as blue-blooded, but it was still quite extraordinary that Charlotte of Mecklenburg-Strelitz was chosen as the bride for the future George III of Great Britain. It can perhaps be explained by the fact that young George (see above) had entered into several unsuitable relationships and his mother Augusta of Saxe-Coburg was so alarmed that she settled for any German princess whom the awkward youngster would accept. In the end, though not by any means beautiful, Charlotte turned out to be an extremely sensible and well-adjusted wife for a king who was prone to regular nervous breakdowns, and all subsequent members of the royal house of Hanover were descended from her. Born in Mirow amongst the Pomeranian lakes of the duchy, she was not even the daughter of the duke but of one of the younger sons, Prince Karl Ludwig (1717-52), brother of Adolf Frederick II. A patron of both Mozart and J.C. Bach, she was collected at Cuxhaven by the Royal Navy and delivered for marriage in London.

Adolf Frederick's second son, Karl (1741-1816), was the first of the family to become a grand duke, though he died very soon afterwards. Born in Hanover, he had served as a field marshal in the British Army and with his Hesse-Darmstadt wife produced the second major personality to emerge from this family. This was the great beauty Louisa (1776-1810) who married Frederick Wilhelm of Prussia. When her husband was defeated and demoralised by Napoleon after the Battle of Jena it was Queen Louisa who inspired a resistance movement and a revival of German patriotism. She also had the charm to manipulate both Napoleon himself and Tsar Alexander I of Russia, who was reputedly infatuated with her. Not only was she the mother of the next two kings of Prussia, one of whom became the first Kaiser, but her daughter, Charlotte, married Alexander's brother, Nicholas I, so she was also the ancestress of all subsequent Romanov tsars.

George (1779-1860), second Grand Duke of Mecklenburg-Strelitz, had vast reserves of land and was extremely wealthy. He abolished serfdom in the region, built schools and was generally progressive, but he and his successors were held back in this respect by the reactionary feudal landlords supposed to be their subjects. The penultimate Grand Duke, Adolf Frederick II, committed suicide in February 1918.

The other Mecklenburg duchies oscillated between the extravagant palaces of Schwerin, Ludwigslust and Güstrow, all reflecting the fact that these tiny states had aspirations far beyond their budgets.

CHAPTER 9

ANHALT-ZERBST AND THE ROMANOVS

This small state was most famous for producing Catherine the Great of Russia. It was founded by Siegfried in 1252, disappeared in 1396 and was resurrected in 1603 in plain countryside north of the Elbe, west of Wittenberg, after the original state of Anhalt had been dissolved. The dynasty was founded by Esiko Count of Ballenstedt who built Aschersleben Castle, latinised as *Ascania*, so that this or Anhalt were assumed as the family name. The castle was between Halle and Quedlinburg, south west of Zerbst.

For a number of years the House of Ascania had prospered, particularly when Albert the Bear became Duke of Saxony in 1139 and even when he lost the dukedom and instead was given Brandenburg. Having first lost Saxony to the Welf, the family next lost Brandenburg to the Hohenzollern and all that was left was a fragment of Saxony round Anhalt. Even this was subdivided into ever more pathetic little enclaves to satisfy the younger sons of each generation, so the resurrected Anhalt-Zerbst was barely viable for a princedom.

When Prince Johann (*d.*1694) took over in 1667 he lost further swathes of territory but he did escape total insignificance by marrying Sophie August of Holstein-Gottorp, thus establishing a link with this better-off family, which was later to stand them in good stead. His son, Karl Wilhelm (1552-1718), built a new castle at Zerbst and the Church of St Trinitatis. In the next generation Johann August (1677-1742) had no children but his sister married Frederick II of Saxe-Gotha-Altenberg, and their daughter, Augusta (see p.76), became the wife of Britain's heir to the throne Frederick, Prince of Wales. Frederick, sadly, died before his father, so he never inherited the throne, but along with Augusta was the ancestor of all subsequent British royalty.

Meanwhile, the heir to Anhalt-Zerbst was Johann August's cousin, Christian August (1690-1747), who had to earn his living in the Prussian army and rose to the rank of field marshal. He married Johanna Elizabeth of Holstein-Gottorp, the sister of the future King Adolf Frederick of Sweden. The couple were stationed in Stettin where Christian August was the military governor when their daughter Sophie was born in 1729. Sixteen years later she was picked as a bride for her cousin, Grand Duke Peter of Russia, whose father was another Holstein-Gottorp. In 1762, shortly after he became Tsar Peter III she was at least tacitly responsible for his murder during a military coup so that as Catherine II she could become empress in her own right, a task she undertook with considerable professionalism for more than three decades. She was also without question the ancestress of all subsequent Romanov tsars, though whether her husband participated in this perhaps dubious honour is seriously open to doubt.

By comparison Sophie Catherine's elder brother, Friedrich August, inherited only the poverty-stricken princedom of Anhalt-Zerbst and had to hire out his small army to the British to act as their mercenaries against the rebel Americans. Anhalt-Zerbst finally disappeared in 1796.

Catherine, before she died that same year, had organised marriages for both her son Paul and grandson Alexander to German princesses, so that a tradition was established which meant that the Romanovs soon became an almost 100 per cent genetically German dynasty. Not only did this encourage their tsars' continued adulation for all things military but it perhaps led them to overcompensate by lavish championship of the Slavs, a tendency which led to the disastrous misjudgements of August 1914 and the Armageddon that followed.

CHAPTER 10

The House of Zähringen

Karl Friedich (1728-1811), First Grand Duke of Baden, was the head of yet another family that did well out of Napoleon, and one of his granddaughters became an empress, the other a queen. He sprang from the House of Zähringen, a castle founded in 1120 and now a suburb of Freiburg. Berthold I (*d.*1078) was made Margrave of Verona in Italy in 1061 and when the family's frontier duties in Italy ceased soon afterwards they conveniently transferred the title to Baden. The properties of the family then went through the usual subdivisions and reunifications until they were consolidated as Baden-Baden in 1771. By this time there had developed fourteen Baden sub-dynasties, some Catholic and some Protestant.

Count Karl Wilhelm of Baden-Durlach (1679-1758), meanwhile, in 1715, was frustrated by French attacks on his home in Durlach and so bored by his wife that he began building a new town and palace for himself and his mistresses, so it was given the name of Karl's Rest, or Karlsruhe. The Baroque palace that he built was bombed in the Second World War but has been reconstructed. His nephew and successor, Karl Friedrich, who reunited the main divisions of the family in 1771, went on to be an effective, paternalistic ruler who abolished serfdom and torture in his territories. He was made an Elector in 1803 and Grand Duke in 1806 by which time he was in his late seventies.

Grand Duke Karl Friedrich's son and heir, Prince Karl Ludwig (1755-1801), had the misfortune not to outlive his elderly father, but he did live long enough to see both of his two beautiful daughters make exceptional marriages. The first, Louisa of Baden (1779-1826), was picked out by no less a connoisseur than Catherine the Great to be the bride of her eldest grandson, the Tsarevich's son Alexander. She was only fourteen and Alexander a year older when she was summoned to St Petersburg for her wedding to the future tsar and rechristened as Elizabeth. There she was shocked by the intrigues and promiscuity of Catherine's court and the unpleasant manners of her new father-in-law, Catherine's heir Paul. It is even suggested that Catherine's latest lover, Platon Zubov, made a pass at her. Nevertheless, she did all the right things, like learning to speak Russian and converting to Orthodoxy, but found her new husband remote and cool. She was still only in her early twenties when Catherine's successor, the Emperor Paul, was murdered with at least the tacit approval of his son, her husband, who now became Alexander I. Their marriage was subsequently an erratic affair with long periods when Alexander ignored her and sought solace elsewhere and others where he came back to her conscience-stricken. Her situation was not helped by the fact that both their children were female and died soon after birth, during periods when she was suffering neglect while Alexander was enjoying intense friendships with both sexes, so that some cynics even cast doubt on the legitimacy of the babies. Alexander then drifted into a fifteen-year affair with a mistress. The unhappy Louisa/Elizabeth died when she was forty-seven.

Louisa's sister, Frederika (1781-1826), was the other royal bride. She married King Gustav IV Adolf of Sweden (see above p.28) in 1797, partly on the strength of her elder sister's success in Russia. She produced five children for him but found his sexual demands excessive, particularly after he had been deposed in 1809. So three years later they divorced and she died the same year as her sister, still only in her mid-forties.

CHAPTER 11

THE TSARINAS FROM HESSE DARMSTADT

The city of Darmstadt was the capital of the Landgraves of Hesse-Darmstadt, later Grand Dukes of Hesse from 1567-1918. They had not been particularly prominent during the eighteenth century because, as so often with German states, their inheritance had been split up, in this case into four main divisions after 1567. During the Thirty Years' War, both the Kassel and Darmstadt branches were strongly Protestant, but one was Calvinist and the other Lutheran so they chose opposite sides.

It was Frederick Landgrave of Hesse-Kassel (1675-1751) who had the perfect opportunity to found a new royal dynasty, for he took as his second wife the temperamental Ulrika Leonora, sister of Karl XII, the Swedish Thunderbolt. On the death of the bachelor King Karl the crown went to Ulrika and within two years she was so disgusted by the restrictions imposed upon her that she handed over the crown to her husband. Unfortunately, despite fathering several children with his string of mistresses, he failed to do so with his wife, so the Hesse dynasty of Sweden ended with his death. Meanwhile, he had left Hesse-Kassel in the hands of his brother, Wilhelm VIII, who had to withstand a French invasion and fought as a general for the Prussian British alliance during the Seven Years' War. He built for himself the Wilhelmsthal Palace and collected Rembrandts.

During the eighteenth century, the counts and dukes of Hesse made money by conscripting substantial numbers of peasants and petty criminals into their armies and then hiring them out to their Hanoverian allies during the American War of Independence. At one point there were 30,000 Hessian troops, mainly from the Kassel and Hanau branches, fighting for the British. Their rough uniform made of cloth like burlap, probably imported from India, thus acquired the name hessian.

The dukes were promoted to grand dukes in 1806 because they chose to side with Napoleon against Prussia. Two of the sisters of the first Grand Duke Ludwig I (1753-1830) married into royalty but not much happiness. Wilhelmina married the Tsarevich Paul of Russia and was renamed Natalia, but she found her husband far from acceptable and took a lover. She died in childbirth in 1776 at the age of twenty-one before she could become empress. Her sister, Frederika (1751-1805), became the second wife of the philandering King Frederick William II of Prussia and was thus the ancestress of all the German kaisers.

Meanwhile, the future Grand Duke Ludwig had made some money by ungallantly surrendering his fiancée Sophia to become the replacement wife for the Tsarevich Paul, so she was the mother of two tsars, Alexander I and Nicholas I. Ludwig instead married his first cousin and they had six children. He gained considerable territory under Napoleon but lost some of it again after 1815 and changed the title of his dukedom to Hesse and by Rhine. During the following century, his family was to produce two empresses of Russia: Marie, the wife of Alexander II, and Alexandra, the wife of Nicholas II.

The second of the Grand Dukes, Ludwig II (1777-1848), had a somewhat unorthodox marriage with his wife, Wilhelmine. There was an eleven-year gap between his first clutch of children and his second, most of whom were generally believed to have been fathered by his wife's lover, a lowly baron called de Grancey. Nevertheless, Ludwig found it convenient to accept official paternity. His daughter from this second batch of children, the delightfully pretty Marie (1824-80), was picked at the age of fifteen by the future Tsar Alexander II as his empress, so she was the grandmother of Nicholas II. It was initially a love-match, for Alexander had to overcome the scruples of his father, Nicholas I, but after fifteen years, in 1857, the tsar began to stray from the marital couch and had a succession of mistresses.

Marie's slightly older brother, Prince Alexander of Hesse (1823-88), served in the Russian army but flouted ducal convention by eloping to contract a morganatic marriage with a Julia von Hauke, a lady-in-waiting to his sister, the Empress of Russia. So since she was of too lowly birth to be either the Tsarinsa's sister-in-law or a princess of Hesse, the couple was found a spare title – Battenberg. The last genuine Battenbergs had died out in 1314 and Battenberg, with its former Kellerburg Castle, was north of Darmstadt in the mountains near Marburg, the original capital of Hesse on the River Lahn. So the title was vacant. Of the couple's children Ludwig Alexander (1854-1921) moved to Great Britain at the age of fourteen and served in the Royal Navy for over fifty years, eventually rising to be First Sea Lord in 1914. It was here that, three years later, he had his name translated into Louis Mountbatten to make himself sound less German. After an affair with the actress Lillie Langtry he married a Hesse-Darmstadt princess, daughter of the fourth Archduke. His son was Louis Mountbatten (1900-97) who also served in the Royal Navy, was the last British Viceroy of India and was murdered by Irish republicans while in his boat in Sligo Bay. His sister married Prince Andrew of Greece and was the mother of Philip Duke of Edinburgh, thus a grandmother of Prince Charles.

One of Prince Alexander's other sons, Alexander Joseph (1857-93) of Battenberg, benefitted from having as his aunt the Empress of Russia and from serving with the Russian army during the Bulgarian campaign of 1877. Two years later the tsar recommended him as the first prince of newly independent Bulgaria. His only problem was trying to please his group of Russian minders and his Bulgarian subjects at the same time, a difficult task for a young man of reasonable intelligence but lacking in political experience.

He made himself an absolute ruler in 1881 and won a great battle against the Serbs in 1885 but was deposed in a military coup in 1886 for being too lenient with them. He was briefly restored but found the conflicting pressures impossible to cope with and abdicated in 1886 when he was still under thirty, and he died seven years later.

His younger brother, Henry, married Beatrice, the youngest daughter of Queen Victoria, and they had a daughter, Victoria Ena (1887-1969), who married King Alphonso XIII of Spain and was the grandmother of King Juan Carlos. Henry was drowned when his ship sank after service fighting the Ashanti in 1896. His sister, Louise (1889-1965), turned down marriage with the Saxe-Coburg King Manuel of Portugal but later became the second wife of King Gustav VI Adolf of Sweden. Sadly, her only daughter died.

Meanwhile, Grand Duke Ludwig IV (1837-92) had married Alice, the second daughter of Queen Victoria, and their younger daughter, Alix (1872-1918), went to Russia to visit her elder sister, Elizabeth, or Ella, who had married the Russian Governor of Moscow, Arch Duke Sergei Romanov. Whilst there, in 1884, she met the impressionable Tsarevich Nicholas, who was twenty-one and currently having an affair with a ballet dancer. Nicholas was sent off on a far eastern trip to get away from them both, but four years later, as his father lay dying, he persuaded his parents to accept Alix as his future wife. Alix, rechristened as Alexandra, was thus twenty-two when she married Nicholas and soon afterwards, on Alexander III's death, she became tsarina. She took with her the haemophiliac strain passed to her mother Alice from Queen Victoria, a factor important in her downfall since it was her only son Alexei's illness that turned her into such a slavish devotee of Rasputin and made her such an unreliable support for her husband as his reign began to fall apart after 1905. A dozen years later, the fact that she was a German also became a severe disadvantage for her as the Russian armies succumbed to defeat at the hands of the Germans. Ironically, all her predecessors had also been Germans, but not at a time when Russia was at war with Germany. She was shot in 1918 in Ekaterinburg and her sister, Ella, was murdered nearby in the forest at about the same time. Alexandra was declared a saint in 2000.

CHAPTER 12

WÜRTTEMBERG AND TECK

Württemberg, a small hill 6 miles outside central Stuttgart, gave its name to another small German state that did well out of the Napoleonic Wars. There, Conrad, the founder of the family, built Rosenstein Castle in 1083. The Counts of Württemberg became dukes in 1495. Duke Karl Alexander (1684-1757), based in his castle at Stuttgart, did well in the Prussian and Austrian armies, particularly in the fight against the Ottoman Turks and was made governor of Belgrade. He was followed by three of his sons in succession: Karl Eugen (1728-93), the patron of Schiller and builder of the massive Baroque palace in Stuttgart, known as the Neues Schloss; Ludwig Eugen (1731-95); and Frederick II Eugen (1732-97).

It was the children of this third brother who took the family to new heights. Sophia (1759-1828), born in Stettin, was, for a cash down payment, gallantly surrendered by her fiancé, Grand Duke Ludwig of Hesse-Darmstadt, to become the second wife of the Tsarevich Paul of Russia and, in due course, briefly his empress with the name Maria Federovna. Paul was murdered soon afterwards but she was the mother of the next two tsars, Alexander I and Nicholas I, as well as the ancestress of all subsequent Romanovs.

Her brother, Frederick III (1754-1816), known because of his height as 'The Great Belly gerent', was rewarded for his support for the much shorter Napoleon by being made King of Württemberg, yet when he sensibly changed sides later in the war he benefitted from being the uncle of the victorious Tsar Alexander and so he kept his title.

The Jubilaumsalle in Stuttgart celebrates the first twenty-five years of his successor, King Wilhelm (1781-1864), who married his cousin, the sister of Tsar Alexander I. Their son, Karl (1823-91), also married the daughter of a tsar, Nicholas I, but was a less than satisfactory husband as his sexual orientation was in other directions. In 1871, he allowed his kingdom to be absorbed into the new Germany, though the kingdom survived in name at least till 1918.

In 1871, the King of Württemberg also revived one of the ancient titles of his family, the dukedom of Teck. There had been a Duke of Teck back in 1187 after the founding of Teck Castle near Kircheim by Adalbert, a brother of Berthold Duke of Zähringen – the castle was destroyed in the peasant wars of 1525 but a replacement castle still stands on the spot 2,500 feet up in the Schwabian Jura. Sadly, this family died out in 1439 and the property was bought by the Württembergs.

It was now convenient to revive the title because Duke Alexander of Württemberg, as sometimes happened, had married an unsuitable lady, Claudine von Kis-Rhede, so the marriage was classified as morganatic and their son Francis was not allowed to inherit the proper title. Giving young Francis the dukedom of Teck was expected to help him catch a rich wife, for his parents left him virtually no money. This strategy worked, for in 1856 he used his charms and impressive new title to woo Princess Adelaide of Cambridge, a granddaughter of George III, and he thus became a minor member of the British royal family, given a 'His Highness' by Queen Victoria soon afterwards. His daughter, Mary, was therefore regarded as suitable material for marrying the Prince of Wales, and when he died she was conveniently passed on, in 1892, to George, the Duke of York, who became king of Great Britain in 1910. Despite her slightly suspect grandmother, she thus became a pillar of the British royal establishment. When at the height of the First World War George V changed the dynastic name from Saxe-Coburg-Gotha to Windsor, the other members of the Teck family wisely took the name of Cambridge and Alexander of Teck became the Earl of Athlone.

PART 2

Travelogue

Despite the ravages of war, a remarkable quantity of the built heritage of the Germanic dynasties survives, some of it very beautiful, some spectacular and exotic. These sites are arranged in the same order as family sections with a short chapter corresponding to the chapters in Part One.

CHAPTER 1

Relics of the House of Oldenburg

IN GERMANY

Oldenburg Castle, now a museum, is the original home of the dynasty that dates back to the original Old Castle, or Altenburg of Eimar, built around 1108 to protect the crossing of the Hunte River in Friesland. From then till 1448 it was the focus of a family that gradually spread its tentacles until its Count Christian became King of Denmark. Thereafter, till 1773, it was under the control of the kings of Denmark. The castle itself, in the moated Altsadt, was remodeled as a horseshoe-shaped Baroque palace in 1607, but the town suffered a plague in 1667 and was sadly neglected by its Danish owners. In 1773, Danish rule came to an end thanks to Tsar Peter III of Russia, and much of the town was rebuilt, including the Lambertikirche, turned into a rotunda like the Roman Pantheon by Duke Peter Ludwig. As capital of the revived independent duchy of Oldenburg-Holstein-Gottorp it kept its status. There are now only the ruins of the wicked Count Otto's castle at Lechtenburg, near the north of the Hunte.

The Oldenburgs took over the neighbouring city of Delmenhorst on the River Delme in 1234, but only the site of their castle remains on the Burginsel.

The quaint Friesian town of Jever has its magnificent pink *schloss* with its 67 metre high tower, which was taken over by the Oldenburgs in 1818. It is now a museum. Eutin, known as the town of roses, was the fortified seat of the Bishops of Lübeck, many of whom were Oldenburgs. One of them, Adolf Frederick of Holstein-Gottorp, was elected King of Sweden in 1751. In 1773, Eutin was released from the control of Denmark and its schloss became a summer home for the part of the Oldenburg dynasty left behind in Germany, the Dukes of Holstein-Gottorp. The castle was remodeled as a Baroque palace and now houses the model ship collection of Peter the Great.

Gottorp, or Gottorf, lies near Schleswig on an island in the fiord, or Bergsee, of the River Schlei, some 40km from the Baltic. Built in 1161, it came into the hands of Kristian I of Denmark in 1459 and was the

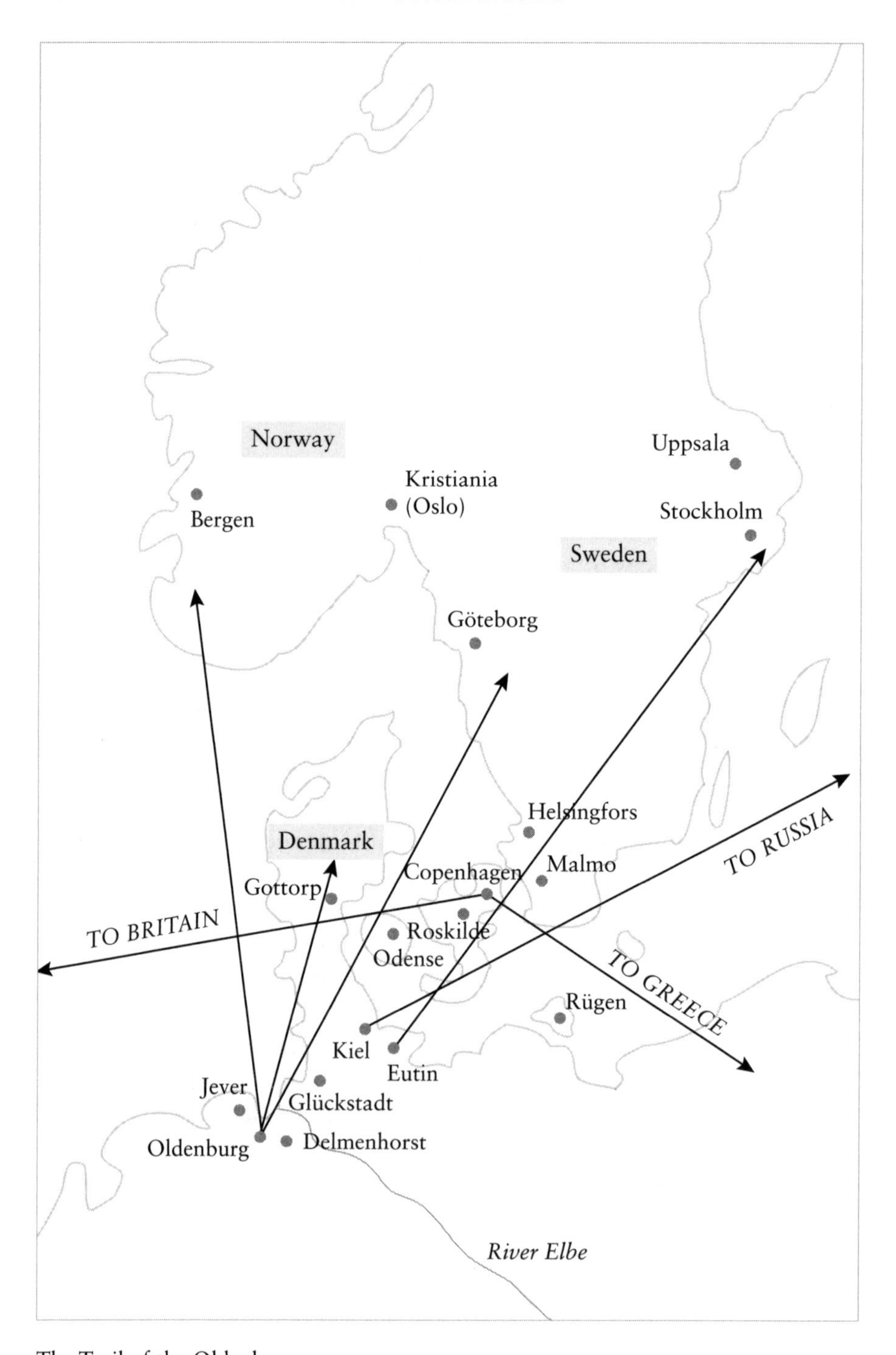

The Trail of the Oldenburgs

favourite residence of Frederik I. From 1544, it was the capital of the new Oldenburg offshoot of Schleswig-Holstein-Gottorp and was rebuilt as a palace by the Swedish architect Nicodemus Tessin in 1697, with a magnificent regal façade. The cathedral, or *dom*, of Schleswig contains the spectacular tomb of Frederik I of Denmark. At least two of the Oldenburg kings of Denmark chose brides from Holstein-Gottorp, a fact that later aided the royal pretensions of this branch of the family. Adolf of Holstein-Gottorp became the King of Sweden in 1751 and his sister, Johanna Elizabeth, who had married Christian August of Zerbst, was the mother of Catherine the Great of Russia who was born in Stettin where her father was acting as military governor for the Prussians.

Glücksburg Castle was built in 1582 in the Flensburg Fiord by Duke Johann, son of Kristian II of Denmark, and is described as Germany's largest water castle. When Schleswig-Holstein, after 1460, was reduced to being only a secondary part of the estates of the Oldenburgs because they were now rulers of Scandinavia, it was agreed that while the family still owned it, it was as a state within the Holy Roman Empire, not a part of Denmark. Thus it became an Oldenburg dukedom, and later, when the Oldenburg dynasty in Copenhagen ran out of heirs, it was their, now distant, cousins in Glücksburg who took over in 1863 as the new kings of Denmark. Flensburg itself was throughout this period the most successful commercial city under Scandinavian control but with the rest of Schleswig-Holstein became part of Germany in 1864 due to the machinations of Bismarck.

Kiel, with its relatively unpretentious *schloss* above the promenade, was the seat of Karl Duke of Schleswig Holstein who in 1727 married Anna, the bookish daughter of Peter the Great. Their son, Peter, was the heir, therefore, not only to Karl's inheritance, which included a possible claim to the crown of Sweden, but also potentially to the Tsardom of Russia. In the end he was persuaded to put Russia first and headed for St Petersburg. Meanwhile, Karl's cousin Karl Friedrich, who later succeeded him as Duke of Holstein-Gottorp, had married and produced a daughter, Sophia, who was also summoned to St Petersburg, changed her name to Catherine and became the frustrated bride of the initially impotent Peter until she lost patience and arranged for his deposition if not murder.

Glückstadt was founded by the Danish Oldenburgs in 1617 as a mercantile port on the Elbe to take business away from Hamburg.

IN DENMARK

Kronborg, in Helsingfors, or Elsinore, at the tip of Zealand and positioned to guard the narrowest entrance to the Baltic Sea, the Oresund, was first built just before the arrival of the Oldenburgs in 1420s but rebuilt in 1585 by Frederik II as a massive fortified Renaissance palace. It was badly burned in 1629 and used from 1739 as a slave prison and to lock up the unfortunate Queen Caroline, sister of the British George III, after she was found to be cheating her husband, the unstable King Kristian VII, in 1772. Also in Zeeland is Frederiksberg Palace, built as a country residence by Frederik IV.

Copenhagen became the capital of Denmark in 1443 when Kristoffer moved here after a fire had damaged Roskilde. Kristian I was crowned here and in 1479 founded the university, which was destroyed in the British bombardment of 1801.

The Amalienborg Palaces are made up of four identical palaces built round an octagonal square by Frederik V in 1744 to celebrate the 300th anniversary of the accession of Kristian I, founder of the Oldenburg dynasty in Denmark.

Frederiksborg was built by Kristian IV – the bath house section of this castle, now a museum, survives from the 1580s and its chapel was used for the coronation of the Oldenburg kings.

Kristianshaven is the harbour area of Copenhagen, founded by Kristian IV, which includes the delightful Church of Our Saviour with its spiral tower, the Stock Exchange, or Børse, with its twisted serpent spire of 1616, a brewery, arsenal and the Holm Naval Church. He also built the pentagram shaped Kastellet fortress in 1626.

Nyborg Castle, birthplace of Kristian II, who after his deposition was imprisoned first at Kalundborg Castle in Zealand then at Sönderborg which he had himself recently extended on the island of Alsen. It was rebuilt by Frederik IV, became part of Germany in 1864 but was returned to Denmark in 1920.

Rosenborg, now in central Copenhagen, was originally built as an out-of-town palace by Kristian IV and in imitation of Louis XIV's Versailles. It contains the Danish crown jewels.

Kristiansborg is a twentieth-century palace used as the main government offices and reconstructed on the site of the original Copenhagen Castle, built in 1369 and demolished in 1731. Remnants of the old castle and its infamous Blätärn, built by Kristian IV, are preserved in the basement of the new building.

Bakken is an amusement park founded in 1583 under Kristian IV, later supplanted by the Tivoli in 1843.

Frederick VIII's Palace and Brockdorff's Palace was bought by Frederik VII in 1767, later used as a military school and then again as a royal residence by Frederik VIII till 1906.

Fredensborg, a hunting seat of Frederik IV in 1719, on Lake Esrum is now used as spring and autumn home for Danish royals.

Odense Palace was built by Frederik IV and nearby is St Kanute's Cathedral.

Roskilde Palace and Cathedral was the original bishop's castle, first occupied by King Kristoffer when he came to Denmark. It was damaged by fire, so he moved to Copenhagen; it was replaced by a palace in 1733. The large twin-spired thirteenth-century cathedral has been the burial place for most Danish kings. Grasten, another Oldenburg hunting lodge was rebuilt in 1759. Kristian I also hugely extended Varberg Castle. Marselisborg at Aarhus was built in 1661.

Hermitage is a two storey wooden framed Baroque hunting lodge built at Dyrehaven north of Copenhagen in a deer park in 1694.

The Trekroner fort dates from 1787. Koldinghus, on the German frontier, was much used by the Oldenburg kings. Fredericia fortress in Jutland was built for Frederik III in 1664.

Greenland remains a part of Denmark, though the original Norse colony was allowed to die out before 1500 by the Oldenburgs, who only encouraged resettlement in 1728 at Nuuk, which has a cathedral from 1849.

The Faroes had a long-term Viking settlement, which was reorganized by Kristian II in 1520 and integrated into Denmark from 1720 till 1948.

In Iceland

Denmark controlled the old Norse colony of Iceland from 1380 but the Oldenburgs, apart from forcing the settlers to adopt the Lutheran Church under Kristian III, largely neglected it as unprofitable until 1660 when Frederik III took more interest. It won home rule in 1874 and became a republic in 1944. The buildings of Reykjavik were largely of wood during the Oldenburg period so little has survived.

In Sweden

The ambitious and extravagant Gustav III, from 1787 onwards, built a series of confections in Haga Park, intending it to be Sweden's equivalent of Versailles. They include the Copper Tent, Temple of Echo, Turkish Pavilion and Chinese Pagoda. The palace was never completed and Gustav was murdered in the Stockholm Opera House in 1792.

Trekroner Slott is symbolic of the union of the three crowns after the Kalmar Union was burned down and superseded by the massive Stockholm Palace, begun in 1692 and rebuilt in 1734.

Rosersberg on Lake Mälaren outside Stockholm was built in the 1630s and given to Karl XIII in 1762.

Uppsala, with its massive cathedral Domkyrka, was where Kristian I was crowned King of Sweden not long after its completion in 1435. It was also the site of Queen Kristina's dramatic abdication and crowning of her ex-fiancé.

Halmstad in southern Sweden was used as the meeting place to renegotiate the Kalmar Union of the three Scandinavian crowns, named after its original venue (1397) of Kalmar Slott. And it was given new fortifications by Kristian IV.

Malmo, now in Sweden, was for a long period Denmark's second largest city. The fortress, or Malmohus, was built in 1434.

Kristian IV founded Kristianstad, with its magnificent Heilige Trefaldighhetskyche in southern Sweden.

Castle Nykoping was a medieval castle rebuilt by Karl IX of Sweden.

Norrkoping in Østrgøtland, the place of coronation for Swedish kings, including Gustav IV at the Church of St Olof, was built in 1750.

In Norway

Trondheim's Nidaros Cathedral, built as a site for pilgrimage for St Olaf, with its superb Gothic west façade, was the scene for the coronation of Kristian I and most subsequent kings of Norway up to 1906, and the royal regalia are kept here. The Stiftsgärden is the local royal palace. Munkholem was a fortress prison built in 1658.

Bergen has Rosenkranz Tower, built in 1560 for the Danish governor. Frederiksberg was built in 1666 for Frederik III. Bergenhus Fortress was built in the 1240s and restored in the 1890s. Frederikstad was founded as a fortified town by Frederik II in 1567 on the River Glomma. Halden has the Frederiksten Fortress from the seventeenth century.

Kristiania, or Oslo, was founded as a new city by Kristian IV in 1642 after its predecessor was burned down. The Oslo Royal Palace was built for the Bernadotte dynasty but used by the Oldenburgs since 1905. Guarding Oslo is the Akershus Fortress, rebuilt by Kristian IV, with its royal mausoleum and also outside Oslo is Bygdøy, taken by the Oldenburgs at the reformation and rebuilt in 1733.

IN FINLAND

Turku Castle, on its rocky island in the River Auru, was captured by the Oldenburgs in 1441 but lost by Kristian II during the Vasa uprising after the Stockholm Bloodbath.

IN ESTONIA

The Oldenburgs held parts of Estonia till 1645, particularly the island of Ösel, now Saaremaa, with the town of Kuressaare, which still has its ducal castle.

IN RUSSIA

Petrodvorets is west of St Petersburg and has the Palace of Peter III, son of a Holstein-Gottorp. It was given to Peter III by the Empress Elizabeth when he became heir to the throne of Russia, and he built his own Peterstadt, or miniature fortress, so that he could drill his pet troops of soldiers.

IN BRITAIN

London has Denmark House, which is now part of Somerset House and was a Tudor royal residence given to his wife Anne of Denmark by King James VI and I, and considerably altered by her with the help of Inigo Jones.

Margaret of Denmark married James III of Scotland and is buried beside him at Cambuskenneth Abbey, Stirling.

IN GREECE

The Oldenburg kings of Greece built a royal palace for themselves in Athens in 1843, and since 1924, it has been the Greek Parliament. George I built a second royal palace in 1868 and it is now the Presidential Palace.

IN INDIA

Tharangambad, south of Pondicherry, still has its Fort Dansborg from 1620 when it was built to defend the Danish colony of Tranquebar, which survived till 1845 when it was taken over by the British. The Danes also held Seranpore.

IN GHANA

Fort Prinsensten, east of Accra, and Fort Christiansborg, near Accra, are two surviving Oldenburg slaving stations.

IN THE WEST INDIES

The islands of St Thomas and St John were taken over by the Oldenburgs in 1671 and 1718 respectively as sugar colonies with slave labour. They were sold to the United States in 1917. Christiansted, now in the US Virgin Islands, was once the capital of the Danish West Indies and still has its fortifications.

CHAPTER 2

Habsburg Relics in Switzerland, Austria, Spain, The Netherlands and America

In Switzerland

Habsburg, or Habichsburg, the original Hawk's castle, built in 1020 some 1,500 feet above sea level on the Wülpelsberg, south of Brugg, was the relatively modest beginning from which the family took its name. Thereafter, they began to build up their fortunes. They founded Muri Abbey, which survives, and controlled Zurich as well as the lucrative exaction of tolls from those crossing the Alpine passes. Altdorf was the scene of the conflict of Albert I of Habsburg and his henchman Gessler against the legendary, perhaps fictitious, William Tell in 1307. On the spot where Albert was murdered his widow founded the Königsfelden Monastery. This became a Habsburg dynastic shrine and where the Habsburg knights killed in the family's greatest setback, the battle of Sempach in 1386, were buried; that heralded their decline as a power in Switzerland.

In Austria

Austria was conquered by the Habsburgs in 1278 during the reign of the first emperor in the family, Conrad. He took over Vienna, which henceforth became the Habsburg capital, and relocated to the original Hofburg. Only the Swiss courtyard survives from this period, but over the next six centuries, the Habsburgs kept adding to the huge palace, especially the Amalia wing and royal chapel, which was installed by Friedrich III, and the Baroque interiors of Maria Theresa, the Kaiser appartments, the Spanish riding school and the treasury with the crown jewels. The Augustinian chapel contains the hearts of the Habsburgs.

St Stephen's Cathedral was rebuilt in its present form in 1359 with its massive latticework spire or Sudturmnick, named Steffl and completed in 1433, dominating the city and rising to 136 metres. It was Friedrich III who made the church a cathedral in 1469 and was buried here in a red tomb. The internal organs of the Habsburgs were buried in the catacombs beneath the cathedral.

From 1619, the main burial place for the Habsburgs was the Kaisergruft beneath the Church of the Augustinian Friars. The imposing Karlskirche was built by Charles VI in gratitude for the survival of the Viennese after the plague of 1713. The Votive Church commemorates the Emperor Franz Joseph surviving an assassination attempt in 1853.

Schönbrunn Palace was built for Leopold I in 1700 as his response to Versailles and greatly extended in Rococo style by Maria Theresa in 1744. Painted her favourite rich yellow, it has 2,000 rooms, a chapel, a theatre and gardens with fountains. Mozart played his first concert aged six in the Mirror Room. Maria Theresa's state coach is in the Wagenburg.

Mayerling is the site of the mysterious death of Prince Rudolf in the Wiener Wald and now has a convent.

The Habsburgs founded a number of important monasteries, for example, Klosterneuburg, on the Danube, rebuilt by Charles VI as a palace; Neuberg in Styria, founded by Otto in 1327; and Gaming Charterhouse, begun by Albert II in 1330.

Graz in Styria is on the River Mur and dominated by the Schlossberg. It became the main residence of Friedrich III whose motto, A.E.I.O.U., is carved in a number of places around the city. Only the bell tower survives of the original castle on Schlossberg. The replacement castle, built for Friedrich in 1435 in the Hofgasse, has its remarkable double-helix staircase, built in 1499, and a sprinkling of Friedrich's favourite slogan. Later it became the court of Ferdinand of Styria. The Cathedral belongs to the same period and next door is the high Baroque Mausoleum of Ferdinand II. The Armoury dates from 1645.

Innsbruck became the capital for the Tirolean branch of the Habsburgs from 1420 and there are many monuments left by the Emperor Maximilian I. The Hofburg, or imperial palace, dates from 1397 but was much refurbished in Baroque and Rococo styles by Maria Theresa, portraits of whose sixteen almost identical looking children abound. It had the massive Giants' Hall, 31 metres long, as its main reception area. The Hofkirche contains the magnificent but empty tomb of Maxilmilian I. The cathedral holds twenty-eight giant bronze statues of the Habsburgs. The Archduke Franz Ferdinand and his wife, both murdered at Sarajevo in 1914, are buried here. Ambras Castle was acquired and extended by Ferdinand II in 1564.

Salzburg has the Heilbrunn palace, originally reserved for Habsburg heirs, and Klessheim Palace, used for the brother of Franz Joseph.

Klagenfurt has its Hochsterwitz Fortress, which was taken over by Friedrich III.

Bad Ischl in Salzkammergut had a reputation for curative waters from 1828 and after Princess Sophie tried them she famously gave birth to Franz Joseph who made the Kaiservilla his summer home.

IN GERMANY

Aachen, formerly Aix la Chapelle, was the original capital of the Holy Roman Empire and its cathedral, or *dom*, and Pfalzkapelle were the scene of imperial coronations until 1560. Charlemagne's palace has gone except for the Coronation Hall.

St Trudpert's Abbey in the Black Forest produced the forged documents that helped Rudolf to create the Habsburg myth, and he gave a relic of Jesus's blood to Weissenau Abbey near Ravensburg in 1283. Frankfurt-am-Main succeeded Aachen as the virtual capital of the Empire for the Habsburgs in 1560 and for the coronation of Ferdinand I. The Electors had met here to 'choose' the new emperors since 1356 and coronations took place in the thirteenth-century *dom*, or cathedral, till 1792. The Gothic façaded Römer in the Römerberg contains the Kaisersaal.

Augsburg was the favoured residence of the Emperor Maximilian I, and only the tower of the Imperial Palace, or Fronhof, survives as part of the Bishop's Residence built in 1743.

IN HUNGARY

Budapest was captured by the Habsburgs in 1686 after a 145-year occupation by the Turks. Buda Castle Szent Gyorgy, the royal palace, survived, as does the Matyas Templom. After the revolution of 1848, Franz Joseph built the Citadel Fortress, but in 1867, power was devolved and Franz Joseph became King of Hungary with a separate parliamentary government. It has the Habsburg Nadori Crypt. The Royal Palace, Budavari Palota, was built for but never really occupied by the Habsburgs. The Habsburgs peppered Hungary with Baroque Catholic churches in the vain hope of imposing Catholicism on the Magyars. Monostori Fortress at Komarom is a huge Habsburg fortress from 1850.

IN THE CZECH REPUBLIC

Prague Castle was rebuilt by the Habsburgs after the fire of 1541, and Ferdinand I built the Belvedere as a summer palace. It was the scene of the calamitous defenestration of 1618 that precipitated the Thirty Years' War. The Emperor Ferdinand V lived here after his abdication in 1848. Terezin, or Teresienstadt, has its great Habsburg fortress from 1757, as does Litomerice. Konopiste Château was bought in 1887

IN SLOVAKIA

Bratislava was the theoretical capital of Hungary from when the Habsburg Ferdinand I acquired what was left of the kingdom in 1526, after the defeat and death of the previous king at Mohacz and till the time the Habsburgs captured Budapest in 1686. They were crowned in Podzony Bratislava at St Marin's Cathedral even after the so-called liberation from the Turks. Bratislava Castle was rebuilt in 1649 and refurbished by Maria Theresa .The Grassalkovich Palace dates from 1760. Zvolen Castle had a Habsburg makeover in 1784.

IN POLAND

Cracow was the capital of the area of Poland acquired by the Habsburgs in 1793 and retained till 1918. Many of their fortifications and other buildings survive.

IN THE UKRAINE

Lemburg, or Lviv, was the capital of Habsburg Galicia from 1792-1918 and many of its historic buildings date from that period.

IN ITALY

Trieste became the main Habsburg seaport in 1382, when its citizens preferred Leopold III to the rule of Venice, and remained so till 1918. Its Castle San Giusto was held by Frederick III, and Miramare was built in 1856 for Archduke Maximilian. Trieste was the main base for the Austro-Hungarian navy and a thriving seaport until transferred to Italy in 1918.

Verona was made the depot area for the Austrian army in the war of 1859 with an additional eight forts, many of which survive, such as Forte Chiero. There were also Habsburg fortresses at Altopiano, Mantua and Legnago. The massive Franzenfeste from 1833 survives at Fortezza.

IN SLOVENIA

Ljubljana was a Habsburg city from 1335 to 1918 and was their capital of Carniola. It had to be rebuilt twice after earthquakes in 1515 and 1895. Its castle and cathedral date from 1701. Rudolf the Founder founded Novo Mesto in 1365.

IN CROATIA

Rjeka or Fiume first went to the Habsburgs in 1471 under Frederick III and was transferred back to Hungary by Maria Louisa in 1809, becoming the only seaport of Hungary till 1918. It has a Habsburg palace.

Zagreb has the Janusevac Castle and Zagreb Cathedral from the Habsburg period.

IN BOSNIA

Sarajevo in Bosnia became a Habsburg province in 1878 and the Austrians put up a number of administrative buildings including the pseudo-Moorish National Library. Latin Bridge was the scene of the murder of Archduke Ferdinand in 1914.

IN BELGIUM

Ghent Castle was the birthplace of the Emperor Charles V, whose Spanish mother had married the Duke of Burgundy, and has St Baaf Cathedral.

IN SPAIN

The Habsburgs ruled Spain from 1516 when Charles took over till 1700. Granada was where Charles V spent his honeymoon at the Alhambra and built his own new palace beside it.

Philip II, the son and successor of Charles in Spain, made Madrid the official capital of Spain, and as a monument for his father built the huge monastic palace San Lorenzo del Escorial on the Sierra Guadarrama where he spent most of his time.

Amongst Philip's other buildings were Valladolid Cathedral, Bisagra Gate at Toledo, where he had first begun his reign in the Alcazar before moving to Madrid, his hunting lodge at El Pardo and his summer palace at Aranjuez.

IN MEXICO

The Habsburg Emperor Maximilian of Mexico was shot by a firing squad on the Cerro de las Campanas by the Queretaro Palace.

IN MADEIRA

Funchal was the final home of the last of the Habsburg emperors Karl and his elaborate tomb is in the Church of our Lady of the Mount at Monte.

CHAPTER 3
FROM ORANGE VIA NASSAU TO THE HAGUE, LONDON, THE FAR EAST AND THE WEST INDIES

IN FRANCE

The Orange part of the Nassau inheritance can be traced back to a tiny princedom, Les Baux, that was founded by Bertrand of Baux in 1180. This dramatic and well-preserved hilltop castle in Provence, some 20 miles south of the old Roman city of Orange and just east of Arles, gave him an impregnable position from which to rule his little state. In due course the family became a trendsetter for the idylls of the troubadours, and by good marriages built up huge land holdings from Châlon to Brabant. Les Baux was left behind and eventually captured after becoming a Protestant stronghold by Louis XIII. In the seventeenth century, the dynasty petered out and its last heiress married Heinrich of Nassau-Breda. Orange was given a new castle by Mauritz but it was captured by the French in 1672.

Château Châlon, Nozeroy and Arlay, south of Bezancon in the Jura, were all held by the Orange dynasty after it left Les Baux and Nozeroy was the birthplace of the last French Prince of Orange.

IN GERMANY

Nassau is the 33 metres high tower of Burg Nassau and it still stands, bristling with Gothic turrets, on the summit of a 120-metre-high cone of rock above the wooded Lahn valley, first built by Dudo, rebuilt by Heinrich III of Nassau in 1220 and the tower completed in 1346.

In Dillenburg little remains of the castle where William the Silent was born in 1533 except the *schlossberg* and the *stockhaus*, or prison, but in the 1870s the Willemsturm was built and houses a museum dedicated to the Orange dynasty.

In Holland

Breda, a medieval town at the junction of the Aa and Mark Rivers, has the twelfth-century Kasteel van Breda, which became the first home of the Orange Nassau dynasty when they moved to Holland. It was rebuilt in 1530 by Count Heinrich III and later became a military academy. The Grote Kerk, with its 100 metres high spire, was the burial place for the family. The Spanjaardsgat, with its two heptagonal towers, recalls the period of warfare between the Dutch and Spain.

Located in the Hague, Noordeinde Palace was originally a farmhouse bought for the widow of William the Silent, Louise de Coligny, and her son, Frederik Hendrik. At one point it was transferred to King Frederick William of Prussia who was a great grandson of William, but Frederick the Great sold it back to William V of Orange in 1754 and it became the main palace for the Stadholders.

Huis ten Bosch was built for the exiled Elizabeth of Bohemia in 1645 and has fine Baroque gardens. It became a favourite of the Stadholders but was badly damaged during the Second World War and has been restored.

In Amsterdam the royal palace, previously the town hall, was built in 1648 on wooden piles by what is now Dam Square and has been the formal residence of Dutch royalty since the war. The Nieuwe Kerk, built in the fifteenth century, has been used for Dutch coronations since 1818.

Het Loo was built in 1684 for William III as a hunting lodge in the forest of Hoge Veluwe and is now a museum. Soestdijk in Soest near Utrecht was originally built as a hunting lodge for William II in 1674. It later became the favourite residence of Queen Juliana.

Amsterdam has its Fortress Ring from 1881 and Muiderslot is one of a series of seventeenth-century fortresses on the Water Lane defence system created by Prince Maurice in the seventeenth century.

In Belgium

In Brussels the Palais des Academies was built in 1823 as a reward for King William of Orange's part in the Battle of Waterloo but not lived in for long as he was deposed from the Belgian part of his kingdom by the revolution of 1830. It was later used by his Saxe-Coburg successors.

IN LUXEMBOURG

The city's sixteenth-century town hall was refurbished for the Orange Grand Dukes in 1817.

IN GREAT BRITAIN AND IRELAND

In London, Kensington Palace was bought by William of Orange in 1689 as it was then out of town and good for his asthmatic chest. He used Christopher Wren to design its refurbishment. He also used Wren to rebuild Hampton Court with a historic mural by Cornhill celebrating the arrival of William in England. He and his wife converted Greenwich Palace into the Royal Hospital.

Scotland's most obvious memorial to the House of Orange is Fort William, the base set up to subdue the recalcitrant clans of the west and from which troops headed out in 1692 to undertake what turned out to be one of William of Orange's greatest public relations disasters, the massacre of Glencoe.

In Ireland, County Meath is the site of the Battle of the Boyne.

IN INDIA

The Dutch colonial enterprise the Vereenigde Oostindische Compagnie, or V.O.C., was founded in 1602 when Maurice of Orange was Stadholder and began a period of extraordinary colonial expansion that has left numerous monuments scattered throughout the world. At least three great modern cities owe their foundation to this activity: New York, Capetown and Jakarta.

Daulatabal Fort is one of a number of Dutch forts surviving from the period of Dutch colonising in India. Also surviving examples of Dutch colonial architecture are the Mattancherry Palace in Cochir and the Masulipatnam Armoury.

Fort William on the Hooghly River at Calcutta was founded during the last year of William III's reign to protect the British East India Company.

IN BANGLADESH

In the silk-making town of Rajshahi the Dutch established a factory that survives and is now known as Barakuthi.

IN SRI LANKA

After capturing the town of Galle in 1640 the Dutch built a large fortified harbour, fortress and town, which became their second largest outpost in the Far East. The fortifications survive, as does their Groote Kerk of 1750.

IN INDONESIA

In Jakarta the Dutch East India Company took over a small British outpost in 1619 and founded their city of Batavia which is now Jakarta. The Stadhuis of the V.O.C. still survives as a historical museum. In the Jakarta Kopa area and Sunda Kelapa harbour there are many Dutch buildings.

Bali has numerous surviving Dutch coffee plantation houses. The Banda Islands have Fort Belgica, built in 1611, and their Run Island was famously swapped for Manhattan in 1667. Ambon in the Moluccas has Fort Amsterdam and Fort Rotterdam, while Ternate has Forte Oranje, built in 1637.

IN SOUTH AFRICA

Capetown was founded in 1652 following the successful survival there of a shipwrecked Dutch crew. The pentagonal Castle of Good Hope, with its Oranje Bastion and Company Garden, still survives, as does the Groote Kerk, built originally in 1678. There are numerous other examples of Cape Dutch architecture, characterised by thick walls, white paint and ornamental gables. The Drostdy Museum in Swellendam and the Boschendal Wine Estate are good examples. The Orange River was named after William III by a British officer.

IN GHANA

Fort Amsterdam and Fort Good Hope, founded in 1705, were Dutch slaving stations.

IN THE UNITED STATES

New York was founded as New Amsterdam in 1624 and taken over by the British only in 1667. The Dutch had hired Henry Hudson to explore the area for them in 1609. The Stockade Historic District of Wiltwyck, now Kingston, 80 miles from New York is now preserved. The ruins of Fort Oranje, founded in 1624 in what is now Albany, were excavated and conserved in 1971 near a motorway interchange. Williamsburg, Virginia, was developed as a replacement for Jamestown in 1698 and named after William of Orange.

IN BRAZIL

Itamaraca near Pernambuco has the well-preserved Fort Oranje that was founded in 1516.

IN THE WEST INDIES

Curacao, one of the five islands of the Netherlands Antilles, is still part of the Kingdom of the Netherlands. Its capital, Willemstad, was founded in 1634, successful as a pirate base and later as a semi-legal slave-trading station. Dutch waterfront buildings survive and plantation houses such as Groot Davelaar. Nassau in the Bahamas was rebuilt in 1695 and named after William III.

CHAPTER 4

From Altdorf to Windsor via Hanover

In Germany

Schöngau Castle has not survived but was the home of one of the first Welf, Warin Eisenbart, or Iron Beard, who, according to legend, had twelve children in one day. One of them was Henry Welf to whom the emperor offered as much land as he could plough in a single day so he had a midget plough made of gold and a relay of horses so that he could claim an unexpectedly huge area. Weingarten, originally called Altdorf, in the valley of the Schüssen in Schwabia was the site of the original castle of Welf Count of Altdorf but was destroyed and replaced by St Martin's Basilica. This is now the largest Baroque church north of the Alps, and as it was known as Weingarten, the name was adopted for the whole town.

Ravensburg to the south was the next home of the Welfs but was lost to the Hohenstaufen in 1191. The castle of Veitsburg was rebuilt in 1751.

Ruined Weinsberg Castle, in the good wine country of Heilbron by the Neckar, is also known as Weibertreu, or faithful wives, because of the legendary siege of the Welfs in 1140 by Conrad III who agreed to let the women escape with all the baggage they could carry – they chose to carry out their husbands, brothers or sons hidden in rucksacks. Hanstein Castle is a massive ruin south of Göttingen.

Henry the Lion was responsible for the founding of two major cities München/Munich and Lübeck as well as the expansion of a third, Braunschweig/Brunswick. Very little survives of Henry's structures in Munich where as Duke of Bavaria, in 1158, he first destroyed an earlier bridge which was not on his land and then built a new toll bridge over the Isar and beside the monastery which gave the city its name, Monks – München. The original versions of the Peterskirche, Heilig Geist Kirche and Frauenkirche, or *dom*, date from this early period but have been subsequently rebuilt. In Lübeck the Heiligen Geist Hospital dates from soon after Henry the Lion as does the *dom* but it was later given a new façade of Gothic brick.

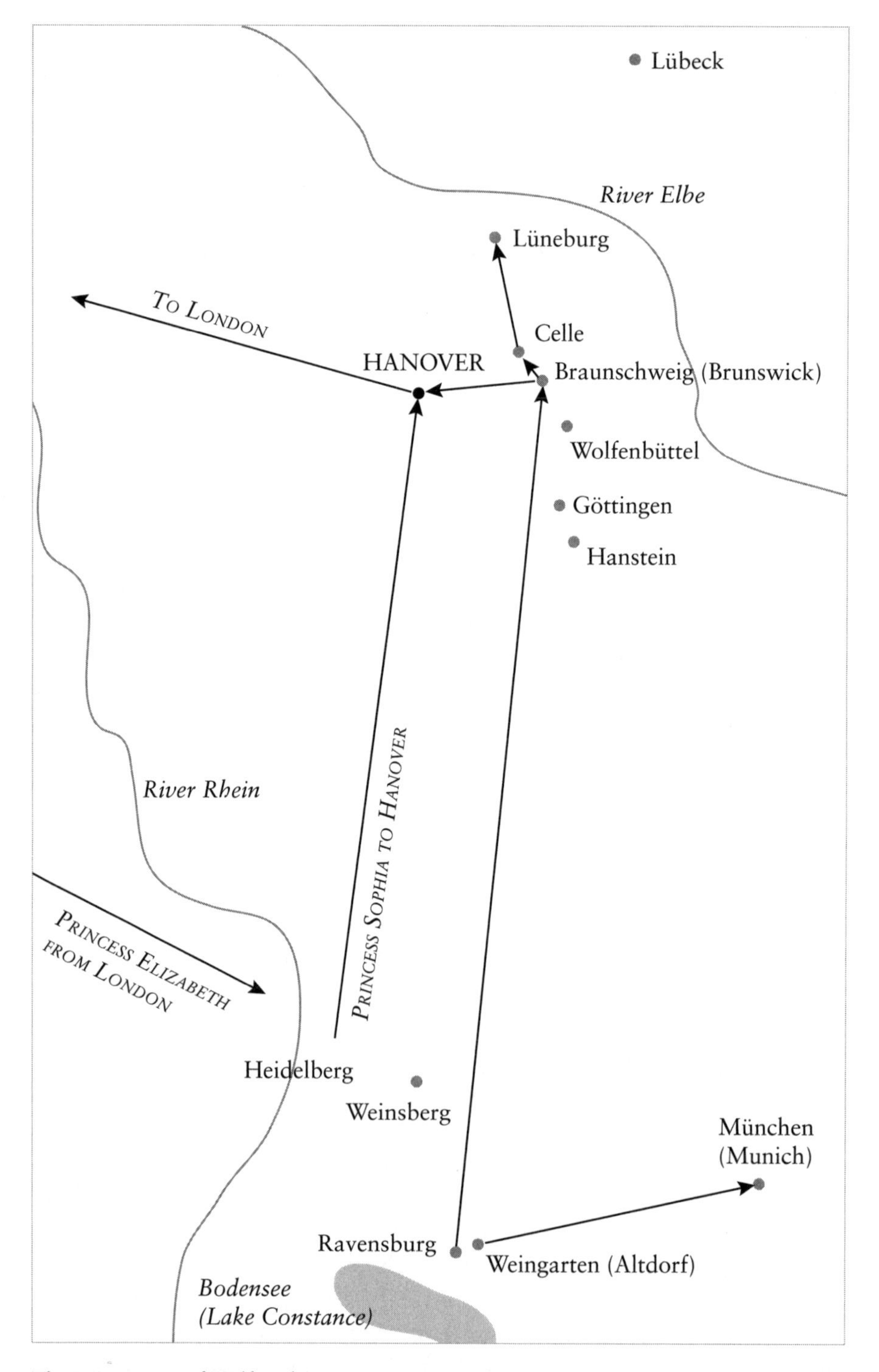

The Migrations of Welf and Hanover

South of Munich is Steingaden Abbey, founded by Welf VI in 1176, which has a Welfenmünster shrine to the dynasty, rebuilt after the Thirty Years' War.

Brunswick was Henry the Lion's favourite residence and as Duke of Saxony he secured its defences by using two arms of the River Oker. His Burglöwe, the emblematic bronze lion perched high on its pedestal, symbolized his ambition and was the first freestanding bronze statue made since the fall of the Roman Empire. In 1173, he founded his new cathedral, the Dom, built more like a fortress than a church, though later a Gothic brick gable was added between the towers. His castle, or Burg Dankwarderode, includes his impressive Rittersaal. In the museum is the cloak of Otto IV, Henry's son and the only member of the Welf dynasty to become Holy Roman Emperor. Duke Anton Ulrich was the other significant member of the family to embellish Brunswick, and he built the first public museum in Germany in 1754, which includes his Rembrandts, Vermeers etc. Holbein the Younger was born and trained in Brunswick. After the fall of Henry the Lion when the family lost both the dukedoms of Bavaria and Saxony the remaining inheritance was an area round Brunswick that included Lüneburg, Celle, Wolfenbüttel and Hanover.

Wolfenbüttel was the seat of one of the Welf splinter duchies from 1432 till 1754 when the duke moved back to Brunswick. The massive four-winged ducal *schloss* was built in Renaissance style and brilliant white stone on the site of the medieval castle and still retains its moat and some of its masonry. It includes a theatre established by an English troop in 1590. Duke August the Younger of Brunswick-Wolfenbüttel built up what was probably the largest library in Europe of its time. It was first built in 1572, rebuilt 1883 and included the exceptional Gospel Book of Henry the Lion.

Lüneburg was a wealthy medieval trading city that profited from its huge salt mines, though these have also caused some subsidence beneath its historic buildings, including the thirteenth-century St Johannis' church, the spire of which has an alarming tilt. The Furstensaal, with its ducal portrait gallery, survives, but the ambitious salt merchants were strong enough to eject the dukes in 1371.

Celle Schloss became the main home of the dukes of Brunswick-Lüneburg when they were forced out of Lüneburg itself by the citizens in 1371. Only the *schloss kapelle* of the medieval castle survives inside the newer Renaissance-style palace with whitewashed walls, built in 1530. Sophia Dorothea was the last heiress of the dukedom and married the future George I in 1680, thus reuniting this part of the inheritance with Hanover so that Celle was no longer the main ducal residence.

Herzberg am Harz, with its massive Welfenschloss, is perched on a huge rock and was the birthplace of Ernst August.

The bishop's palace at Osnabrück was the birthplace of George I as his father was, at the time, its Prince Bishop, and George also came back here to die in 1727. St Peter's Cathedral survives as does the Heger Tor, a memorial to the Elector George's German legion, which fought at Waterloo.

Hannover (Hanover), which was bought by the Welfs from the previous ducal family in 1241, has few remains of the medieval period apart from the Beginenturm, part of the old walls. In 1490, the local citizens, led by the 'Seven Spartans', beat off a siege by Duke Henry. The Dukes of Calenberg moved here in 1636 to take advantage of the protective walls during the Thirty Years' War. They took over a monastery by the River Leine and converted it into the Leineschloss, which was all but destroyed by allied bombing, but rebuilt in 1957 as the regional parliament.

Ironically, the great Herrenhausen Palace, built for the newly promoted Elector of Hanover in 1690, was destroyed by allied bombing during the Second World War (Volkswagen announced a plan to rebuild it in 2008). However, the Orangerie and Galerie survived as did many areas of garden, including the Grosser Garten laid out by the Electress Sophie, grottoes, waterfalls, Grosse Fontäne and many botanical features. The Fürstenhaus contains a museum of the House of Hanover. The Leibnizhaus recalls the residence of Leibniz here under the patronage of George II's wife, Caroline. The Wragenheim Palace was rebuilt for George V of Hanover in 1851.The Welfenschloss and Welfengarten also survive.

Calenberg, west of Hildesheim, has the ruins of the Welf ducal castle held by them from 1485. Ahlden Castle stood on the Lüneburg Heath and is where George I's allegedly adulterous wife, Dorothen of Zell, was incarcerated from 1694-1727.

Göttingen University was founded by George II, and much of the Altstadt has been preserved.

IN SWITZERLAND

Kreuzlingen in Thurgau has the former monastery founded in honour of the Welf saint, St Conrad who procured a piece of the True Cross.

IN GREAT BRITAIN

The first two Georges mainly used St James's Palace and Kensington Palace as their places of residence but George II's heir Frederick had Leicester House – now demolished – in what is now Leicester Square. His son

George III, in 1760, bought Buckingham House, which was refurbished as Buckingham Palace by his son George IV. George III also spent many years (1718-28), particularly during periods of nervous breakdown, at Kew Palace surrounded by the gardens that his mother and wife did much to lay out. Clarence House was acquired in 1825 for the future William IV.

Windsor Castle was substantially remodeled in Gothic style during the 1820s by George IV, who festooned it with turrets.

Brighton Pavilion was the exotic creation of George IV as prince regent with a medley of architectural styles.

The most obvious relics of the Hanoverians in Scotland are the huge barracks they erected during the Jacobite crises from 1715-46. These include Ruthven Barracks on their imposing mound near Kingussie, Bernera Barracks in Glenelg and the massive Fort George on the shores of the Moray Firth.

IN THE UNITED STATES

The Hanoverians ruled most of Canada and the American colonies for sixty-two years, from 1714-76, and during the Seven Years' War they added substantially to their holdings by defeating the French, but when they tried to recoup the cost of the war from the colonists they provoked the revolution that led to the founding of the United States. Most of the relics of this period are, therefore, military.

The largest town in Hanoverian times was Boston, which in 1720 had a population of 12,000.

Ticonderoga, the much fought-over fort built in 1755 on the narrows of Lake Champlain and previously known by its French name of Fort Carillon, has been reconstructed. Fort William Henry on Lake George dates from the same period. The walls are still standing of the fort at Crown Point near Burlington, which was rebuilt as a Hanoverian base in 1759 and captured by the Americans in 1775. Buildings of the Hanoverian period survive in the historic town of Yorktown where the British finally surrendered to Washington.

Savannah and the colony of Georgia were founded in 1733 by James Oglethorpe with the support of George II and were the largest new settlement attributable to the Hanoverians.

The town of Baltimore was founded in 1729 and was a mainstay of the sugar trade in Hanoverian times.

NOTE: Some later British royal residences will be dealt with under the Saxe-Coburg section.

IN CANADA

The site of General Wolfe's defeat of the French at Quebec in 1759 is preserved as are many of the reconstructed French barracks and the massive forty-acre star-shaped Citadel begun by the Hanoverians in 1775 to prevent American attack and finished in 1821. Toronto was developed in 1794 and called York after George III's son the Duke of York, but changed back to Toronto in 1834. Meanwhile, it was badly damaged by an American attack in the war of 1812 and had to be re-built. Fort George, the hexagonal fort, was built in 1796 to guard Niagara.

IN THE WEST INDIES

During Hanoverian times, a very substantial portion of the nation's wealth came from the West Indies. Jamaica still has the Port Royal Naval Dockyard, the base for the Hanoverian navy, Fort Charles and Fort George built in 1729 at Port Antonio. St Kitts has Brimstone Hill, a rock-top fort held from 1752-1851.

IN AUSTRALIA

Australia was first settled by the British during the reign of George III in 1786 when it became a useful new destination for convicts.

Parramatta still has cottages dating back to the earliest period of Hanoverian settlement in Australia.

Sydney's Hyde Park Barracks, dating from 1819, was originally built to house convicts and what is now the State Parliament building was previously part of a hospital built in 1810 for Governor Macquarie.The typically Victorian Gothic Government House was begun in 1837 to replace its predecessor.

Melbourne is the site of Trobe's Cottage, home of the first governor that dates from 1839.

Perth is where the old courthouse can be found. It dates from 1836, and Fremantle's Round House was used to house incoming convicts from the 1830s.

CHAPTER 5

From Hohenzollern to Berlin, Bucharest and Beyond

The original castle of High Zolle, or Burg Hohenzollern, built by Burchard in 1061, stood 2,500 feet above sea level on an isolated rock in the Schwabian Jura, 3 miles south of Hechingen. It was largely destroyed during a siege in 1423, and of its replacement, built in 1454, only the St Michael-Kapelle survives, cocooned inside a nineteenth-century pastiche that was erected on the orders of King Friedrich Wilhelm IV. It is huge and evocative but was never lived in by any senior member of the dynasty.

Nürnberg (Nuremberg) became the main focus for the family's attentions in 1192 when Friedrich III of Hohenzollern married the daughter of the Burgrave and soon afterwards took over his duties. This meant that he was responsible to the Holy Roman Emperor for the Kaiserburg, the huge imperial castle that dominated the city. It was one of the emperor's main bases, a place where he held diets or consultations with his princes and where he also kept reserves of money. The Fünfeckturm, or pentagonal tower, belongs to this period but the slightly later Luginslandturm reflects the declining relationship between the local townspeople and the ambitious Hohenzollern burgraves, for it was put up to keep them from taking over the town. In the end the townspeople succeeded, so the Hohenzollern had to look elsewhere to satisfy their lust for wealthy properties.

In 1254, some seventy years after their promotion to Nürnberg, the Hohenzollern family acquired most of Ansbach, which soon afterwards became the capital of their first dukedom. A Gothic hall from their original moated castle here survives as part of the later palatial Baroque Residenzschloss, which was built in the seventeenth century. The Church of St Gumberus contains the Schwannenritterordenkapelle, or the Chapel for the Knights of the Order of the Swan, which was founded by Margrave Albert Achilles in 1465. Caroline of Ansbach, a member of one of the Hohenzollern families that stayed here after the main branch moved to Brandenburg, became the wife of the future George II of Great Britain and Hanover.

The other town acquired at about this time by the Hohenzollern was Kulmbach, near where the White and Red Mains join. It had a large castle

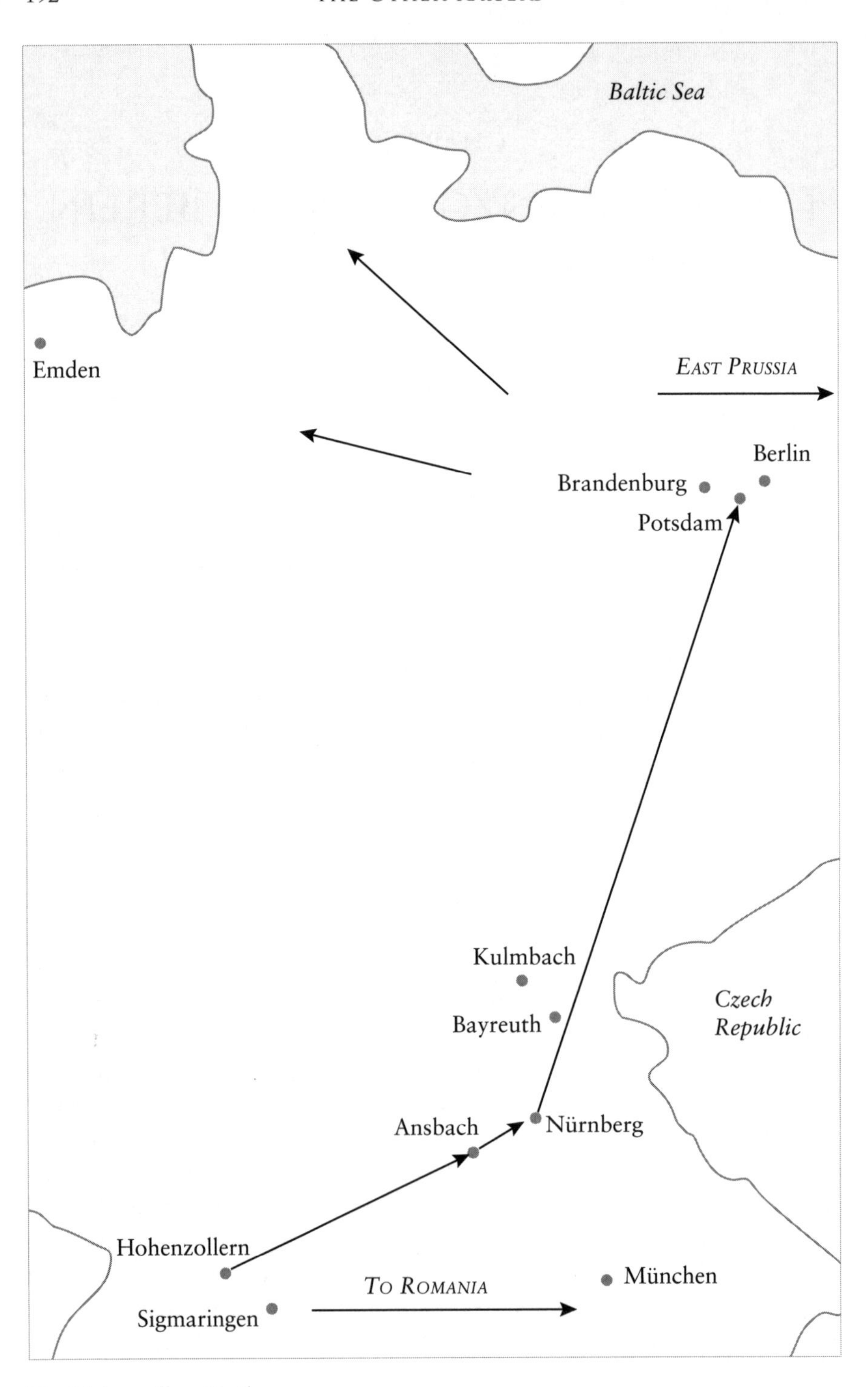

The Hohenzollern Trail

– Plassenburg – that has been rebuilt as a Renaissance ducal palace. The lower castle, or *niederburg*, has huge defensive walls whereas the upper castle, or *hochburg*, is elaborately embellished with dynastic symbolism. This was the headquarters of a branch of Hohenzollern princes from 1398 until 1553 when it was badly damaged after a siege caused by the ambitions of Margrave Albrecht Alcibiades who had tried to snatch the whole of Franconia, failed and was deposed.

In 1603, the family shifted their base to Bayreuth. Here they had an octagonal Renaissance tower above the Altes Schloss, most of which the Margrave Friedrich accidentally burned down in 1753. His wife was his cousin, the ambitious Wilhelmina of Prussia, elder sister of Frederick the Great, who had at one point been intended for the Prince of Wales, and commissioned numerous extravagant new buildings. These included the exotically Rococo Neues Schloss, which replaced the old tower (it passed to the Ansbach Hohenzollerns in 1769 since the couple left no sons) and the Opernhaus and Heremitage. The Italienisches Schlösslein was added by Friedrich's second wife, Caroline. We will return to Bayreuth in the Wittelsbach chapter for the era of Ludwig II and Wagner.

The Hohenzollerns were promoted to Margraves of Brandenburg in 1415. However, they did not stay long in the province's original capital, Brandenburg, which had been founded on three islands in the River Havel by the Slav Wends and did not become an official imperial province till 1157. The Neusstadt Island still has its large Gothic Katherinenkirche from the early Hohenzollern period. The Dominsel, as its name suggests, has the cathedral and the Aldstadt – the remains of part of the city's medieval fortifications. The Rococo Rheinsberg Château, situated on the picturesque Grienericksee, was rebuilt in 1734 by Friedrich Wilhelm I for his son the future Frederick the Great.

Instead of remaining in Brandenburg itself, the Hohenzollerns moved their capital east to Berlin where they took over a castle on Fishers Island in the River Spree at Kölln. Soon afterwards, in 1453, Friedrich II had it rebuilt as his Stadtschloss in more palatial style and there followed a series of demolitions and rebuildings until the communist regime finally got rid of it as a symbol of imperialism in 1950. A pathway lined, in the 1640s, with lime trees from it to the margrave's hunting area at Tiergarten became later the boulevard Unter den Linden with a monument to Frederick the Great in its centre. Of the surviving residences of the Hohenzollern in or around Berlin, the Zitadelle of Spandau was one of the original fortresses and much strengthened in the sixteenth century by the Hohenzollern. Red-roofed Schönhausen was bought by Friedrich III in 1691 and he used it as his main base when he made himself king in Prussia ten years later. The Schloss Charlottenburg was founded by Queen Sophie Charlotte in 1695 and subsequently extended as the summer home of the Prussian kings, including Frederick the Great who added the Knobelsdorff-Flugel. The Baroque Kronprinzenpalais was, as its name suggests, for the heir to the throne, and the Italianate Schinkel Pavilion was the favourite of Friedrich Wilhelm III who, amongst others, was buried in the nearby Mausoleum.

The massive Baroque Zeughaus, or Arsenal, was built for Friedrich Wilhelm in 1695 as part of the build-up of Prussian military force, and it was decorated with numerous symbols of victory and the noble death of warriors.

Amongst Frederick the Great's other contributions, are the Gendarmenmarkt, a huge public square, and parts of the neighbouring Französische Friedrichstadtkirche, built for the use of the Huguenot immigrants and balanced by the St Hedwigs Kathedrale, which he provided for Berlin's Catholic minority.

The early twentieth-century replacement *dom* contains the elaborate tombs of the Hohenzollern royals and of similar vintage is the bombed shell of the Kaiser-Wilhelm-Gedächtniskirche. The Siegessäule is a column commemorating the Prussian victories of the Bismarck era that led to the founding of the Kaiserreich, while the Brandenburg Gate was a somewhat premature triumphal arch erected in 1791 shortly before Prussia's severe defeats at the hands of Napoleon.

Potsdam first came to prominence when Friedrich Wilhelm built a summer palace here in 1660. Later came Frederick the Great's elegant single-storey Rococo palace Sans Souci meaning 'without care' to which he could escape from Berlin, which he hated, and his wife, whom he preferred to avoid. It is set in vast ornamental gardens, which also include the Neues Palais, built to celebrate Frederick's victory in the Seven Years' War. It has the Marmorgalerie, imitating the Versailles Hall of Mirrors, a theatre for private opera performances, numerous galleries and a monument to his sister Wilhelmine, perhaps the only woman that he ever loved.

Other additional towns acquired in this area were Cottbus (1445) and Zossen (1490).

The Ruppin area west of Berlin was added in 1524 and the towns of Beeskow on the River Spree and Storkow as a gift from Bohemia in 1571. Frederick II founded two new towns of Philadelphia and Neu Boston nearby to annoy the British in 1776.

East Friesland, with the port of Emden at the mouth of the River Ems, were acquired by Frederick the Great in 1744 to add to two existing properties in the Ems area, Minden (1648), Lingen (1702) and Ravensberg, which had been part of the package after the Elector Johann Sigismund's wife became heiress of Jülich-Cleves in 1609. Ravensberg has its Sparrenburg Castle now in the outskirts of Bielfeld. After a brief war, the Hohenzollern took over Gelders and Kleve (Cleves) in this area giving them a useful foothold in the Rhineland. Both Kleve and Jülich were almost obliterated by bombing in 1944 but the Schwanburg has been rebuilt at Kleve. Jülich's Citadel fell to Napoleon and was not recovered in 1815. Eventually, the group of Rhineland enclaves was consolidated as part of Prussia

Magdeburg on the River Elbe, the scene of the horrendous siege of 1631, became part of Brandenburg-Prussia in 1680 but was lost to Napoleon in 1806. The ruins of the huge Prussian fort survive, and the cathedral was rebuilt after 1945.

The secularised bishopric of Halberstadt in the Harz came in 1648 with its fine cathedral and a large Jewish population.

The Kaiser Wilhelm Kanal reopened in 1914 with the increased width to cope with Dreadnought size battleships – an achievement which sadly made it more likely that the Germans would risk a major war. Kiel had been acquired by the Prussians in 1865 and six years later became the chief base for the new German Navy. Meanwhile, Wilhelmshaven – also in former Oldenburg territory – had been founded by Wilhelm I as the second major new naval base. Johannisthal was the site in 1900 of the first German attempts to develop aircraft for military use.

Despite the success of the Brandenburg branch of the Hohenzollern family, the original branch which had stayed in the ancestral home in Schwabia had made little progress. Until 1846, they did not rebuild the castle, which was anyway in a most inaccessible location, but had built a new one down the hill at Hechingen. This Altes Schloss was refurbished in the usual way as an ornate Baroque palace in the seventeenth century and displaced the Neues Schloss. As so often happened, the family divided itself into three in 1576 creating three new counties: Hechingen, Haigerloch and Sigmaringen. Haigerloch 1,500 feet up in the Eigach valley, has its castle and castle church but is mainly now remembered as the home of the Nazi attempt to build an atom bomb in 1944-5.

Sigmaringen had its Residentzschloss founded by its first count, Karl, in 1579, and in 1623, the counts were promoted to princes, so the castle had to be rebuilt as a Renaissance style, red-roofed palace perched on a cliff above the Danube just north of Lake Constance. In 1866, this was the home of another Karl, the Hohenzollern, who changed his name to become King Carol I of Romania.

IN POLAND

Malbork, in the Massurian Lakes south of Gdansk on the River Nogat, is the scene of Marienburg Castle, the huge red-brick fortress of the Teutonic knights whose last grand master, Albert of Hohenzollern, was based in its Grand Master's Palace. During the reformation, he dissolved his own order and procured for himself its province of East Prussia as a duchy for himself and his successors. However, the area known as West Prussia remained part of Poland till 1772 under Frederick the Great, was lost again in 1824 and then regained from 1878-1919. Gdansk (Danzig) became Hohenzollern in 1793 till 1918. Other castles include Blaga at Vesyolye. Boyen Fortress at Gizycko is a surviving Prussian base from 1844.

Krosno Ordzanskie, or Krossen, became part of Brandenburg in 1482 and was ethnically cleansed when it became Polish in 1945. Kostrzyn has the meager ruins of Kustrin Castle where Frederick the Great was held prisoner after his attempted escape to the west. It was badly damaged during the Second World War. Lebork, or Lauenburg, in Pomerania was another Hohenzollern outpost.

Szczecin, or Stettin, the capital of West Pomerania, became part of Brandenburg when bought from the Swedes in 1720 and remained so till 1945. The castle of the dukes of Pomerania was converted into a brewery by the Prussians. The walls of the Maiden's Tower are 4 metres thick. The royal gate is also known as the Gate of Prussian Homage.

South Prussia, acquired in the Second Partition of 1793, was lost to Napoleon and then to Russia in 1815 but regained from 1848-1918. The main Germanic city is Poznan, which still boasts a large imperial palace.

New East Prussia, including Warsaw, which came to the Hohenzollerns in the Third Partition of 1795, was held only briefly till 1806 when the Poles were helped by French troops to drive out the Prussians. It is now spilt between Poland and White Russia.

Silesia, now partially in Slovakia but mainly in Poland since 1921, was the first major conquest of Frederick the Great in 1740 and he bought for himself Breslaw Palace in its main city of Breslau or Wroclaw which also has the fine Centennial Hall erected by the Germans in 1911. The city endured a horrific siege by the Russians in 1945 and the German inhabitants who survived were mainly ethnically cleansed to the west.

In Lithuania

Memel, now known as Klaipeda, was from 1525 part of the East Prussian duchy created by Albert of Hohenzollern, which was part of Brandenburg from 1618. It was a successful port and was captured by the Russians from 1756-63, and was then Prussian again until 1918. Memelburg castle had been a major Prussian base.

In Russia

Kaliningrad, or Königsberg's Castle of the Teutonic knights, was destroyed by the Russians in 1945, but the cathedral survives with its statue of Albert of Hohenzollern, the first Duke of Prussia, as do some remnants of the old Prussian port's fortifications. Friedrich III was crowned here as the first king in Prussia. There is a Prussian fort at Polessk.

The ethnically German populations of Prussia, descendants of farmers who had followed in the wake of the Teutonic knights, were mostly deported from both Poland and Russia back to Western Germany. Many settled in areas like Hanover, which had lost many of its inhabitants during the war.

In France

Versailles, with its Hall of Mirrors, was the scene of the foundation of the Kaiserreich in 1871 after the Prussian victory over Napoleon III at Sedan, so that King Wilhelm became Kaiser Wilhelm I.

In Romania

Bucharest's Royal Palace is now the National Museum of Art. It was remodelled by the Hohenzollern Carol I after 1866 and again by Maria and Carol II. The other favourite summer residence for the Hohenzollerns in Romania was Peles in Sinaia, high up in the Carpathian mountains. It was built with an exotic mixture of styles: half-timbered, Renaissance and romantic. Nearby Pelisor was the favourite of Ferdinand and Maria, as was their hunting lodge at Foisor.

In Greece

The delightful Achilleion Palace on Corfu was originally built by the Habsburg Empress Eilzabeth, but taken over in 1907 by Kaiser Wilhelm II.

In China

Kiautschou/Qingdao was captured during Wilhelm II's reign and visited by Tirpitz as he prospected for a Pacific base for the German Navy. The fortified Governor's mansion and Guest House survive as do a number of German buildings in Ba Da Guan as well as the successful German Brewery at Tsingtao.

IN NAMIBIA

Swakopomund still has Die Alte Kaserne and Hohenzollern Hause from the period of brutal German occupation after 1892.

IN TANZANIA

Bagamoyo has its German Boma and German Hanging Place from the period when it was the capital of the German colony.

IN CAMEROON

Ambam, its colonial capital in 1884, has a number of public buildings, railway bridges etc. from the German period.

IN PAPUA NEW GUINEA

Rabaul, then called Simpsonhafen, was the capital of the German colony of New Guinea from 1884 till the Australian army captured it at the beginning of the First World War. Most of its buildings from that era were destroyed in the volcanic eruption of 1994.

MARSHALL ISLANDS

The Germans had a colony here on Likiep Atoll from 1885 and a number of their buildings survive.

CHAPTER 6

From Wettin via Meissen to Balmoral, Lisbon, Brussels and Sofia

In Germany

Wettin Castle itself has been completely rebuilt but perhaps bears some vague resemblance to the original, for it is perched on a rock above the town and would have to use the same contours. It was acquired by Dietrich Count of Hosgau and Liesgau after the conquest of the area from the Wends in 982 and passed on to his two sons. Looking down on the River Saale, it is high in the wooded mountains of south-eastern Thuringia.

In 1089, the family of Wettin were promoted to be guardians of the new eastern frontier, or Margraves of Meissen, on the River Elbe west of Dresden. Here, in 1423, they were promoted to Electors of Saxony and the two brothers split the titles between them, Ernst being the Elector and Albrecht the Duke of Saxony, yet they decided to share the building of a new castle at Meissen. This remarkable and pretentious fortified palace, the Albrechtsburg, was built ingeniously on the rock overlooking the town, so that the outlying parts are six storeys high. The cathedral, or *dom*, is sheltered in its massive courtyard as is the Fürstenkapelle. Sadly, before the building was finished the heirs of the two brothers began to fall out and the family endured a prolonged split. Meissen still has a porcelain factory, as it was the first place in Europe where genuine porcelain, often referred to as Dresden, was produced, and all because Augustus the Strong had imprisoned his pet alchemist Johann Böttger in order to bully him into making gold.

Around 1200, Dietrich of Meissen captured the trading city of Leipzig but his castles have disappeared. Thomas Kirche, where J. S. Bach served as kantor for twenty-seven years, survives.

In 1283, the Wettin family had taken over the county of Thuringia, one of whose towns was Gotha. Here the Wettin dynasty built the massive Schloss Freidrichsthal and Schloss Friedenstein, a massive Baroque palace with huge square towers at its corners. Its elaborately decorated interior now includes a museum, the former ducal theatre, dating back to 1774, and the *schlosskirche*, which contains murals boosting the image of the

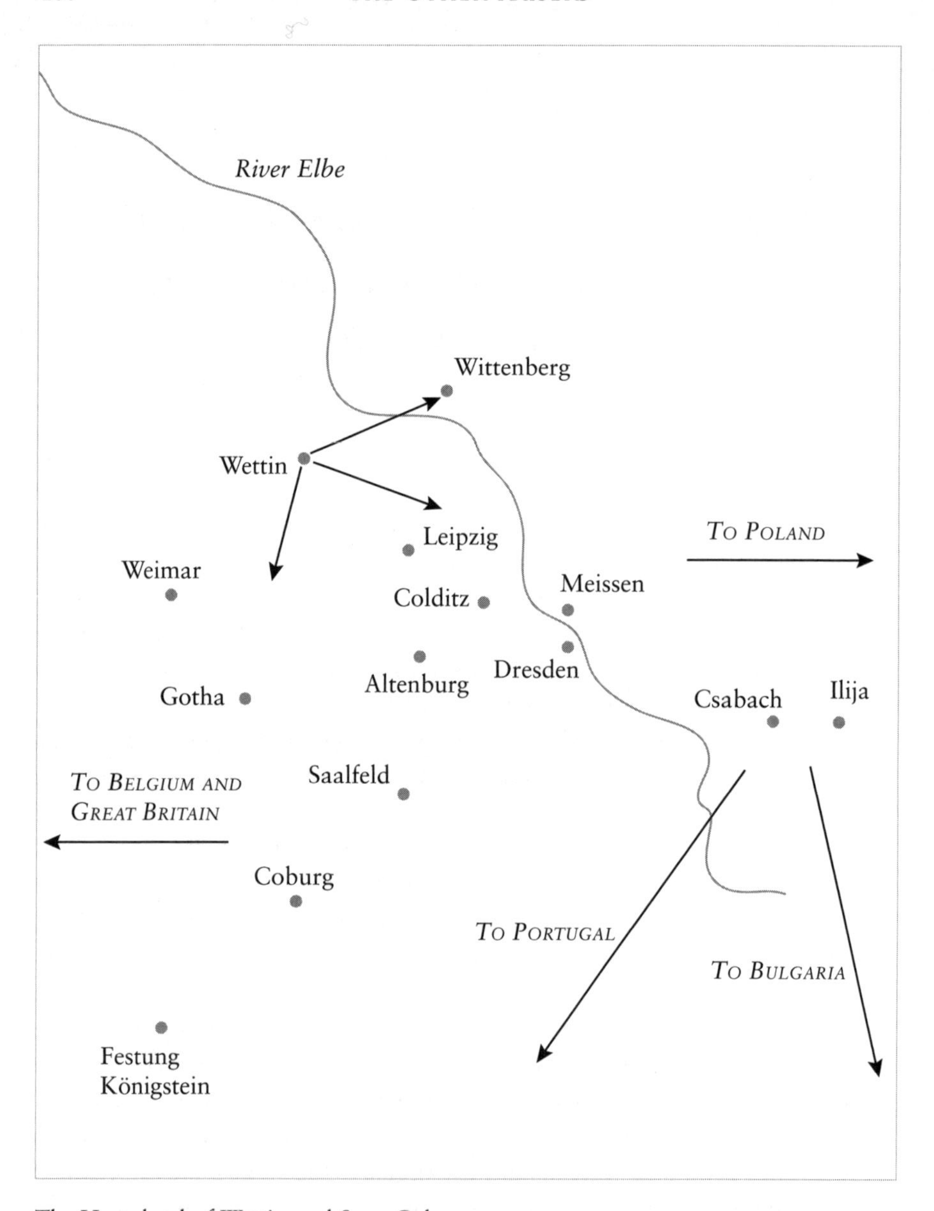

The Homeland of Wettin and Saxe-Coburg

dynasty of Saxe-Gotha. In the town there is also an Orangerie, the exotic folly Teeschlösschen and the former home of Lucas Cranach.

The town of Coburg is well to the south of Gotha in Bavaria yet linked with it as the best known of the ducal titles of the Wettin dynasty who took it over in 1353. High above the town stands the Veste Coburg, one of the largest surviving medieval fortresses in Germany and most of it rebuilt after a major fire in 1499. It includes a bear pit, or Bärenbastei, and the half-timbered princely residence, or Fürstenbau. The Elector John the Steadfast famously offered a safe retreat here to the outlawed Martin Luther when he might otherwise have been executed as a heretic, and the Lutherkapelle commemorates his six month stay here, much of which he spent in the castle's heated stone chamber translating the bible into German. John the Steadfast's portrait by Lucas Cranach recalls the patronage given to the artist here and in Gotha, and the propaganda work that Cranach undertook for Martin Luther. The armoury has the armour worn by Johann Casimir, the first duke of Saxe-Coburg, and beside it the armour of his dwarf. In 1540, not content with Veste Coburg, the dukes soon began a new Renaissance palace, the Schloss Ehrenburg, which after the usual convenient fire in 1690 had to be elaborately refurbished in Baroque. It has its Hall of Giants, or Riesensaal, glorifying the house of Saxe-Coburg and a throne room copied from Napoleon's in the Tuileries. Even at this period this apparently minor branch of the Wettin dynasty, with its small duchy and massive palaces, showed a gift for self-promotion which later won it four kingdoms. They had the ducal mausoleum in the Church of St Moriz and another two castles: the massive Schloss Callenberg, which Duke Ernst turned into a medieval pastiche, and Schloss Rosenau, which the dukes bought and refurbished in 1805 and where Prince Albert was born in 1819.

Colditz is now more often remembered as a high security gaol, or Oflag IV C ,for prisoners of war during the Nazi period but came into the hands of the Wettin by purchase in 1404 and was rebuilt after the usual fire in 1506 along with its own large private zoo. Once abandoned by the dukes in 1826, it spent a century as a mental institution.

Altenburg, which was part of the Thuringian inheritance and was captured by Friedrich Margrave of Meissen after a battle in 1307, has a vast hilltop castle, yet it did not help the two sons of Friedrich the Wise who were kidnapped from here in 1455 during the inter-family war. In the family split of 1485 it went to the electoral branch of the Wettin, then in 1672, to the Saxe-Coburg-Gotha branch of the family and finally, in 1826, to the Saxe-Altenburg dukes, the last of whom abdicated in 1918. The medieval castle was refurbished as a classical palace. During the Second World War, the town had a number of slave labour sub-camps of Buchenwald concentration camp.

Dresden became the capital of the descendants of Albrecht in 1485 when they had to leave Meissen, and Dresden soon overtook Meissen in terms of urban growth. Many of its historic buildings were virtually destroyed in the infamous bombing raid of 1944 but most have been reconstructed. This includes the Zwinger, an elegantly Baroque palace built by Augustus the Strong. He turned Dresden into one of the most fashionable cities in Europe albeit his court was widely regarded as a den of iniquity. Helped by his considerable wealth, he spent vast sums on building and planned the amazing porcelain menagerie for his Japanese Palace. He cultivated his image as a strongman by telling his servants to release wild boars for him to wrestle with, but perhaps neglected to hone his political skills, for his dynasty did not long survive him in Poland. Among his other building projects were the magnificent Brühlsche Terrasse in Dresden, the Moritzburg Palace, a vast square *château* set on an island in a lake east of Meissen, the Grossedlitz Garden and Orangery at Heidenau, and the Pillnitz Palace, which is elegantly situated on the banks of the Elbe outside Dresden and was given as a present to one of his many mistresses. One of his other mistresses, Anna Constantia, had the less happy fate of being locked up in the forbidding medieval keep of the Wettins at Burg Stolpen.

The capital chosen by the descendants of Ernst, the electors of Saxony, was Wittenberg, which is also famously associated with the protection afforded by the family to the outlawed rebel monk Martin Luther whose former monastery is now the Lutherhalle. Most of the once magnificent ducal Residenzschloss has been destroyed in successive wars but part survives as a youth hostel and its *schlosskirche* has the famous doors to which Luther nailed his ninety-five theses in 1519.

When Friedrich the Magnanimous was driven out of Wittenberg in 1547, he built himself a new palace at Weimar of which the magnificent Renaissance tower survives, as do works of Cranach whom he sponsored here. The *schloss* was remodeled in classical style and Duke Ernst of Saxe-Weimar, also in 1724, built the Baroque Schloss Belvedere as his pleasure palace – Lustschloss. Weimar became a major cultural centre that attracted Goethe, Schiller, J. S. Bach, Franz Liszt, Richard Strauss and Friedrich Nietzsche.

Torgau on the Elbe had another fine Wettin castle at Hartenfels.

Saalfeld, an old fortified mining town on the River Saal, became the home of a sub-branch of the Saxe-Coburgs, which made itself rich by marrying a wealthy Hungarian heiress. This marriage required them to become Catholics but this proved useful when one of them had the chance to marry the Queen of Portugal and another to be given the princedom of Bulgaria.

IN SWITZERLAND

Festung Königstein was the prison where August the Strong imprisoned the luckless alchemist Bottger who accidentally discovered how to make fine porcelain when he was supposed to be making gold.

IN POLAND

The Elector of Saxony and King of Poland Augustus the Strong built the magnificent Baroque Saski (Saxon) Palace for himself in Warsaw to match the one he had in Dresden. It was badly damaged during the uprising against the Russians in 1794 and on several other occasions, so only the central arcade and gardens survive.

IN BELGIUM

Palais Royal de Bruxelles had been built by the Orange family but was taken over by the Saxe-Coburgs in 1830. Laeken castle in the outskirts of Brussels was built in 1782 for the Habsburg rulers of the Austrian Netherlands, and Belvedere in its grounds was used by Albert II.

IN SLOVAKIA

The two now ruined fortresses of Sitno (Ilija) and Cabrad (Csabrach) belonged to the Kohare family whose wealthy heiress married into the Saxe-Coburgs and gave them Catholicism as well as the muscle they needed to win the crowns of Portugal and Bulgaria. They moved to Svaty Anton, which survives.

IN GREAT BRITAIN

The Crystal Palace was built at Prince Albert's instigation for the Great Exhihition of 1851 and was his crowning achievement. The Albert Hall was built in his memory and completed ten years after his death in 1861.

Sandringham in Norfolk was acquired by Queen Victoria in 1862 for her son, the future Edward VII, and his new wife, Alexandra, who rebuilt it as a large brick country house. York Cottage in the grounds was a favourite of George V.

Frogmore House, an elegant white mansion built in the grounds of Windsor Castle, was a favourite retreat for Victoria and Albert and has their joint Mausoleum in its garden.

Osborne House on the Isle of Wight was bought by Victoria and Albert in 1884, demolished and rebuilt with Italianate towers. Victoria died here and her successor, Edward VII, preferred Sandringham, so it was soon given over to other uses and is now run by English Heritage.

Balmoral on Deeside is the estate first rented by Victoria and Albert in 1848, and they liked it so much that they bought it four years later, rebuilding the house as a typical Saxe-Coburg schloss except that the area is relatively flat.

IN PORTUGAL

Lisbon's neoclassical Ajuda Royal Palace, though begun by the previous dynasty, was first used in 1861 by Luis I of Saxe-Coburg and his wife. It is now a museum. Luis was also responsible for the founding of Lisbon's pioneering aquarium.

Castelo da Pena was built in 1839 on the orders of Fernando I, the first of the Saxe-Coburg kings of Portugal. He bought the ruins of a rocktop monastery here, Nostra Senhora da Pena, and replaced them with a fantasy Germanic castle with red turret-topped towers reminiscent of a colourful Balmoral and a mix of decorative styles including Moorish.

Bucaco Palace was also built on the site of a former monastery but only completed in 1907 three years before the last king was deposed.

IN BULGARIA

The Royal Palace of Sofia in Battenberg Square is now an art gallery. It was begun in 1880 for the ill-fated Alexander of Battenberg but taken over by his successor Ferdinand of Saxe-Coburg who added the East Wing.

Ferdinand bought Alexander's hunting estate of Vrana where he built a hunting lodge in 1904. Many years later it was re-occupied by ex-Tsar Simeon II after the fall of communism. Vrana Palace was built in 1909. The summer palace of Euxinograd on the Black Sea coast was begun by Alexander in 1882 and finished under Ferdinand.

IN AFRICA

In the early twentieth century, three of the Saxe-Coburg dynasties between them, albeit as constitutional monarchies, held a massive proportion of the African continent. With the Belgians' massive presence in the Congo, the Portuguese in Angola and Mozambique, plus the monster portfolio of British colonies, all other dynasties were dwarfed by comparison.

IN THE CONGO

Henry Stanley founded Kinhasa as Leopoldville, a port on the River Congo. He had been hired by Leopold II who turned the Congo into a personal fiefdom, and extracted its wealth with considerable ruthlessness amounting to genocide.

IN INDIA

Here the Saxe-Coburgs won their fifth crown, for after the last of the Moguls had been formally dethroned for his failure to prevent the Indian Mutiny in 1867 Queen Victoria was declared empress of India. There are numerous buildings from this era but perhaps the most typically Saxe-Coburg example is the enormous Chatrapati Shivaji Terminus in Mumbai – a railway station that resembles a massive German *schloss*. In New Delhi, itself a Saxe-Coburg creation, is the Rashtrapati Bhavan, a huge classical vice-regal residence built in 1912.

CHAPTER 7

From Wittelsbach to Munich, Stockholm and Beyond

In Germany

Of Wittelsbach Castle, itself built by the local Count of Dachau and destroyed in 1209, nothing remains except a memorial stone marking the spot. Its then count, Otto, had dared to challenge the king and suffered the consequences. It stood just outside the village of Aichach on the Paar River 20 miles north-west of Munich. It was replaced by a new castle at Trausnitz, which had been built only five years earlier and stands in Landshut near the north-east of Munich on the River Isar. This was the base for the family as they served from 1255 as dukes first of lower Bavaria, then from 1503 of the whole of Bavaria. The first Renaissance palace north of the Alps, it still has its high Wittelsbach Tower, its Fools Staircase and its Knights Hall. Landshut itself has St Martin's church, which eventually became the tallest brick building in the world. Haziga of Aragon, the wife of Count Otto of Scheyern and an early member of the family, founded Scheyern Abbey at Petersberg in 1099, and it became the burial place for the family. It was rebuilt nearly nine centuries later by Otto's descendant, King Ludwig I of Bavaria, who also built the Freedom Palace at Kelheim.

Dachau was also one of the original properties of the family, and their early castle there was replaced by a Renaissance *schloss*, of which only the Festsaal and gardens survive. Outside the town is the notorious Konzentrationslager. Meanwhile, the family received further rewards, for in 1214 Frederick of Wittelsbach was made Count Palatine of the Rhein and this brought them two new cities, Heidelberg and Mannheim.

Heidelberg Castle, sitting half way up the Königstuhl, was first occupied by the Wittelsbachs in 1225 when Count Ludwig I persuaded the local clergy that they needed him to protect the trade route up the Neckar. The family added a second castle in 1294 but the upper one was destroyed by lightning in 1537. It was rebuilt and in 1619 was the seat of the Elector Friedrich V. He had married Elizabeth Stuart, daughter of James VI, and was himself, at this point, offered the Protestant crown of

The Spread of the Wittelsbachs

Bohemia. Disastrously, he accepted, and the castle was twice besieged and badly damaged in the Thirty Years' War that followed. It was rebuilt in 1649 but again twice besieged in 1688 and 1693, this time by the French. The Electors Palatine finally moved out in 1720 and the castle suffered a double lightning strike in 1764, which many, including Victor Hugo, interpreted as a sign that it was doomed. Nevertheless, the ruins are now regarded as one of the finest Renaissance buildings north of the Alps. They include some additions made by the Scotswoman Queen Elizabeth of Bohemia, the Winter Queen and ancestress of the British House of Hanover.

The new capital chosen by the Elector Palatine in 1720 was Mannheim, which had been founded as a fortress in 1606 at the junction of the Rhine and Neckar rivers. It is also where, in due course, the new Residenzschloss, the largest Baroque palace ever built in Germany, was situated. Its *schlosskirche* and *jesuitenkirche* reflected the fact that the Palatine Wittelsbachs had reconverted back to Catholicism. However, Mannheim remained the capital for less than sixty years, for in 1777 the Palatine branch of the Wittelsbachs inherited the Bavarian dukedom from the southern branch of the family, which had run out of male heirs, so Munich became their preferred residence. The fine Palladian-style façade of the palace has been restored since the bomb damage of the Second World War, but only part of the interior – the Rittersaal, as a concert hall and the reception rooms, now a museum. The Electors were great patrons of music here and, amongst other novelties, sponsored the development of the clarinet.

Pfalz, the picturesque, eponymous Palatine castle on its island in the Rhine at Kaub, was a profitable toll collection point for river traffic. It came to the Wittelsbachs in 1277 and went back briefly to the Katzenellenbogen family in 1477.

Overlooking the Rhine Rift, the ruins of the once important Schloss Landskron at Oppenheim south of Mainz date from 1204.

Neuburg on the Danube still has its fourteenth-century town walls and its Wittelsbach castle, founded in the thirteenth century, was rebuilt in 1530. There is also the Hofkirche from 1608 and nearby is the huge, elegant and once moated hunting lodge of Schloss Grunau, dated 1555. Also on the Danube is Straubing, developed by Duke Ludwig I from 1218, where the Herzogschloss stands by the river and the commoner wife of Duke Albert III, Agnes Benauer, was cruelly drowned as a witch on the orders of his father in 1432.

Regensburg, or Rattisbon, has an extravagantly nationalistic Walhalla monument erected by Ludwig I.

Pfalz Neumarkt in Oberpfalz, south-east of Nürnberg, was the home of a branch of the family who found fame in Denmark. Amberg, east of Nürnberg, still has some of its medieval walls and a Wittelsbach castle. Nearby was their Deinschwang hunting lodge.

Munich/München was founded in 1158 by the Welf magnate Henry the Lion as a tax collection point on the River Isar but on his fall in 1180 it passed to the Wittelsbachs. It was the capital of the northern part of their divided duchy from 1255 and from 1503 capital of a united Bavaria. Little survives of the Altstadt except three of the town gates from the fourteenth century and the court brewery, from 1589, which became the famous Hofbräuhaus, favoured by Hitler, while the Augustinerbräu dates from 1328. The Frauenkirche contains one of the two Wittelsbach emperors, Ludwig IV. Wilhelm V had the Jesuit St Michael's church built in 1597 and it has the tomb of mad King Ludwig II in its crypt. The Wittelsbachs moved in the late fourteenth century from their old town Alter Hof, built originally in the thirteenth century but now an office, to the north-east of the city where they built first a fortress and then after 1570 the palatial Residenz, part of which is now a museum. The Turm Herzog-Maximilian-Burg is all that is left of the castle built in 1593 by Wilhem V. The Residenz has Ahnengalerei with over a hundred Wittelsbach portraits, Grottenhof, Goldener Saal, *kurfürstenzimmer* or Elector's Rooms, two chapels and Wagnerian Niebelungensäle.

At Theresienwiese is the colonnaded Rumeshalle, a glorification of Bavaria paid for by Ludwig I, overlooking the site of the Oktoberfest.

As a summer residence the Wittelsbachs, in 1664, began to build the Italianate palace which later grew into the huge Schloss Nymphenburg 3 miles outside the city centre. It includes, from 1761, a porcelain factory, the Rococo Grosser Saal for grand occasions and the *schonheitengalerei* with portraits of Ludwig I's favourite women, including the dangerous Lola Montez. Outside is the magnificent Schlosspark with its pavilions, a hermitage, pagoda and other follies. A third Wittelsbach three-palace complex was the Altes Schloss Schleissheim built by the pious Duke Wilhelm V in the seventeenth century, the massive Baroque Neues Schloss and the smaller Schloss Lustheim.

Schwangau, north of Füssen, is the centre of the group of fantasy castles built by the last Wittelsbach kings who were obsessed with Swans. Schloss Hohenschwangau was begun by Crown Prince Maximilian in 1830 as a mock Tudor fantasy. Its *hohenstaufensaal* contains the square piano used by Ludwig II and Wagner.

Schloss Neuschwanstein, an obscenely extravagant grey-granite monstrosity towering above the countryside below and verging on Disneyland, has the remarkable Marienbrücke crossing the Poellat Gorge. There are also the smaller but unfinished Linderhof with delightful gardens, a Venus Grotto as a set for Tannhäuser and Moroccan house opium den and Herrenschiemsee, a miniature Versailles to add to the extraordinary collection of buildings. Falkenstein was the site of another extraordinary castle building project and there is the mountain hunting lodge of Schachen.

Ingolstadt, north of Munich on the Danube, became a major Wittelsbach fortress with well-preserved medieval walls and towers. The thirteenth-century Altes Schloss is now a library. Duke Ludwig VII the Bearded of Bavaria built the French style Neues Schloss castle here, now a museum of armoury.

Simmern near Meisenheim has its Schinderhannes Turm perched high on a rock, castle of the local Wittelsbach dukes. Nearby the family provided land for vine growing in 1464, and the Rheingau wines of Hattenheimer Mannberg are still popular.

Zweibrücken, as its name suggests, has two bridges and is famous for its roses. The area in the Saar was bought by the Wittelsbachs in 1140 and this branch of the family later produced three kings of Sweden. The town was destroyed in 1635 and 1677, and then became a province of Sweden till 1718. The large Baroque palace of Duke Leopold built in 1720 is now a courthouse. The Alexanderkirche was the family burial place. The massively extravagant Baroque castle of Karlsberg – it even had a pineapple greenhouse – on the Buchenberg was built in 1778 and destroyed by the French in 1793. All that survives is a farmhouse, now owned by the brewers of the same name. The Sulzbach division of the family ultimately took over the Palatinate and Bavaria. Sulzbach-Rosenberg is a Bavarian hill-town still with its Wittelsbach castle and iconic lion in the square.

The Wittelsbach share of the duchy of Jülich-Berg included Bensberg where they built the huge early eighteenth-century Neues Schloss, now a luxury hotel overlooking Cologne.

IN SWEDEN

The Tre Kronor Castle was rebuilt in Baroque palatial style in 1692 for the belligerent Palatinate King Karl XI but burned down five years later just before his death. A gallery in his name survives in the massive replacement palace with 609 rooms. It was built in 1734 under King Fredrik I from Hesse-Kassel, the husband of Ulrika Leonora who was the tempestuous sister of Karl XII, the Swedish Thunderbolt, who had himself been away fighting for most of his reign and never had time to consider palace-building. As they had no children, this couple marked the end of the Palatinate/Wittelsbach dynasty in Sweden.

Drottningholm Palace, with its superb Baroque gardens, just outside Stockholm had been built in 1580 under the Vasas but burned down in 1661 just after the death of Karl X Gustav. His widow, Hedwig Leonora had it rebuilt while acting as regent for their son, Karl XI. It was later refurbished in Rococo style by Louisa Ulrika, wife of the first of the new Holstein Oldenburg kings, Adolf Fredrik, in 1751.

CHAPTER 8

From Mecklenburg to London and Berlin

Micklingburg/Mecklenburg in West Pomerania lies in a large plateau of interconnected lakes interspersed with flat, often boggy peatlands and rich farmland. Only a few ruined ramparts remain of the original castle which stood on a peninsula jutting into one of the many lakes. Mecklenburg Castle Domitz, with its star-shaped moat, was built in 1559 by Duke Johann Albrecht to control the crossing of the Elbe.

Strelitz, east of the Muritzsee, is Germany's second biggest lake after Lake Constance and became capital of one half of the divided duchy in 1701. Both town and castle were destroyed by fire in 1712 but the duke moved to his hunting lodge on the Zierker See and Neustrelitz grew up around it as a replacement, a planned eighteenth-century new town with well-ordered Baroque buildings. The Baroque palace was destroyed by bombing in 1944, but its gardens, Orangerie and chapel survive.

Ludwigslust was begun with a ducal hunting lodge in 1757 and like Neustrelitz, was a planned town. The exotic and imposing Baroque *schloss* survives, though the duke was short of money and the stone façade hides the fact that the main structure is of brick.

Schwerin, on the Schweriner See and nine other lakes, was founded in 1160 by Henry the Lion as part of the 'Drang nach Osten' and still has its medieval cathedral. It became capital of the grand duchy in 1837 and on the site of the ancient castle on an island in the lake the duke built a French-style château with golden domes, which now houses the regional parliament, where Angela Merkel first made her name as a politician. The network of lakes and rivers was used to help form the Hamburg-Berlin Canal system

Mirow on its lake of the same name was the birthplace of Queen Charlotte Sophia, wife of George III as her father, one of the duke's younger brothers, was Prince of Mirow.

Gustrow was the summer residence of the Dukes of Mecklenburg and their superb Renaissance palace, built in 1589, survives, as does the brick Gothic cathedral dating from 1226.

CHAPTER 9

FROM ANHALT-ZERBST TO ST PETERSBURG

Aschersleben Castle, latinised as *Ascania*, was the starting point for the dynasty that held Brandenburg before the Hohenzollern and later went on to produce Catherine the Great of Russia, previously known as Sophia of Anhalt-Zerbst. The town 15 miles east of Quedlinburg was the capital of Anhalt from 1252-1315. Much of the historic old town survives but not the old castle. Castle Ballenstedt at Roseburg still survives in a ruinous state as well as the later Baroque Ballenstedt ducal palace. Walsrode Monastery, founded by the family to guard the ford over the River Boehme in the tenth century, is still in use.

Zerbst is 17 miles south-east of Magdeburg. Much of the old town walls are still in place and a number of medieval monasteries and other buildings survive. The ducal palace, childhood home of Catherine, was built in 1681 and now partially ruined though parts used for archive storage.

Kothen was the scene for the first performance of Bach's Brandenburg Concertos in 1721.

IN POLAND

Szczecin/Stettin is at the mouth of the Oder on the Baltic coast. It was the birthplace of Catherine the Great, as in 1729 her father was garrison commander for the Prussians.Tthe palace of the dukes of Pomerania was destroyed by bombs in 1944 but was rebuilt in the 1980s.

IN RUSSIA

St Petersburg and its surrounding areas have a large number of exotic buildings, which Catherine the Great had built, but perhaps the best known is the Hermitage annexe, which she commissioned in 1764 to house her paintings. She also completed other parts of the Winter Palace;

there are also the Marble Palace, built for one of her earliest lovers, Grigori Orlov, and the Tauride, built for one of her last, Grigori Potemkin. In Petrodvorets she built, amongst others, her Chesme Hall, and at Tsarskoe Selo she rebuilt the Catherine's Palace and added the famous Cameron Gallery.

CHAPTER 10

From Zähringen to Moscow

In Germany

Zähringen, which is just outside Freiburg on a hill overlooking the valley of the River Dreisam, has the ruins of the original castle of the ancestors of the Baden dynasty. It was founded in 1128 by Berchold who became its duke. He also founded Berne in what is now Switzerland but was then part of his duchy.

Karlsuhe was founded in 1715 when the markgraf Karl Wilhelm of Baden began a country palace for himself in the Hardter Wald as a place where he could dally with his mistresses and his artistic friends away from his nagging wife; hence the name of the city, Karl's Rest. It became the capital of a reunited Baden in 1771 and grew further when Napoleon promoted the counts to Grand Dukes. The *schloss* was rebuilt in the 1750s and was severely damaged in the Second World War but has been restored as a museum. It includes a reconstructed *thronsaal* with the crown jewels of the grand dukes. Karl Wilhelm's pyramid grave survives, as does his obelisk in the centre of the Marktplatz. The *palais* is now a bank. Just outside the city is the former home of the counts at Durlach where the replacement Baroque Schloss Karlsburg, begun after the French destroyed its predecessor in 1688, was never quite finished and now houses a museum.

In Russia

In Taganrog is the Alexander I Palace where the neglected Tsarina Elizabeth, Louise of Baden, nursed her dying husband. It is now a sanatorium.

CHAPTER 11

From Hesse to St Petersburg and London

Darmstadt was the capital of the Landgrafs of Hesse-Darmstadt from 1567 and of their Grand Duchy from the days of Napoleon. Much of the built heritage was destroyed in the bombing and firestorm of 1944, but the Ludwigsmonument survives, the huge column for the Grand Duke Ludwig I, as does the fifteenth-century Weisserturm. The huge *schloss* complex had medieval, Renaissance and Baroque makeovers but was severely damaged by bombing in 1944 and has been recycled as parts of the university and library. The Prinz-Georg-Palais, set in its own Rococo gardens, houses the ducal porcelain collection. The Russische Kapelle, a traditionally gilded Russian orthodox church, built in 1898, recalls one of the duchy's most famous exports, Alexandra, the wife of Nicholas II who had it built for her.

The other tsarina to be born here was Maria, wife of Alexander II, though notoriously at the time of her birth her father and mother had been separated for a number of years, so alternative paternity was alleged.

Kassel was badly damaged in 1943, but outside it survives Count Wilhelm IX's Wilhelmshöhe, built in 1786, and his quasi-medieval Löwenburg, later used as German army headquarters during the First World War. There are the usual Baroque gardens full of follies and cascades plus the Karlsaue Orangerie.

Wilhelmsthal Palace in Kronach was built by Landgraf Wilhelm VIII in the 1740s after his brother became king of Sweden.

The tower of Battenberg has survived.

In Russia

Yekaterinburg now has a shrine at the place of execution of the Tsarina Alexandra and her family.

CHAPTER 12

From Baden and Teck to Russia and Britain

Württemberg itself is a steep hill outside Stuttgart, which gave its name to the dukedom, later after 1806 a kingdom. In Stuttgart the Altes Schloss was built in the tenth century to protect the stud farm that gave the city its name, and it was replaced by a moated castle, some of which survives, followed by an elegant Renaissance palace now used as a museum and concert venue. The massive Baroque Neues Schloss now houses government offices. The Jubilaumsäule in the Schlossplatz commemorates the silver jubilee of King Wilhelm I of Württemberg.

Schloss Rosenstein on the outskirts of Stuttgart is the former country residence of the Württemberg kings; it is set in a stylized garden and is now a museum. Similarly, Schloss Solitude to the west is a very stylish oval palace, built in the 1760s as another country retreat for the Württemberg dukes.

Ludwigsburg is perhaps the greatest example of the extravagance of minor German heads of state. It has the largest Baroque castle in Germany, the Residenzschloss, built in 1704 by Duke Eberhard Ludwig on the site of an older hunting lodge destroyed by the French in 1688. He then went on to build another two smaller palaces, Favorite in 1713 and the octagonal lakeside Seeschloss Monrepos. As the duke made Ludwigsburg his capital he had to create a new town to house his subjects. Urach also has a Residenzschloss for the dukes of Württemberg.

The dukedom of Teck came to an end in 1187 soon after the founding of Teck Castle by Adalbert, a sibling of the Zähringen. The castle was destroyed in 1525 during the Peasant Wars, but the title was revived in 1871 by the King of Württemberg for Francis, a spare and not quite suitably-born nephew, in the hope that it would help him find a rich wife. He did, Princess Adelaide of Cambridge, granddaughter of George III, so he transformed himself into a thoroughly English minor royal and fathered Mary of Teck who became the wife of the future George V. A new castle of Teck had been built and survives 2,500 feet up in the Schwabian Jura.

Bibliography

Arnold, Benjamin, *Princes and Territories in Medieval Germany*, Cambridge, 2003

Arnold, Jacques, *Royal Houses of Europe, The Hohenzollern Dynasty of Prussia*, London, 2005

Bain, R.N., *Scandinavia – A Political History of Denmark, Norway and Sweden*, London 2002

Black, J., *The Hanovers*, London, 2004

Blackburn, Doris, *History of Germany 1780-1918*, Oxford, 2003

Blom, J.C.H. and E. Lambert, *History of the Low Countries*, London, 2006

Clark, C., *Iron Kingdom – The Rise and Fall of Prussia*, London, 2007.

Elliot, J.H., *Imperial Spain*, London, 1983

Feuchtwanger, E.J., *Albert and Victoria*, London, 2006

Fulbrook, M., *Concise History of Germany*, Cambridge, 2004

Grattan, T.C., *Holland*, London, 2007

Hüttl, L., *Das Haus Wittelsbach*, Heyne, 1980

Jespersden, K.J.V., *History of Denmark*, London, 2004

Kitchen, Martin, *Cambridge Illustrated History of Germany*, Cambridge, 1996

Krickmann, P., *The Wittelsbach Palaces*, London, 2001

Longford, E., *Victoria*, London, 1964

Mclachlan, G., *Rough Guide to Germany*, London, 2004

Mouritsen, L., *Rough Guide to Denmark*, London, 2007

Morby, John E., *The Dynasties of the World*, Oxford, 2002

Nelson, W.H., *The Soldier Kings – The House of Hohenzollern*, London, 1921

Plumb, J.H., *The First Four Georges*, London, 1956

Proctor, James, *Rough Guide to Sweden*, London, 2006

Roy, J.C. and Amose Elon, *The Vanished Kingdom – Travels Through the History of Prussia*,

Taylor, Edward, *The Fall of the Dynasties*, London, 1990

Thomson, Oliver, *The Romanovs*, Stroud, 2008

Wedgwood, V., *The Thirty Years' War*, London, 1957
Wedgwood, V., *William the Silent*, London, 1960
Wheatcroft, Andrew, *The Habsburgs*, London, 1996.
Witte, E., J. Craebeckx and A. Meynen, *Political History of Belgium*, London, 2000